EDUCATION AND PSYCHOLOGY OF THE GIFTED SERIES

James H. Borland, Editor

Out of Our Minds

Anti-Intellectualism and Talent Development in American Schooling

Craig B. Howley
Aimee Howley
Edwina D. Pendarvis

 Teachers College
Columbia University
New York and London

Published by Teachers College Press, 1234 Amsterdam Avenue, New York, NY 10027

Library of Congress Cataloging-in-Publication Data

Howley, Craig B.
　　Out of our minds : anti-intellectualism and talent development in
American schooling / Craig B. Howley, Aimee Howley, Edwina D.
Pendarvis.
　　　　p.　cm. — (Education and psychology of the gifted series ; 9)
　　Includes bibliographical references (p.) and index.
　　ISBN 0-8077-3417-9 (cloth: alk. paper). — ISBN 0-8077-3416-0 (pbk. :
alk. paper)
　　1. Gifted children—Education—United States.　2. Education—
United States—Aims and objectives.　3. Learning, Psychology of.
I. Howley, Aimee　II. Pendarvis, Edwina D.　III. Title.
IV. Title: Anti-intellectualism and talent development in American
schooling.　V. Series.
LC3993.9.H69　　1995
371.95′0973—dc20　　　　　　　　　　　　　　　　94-44979

ISBN 0-8077-3416-0 (paper)
ISBN 0-8077-3417-9 (cloth)

Printed on acid-free paper

Manufactured in the United States of America

02　01　00　99　98　97　96　95　　8　7　6　5　4　3　2　1

Contents

Foreword

My first encounter with the work of Craig Howley, Aimee Howley, and Edwina Pendarvis came when I received a copy of *Teaching Gifted Children*, the textbook they published in 1986. As a university professor, I routinely receive complementary copies of new publications, and, amid the flurry of books on this topic that came my way in the late 1980s, this one had no particular claim on my attention, especially since I had never heard of the authors. I did not have to get too far into this book, however, to realize that here was something different, a textbook whose contents reflected the results of three wide-ranging, penetrating, and reflective intellects brought to bear on a host of topics that had previously been given the same tedious treatment in textbook after dreary textbook. I was similarly impressed by their subsequent book, *The Abilities of Gifted Children* (1990), by their journal articles, and by my conversations with them. I was thus very eager to have Craig, Aimee, and Eddy contribute to the *Education and Psychology of the Gifted* series, and, having read this book at various stages of its development, I am more than happy with the result.

With *Out of Our Minds: Anti-Intellectualism and Talent Development in American Schooling*, Craig, Aimee, and Eddy have made an important contribution to the current discourse on schooling, intellect, and the construct of giftedness, which is emotionally and politically heated, yet often intellectually tepid. Theirs is a disturbing book, in the best sense of the term, one that will not gain easy acceptance either by those critics of "gifted education" who view all provisions and programs for gifted students as irredeemably elitist and anti-egalitarian, or by those steadfast defenders of the faith who regard any challenge to "gifted programs" as typically constituted in educational practice as errant and pernicious nonsense. Although this might suggest the existence of a significant audience of potential readers and thinkers who occupy a vast middle ground between these two positions, such is the nature of the debate on these issues today that most individuals, at least those with the most conviction and publications, seem to occupy the polar regions of the continuum. This book does not fit easily into either position, which is one of its many conspicuous assets.

I will leave it to the reader to discover and appreciate the book's arguments and analyses and the literate and graceful manner in which they are developed, but I do want to call attention here to a few of the ideas found on the following pages. I think that the idea that is at the core of the web of ideas set forth in this book is that the "stewardship of the intellect" is the most basic and important mission of the schools. As the authors write in the Preface, "We like to think of schools as the institutions charged with caring for the intellect." That this statement could be regarded as exceptionable in any way is reflective of a remarkable and disconcerting state of affairs in contemporary education. Nonetheless, the idea of schools primarily conceived as stewards of the intellect is anathema to many critics and proponents of special programs for gifted students. The authors' analysis and interpretation of how and why this came to be is one of the strengths of this book.

Rather than merely decrying the anti-intellectualism that pervades education today, the authors look for its cause, finding it in "the things to which the economy, the polity, and the society ascribe value; in short, in the organization of production, governance, and social relations, rather than in individuals." Moreover, in looking at how class, race, ethnic, and gender conflicts are played out in the educational sphere, they "locate the source of such troubles in the goal of economic domination characteristic of . . . capitalism." This sort of systematic analysis of how economic systems and imperatives determine the societal structures and organizations that schooling subserves is suggestive, in its breadth and intent, of Marx's historical materialism, although the authors of the present work find such constructs as Marxist class categories to be inadequate for their purposes. The point is that Craig, Aimee, and Eddy, unlike most of us writing in this field, have applied a rigorous (a word I use gingerly in light of the discussion of rigor in Chapter 1) and systematic analytical framework to the issues and problems surrounding the education of gifted students. This framework acknowledges the embeddedness of "gifted education" in the larger system of schooling and the embeddedness of that system in the dominant structures and ethos of the prevailing economic system. Whether or not one agrees with these conclusions, this is a significant contribution, especially when contrasted to the ad hoc musings that characterize so much of the writing on this subject.

Equally important, with this book, Craig, Aimee, and Eddy have carved out a position on the issues of education and giftedness that offers a haven for those of us uncomfortable with the forced dichotomy of the current debate to which I referred previously. It seems that today one is expected to choose sides, casting one's lot either with self-professed liberal or radical critics of programs that represent an acknowledgment of and response to individual differences or with conservative advocates of separate and unequal programs whose rationale for such programs does not seem to be that far removed from social Darwinism. Of course, these stereotyped positions are not the only options available, but it often seems that, under the terms of the current debate, those are the choices. What one encounters in this book, however, is a view that is decidedly critical and interpretive, with the implications for egalitarian societal transformation that are inherent in that position, and that also acknowledges individual needs deriving from individual differences (without the biological determinism). This a welcome sign for those of us who are unwilling to pretend that all children are equal with respect to academic ability and educational need but who are uncomfortable with placidly accepting the societal inequities that partly contribute to individual differences and the programs that frequently serve to strengthen and reproduce these inequities.

There is much that is provocative, compelling, disquieting, encouraging, and persuasive to be found in *Out of Our Minds*. Craig, Aimee, and Eddy raise troubling issues that we often leave to others outside our field to articulate, placing us in a reactive and defensive position that badly serves both the educational profession and the children whose needs it serves. It is time we took the initiative in advancing the discourse on the topics of this book, which are issues of great concern and moment in the larger field of education and in society today.

The outcome of the debate on these issues, especially that of the role and the fate of the intellect in American education, is clearly of major significance. As the authors write in the Preface, "Intellect most cogently represents the practices and artifacts that go by the name of 'culture.' But too many are fearful of intellect, possibly as elitist, amoral, or immaterial. We hope that the consideration that follows will help people understand why the fate of intellect will decide whether or not a true education can arise in the institution of schooling." This is a question of critical importance, and this is a book worthy of that question.

James H. Borland

REFERENCES

Howley, A., Howley, C. B., and Pendarvis, E. D. (1986). *Teaching gifted children: Principles and strategies*. Boston, MA: Little, Brown and Company.

Pendarvis, E. D., Howley, A. A., and Howley, C. B. (1990). *The abilities of gifted children*. Englewood Cliffs, NJ: Prentice Hall.

Preface

The fate of intellect is the principal idea in *Out of Our Minds* because we have for so long worried about how Americans school gifted children. Our interpretation draws on our experiences in working with academically able children, their families, their teachers, and the schools they attend. It also emerges from our own experiences as students in schools and as parents. But this book is not about gifted education in the usual way, as a variety of "instructional technology"; rather, it interprets the intellectual and cultural contexts of gifted education.

We have been troubled all along by how difficult it is for American schools to respond appropriately to the gifted. In seeking to explain why schooling so seldom does what it ought to do *even for bright students from advantaged circumstances*, we have been led to consider how and why U.S. schooling fails to care for intellect and develop the talents of all children. It is past time, in our view, to consider gifted education in the wider context of educational purpose. Thus, our more general topic is schooling, and why it is as it is, and what ought to change.

With few exceptions, however, the most widely considered proposals for making schools better have *nothing* to do with education. Instead, they are about greed — corporate, state, and individual. If we could admit more widely that this is the covert aim of schooling, more of us might experience an anger that leads us to resist such influence. But, as some of the sources in this book insist, we are rapidly losing the ability to talk about such things as greed and its relation to our own intellectual and moral well-being. The fault, in part, is our schooling. In this book we pose an alternative in stewardship of the intellect. This doesn't sound very practical, but it is of much greater worth than a relentlessly instrumental schooling in which greed deflects every higher purpose.

We all had good teachers, after all; we remember who they were and what they did for us. They respected our minds, whatever state of disorder or confusion reigned inside. They helped us understand difficult matters. They disclosed things to us that were hidden before. And they extended themselves in just these ways toward many more students, and through such generosity modeled an alternative to greed. This is what stewardship of the intellect looks like in the institution of schooling. We find considerable hope in the fact that many of us *do* experience good teaching even with things the way they are.

These brief statements simplify matters too much for people particularly concerned with education, which is why we offer the longer interpretation between these covers. We have been writing this book for at least 10 years, and maybe much longer than that, maybe since we were adolescents trying to make some sense of things in three quite different American high schools. Though obscurely, this book represents who we are now and how we got that way. It captures the anger and arrogance that permit us to write about these matters at all. But that anger and arrogance ought not to disguise who we are in ordinary life: We have regular jobs, we have the usual troubles, we are too seldom able to do the right thing in terms that approach what we truly believe. We bite our tongues too often, despite the sharpness of our critique in this book. The dilemma we are writing about is our own.

AN INTRODUCTION TO THE STORY WE TELL

Our previous books were textbooks. Such books are designed exclusively for a captive audience. The object in writing textbooks is to give a detailed summary of a certain literature—in our case, and for the most part, empirical studies of gifted education. The role of interpretation is limited mostly to explaining the results of individual studies, combined with an effort to integrate results in a way that might help readers grasp important themes in the research. Judgment comes into play, but the form of the textbook imposes a variety of stringent limits on expression. Much more heartache than might be imagined goes into forging from one's own experience and commitments textbooks that sound so remote and neutral.

Out of Our Minds is an entirely different affair, however. Here, the emphasis is on interpretation, though we hope that we have also provided a fair account of how matters stand in the world. We cannot be certain, though. We have come to this task with assumptions and commitments little different from those with which we approached the writing of textbooks, but our object here is much more ambitious and much more personally based.

In this book we aim to present a cultural reckoning from one perspective (ours); other such accounts of the place of intellect in American schooling are not merely possible, they are essential. Our words—considered as best we can consider them—are part of a conversation begun long ago and that must continue well into the future. Readers are part of this conversation, even if they write not a word, because the conversation continues in their minds, and they draw others into it as they think, and speak, and act — and as they labor in schools.

This work rests on some premises, which parallel the chapter-by-chapter organization, and that should be made clear at the outset in deference to our readers. The premises disclose our commitments and also our limitations.

First, we like to think of schools as the institutions charged with caring for the intellect. For many reasons the phrase "like to think" is a necessary qualification, for it does not seem to us that what we like to think is usually the case. Schools, it seems, are doing something other than caring for intellect. (Chapter 1 attempts to explain what intellect is and how it differs from intelligence, and why it is so important to a true education.)

But as for the dissonance between what we "like to think" and what we happen to see in school practice: It is the essential motive for this work. It is incredible to us that schools (of all places!) refuse to claim an intellectual mission. Some few do, of course, but schooling is a system; it is more, and also much less, than the sum of its parts. Schools, lacking even the autonomy of individuals, rarely have options or the wherewithal to exercise them. They "behave" as part of the system of which, indeed, they *are* a part.

And so, our second premise is that the system of schooling is so constructed — so arranged — as to devalue intellect. We might, further, claim that schooling quite concertedly debases intellect. This shortcoming is most striking, for us, in the case of the gifted. The institution of schooling, we believe, functions more to "socialize" students than to nurture intellect (even in the case of those very students it identifies as most talented), as if an unusual intellectual capacity must be deflected, hobbled, and normalized for officially sanctioned purposes. The fault, we stress, lies in the things to which the economy, the polity, and the society ascribe value; in short, in the organization of production, governance, and social relations, rather than in individuals. (Chapter 2 elaborates this interpretation; some reviewers complained that early drafts of this chapter constituted "teacher bashing," and this is not at all our intention. But the result of the organization of schooling is that the intellect of teachers, as of students, is neither widely valued nor widely cultivated.) It is important, in the context of this critique, to remember also that individuals will always persist in developing their idiosyncracies, even when schooling disrespects their capacity to do so. There is, in short, always an objective basis for hope.

We also believe — and this is a predictable premise for a work in this series — that unusual degrees of talent exist and can be taken into account rather early in students' schooling, though a surprising number of educators dispute this view. But we also think that the largely verbal abilities we call "giftedness" are rarely, if ever, inborn. Rather, they develop rapidly in young children who have the good fortune to be born into affluent homes or homes where the adults sponsor certain sorts of verbal expression. Though the institution of schooling also credits the existence of unusual talent, its response is oddly anti-intellectual. Schooling more often destroys than nurtures talent, and this observation applies particularly to the talents of able children. (Chapter 3 considers the ways in which such destruction occurs.)

Can anyone fail to believe that life in the United States is afflicted with class, race, ethnic, and gender troubles? Probably not. The source and significance of such troubles comprise the substance of much debate, and our fourth premise reflects where we stand on the issue. Some people, probably many, would locate the source of troubles in an unchangeable human nature that encompasses evil, or at best seeks to maximize individual pleasure. Others would see the troubles only as evidence of poor social engineering. We, by contrast, locate the source of such troubles in the goal of economic dominion characteristic of (if not necessarily endemic to) capitalism.

Michael Apple (1993, p. 236) sums up the threat that this goal for public education poses for the commonweal:

> This transformation [of the purposes of education in the last 15 years] involves a major shift — one that Dewey would have shuddered at — in which democracy becomes an economic, not a political, concept and where the idea of the public good withers at its very roots.

Our concern over the fate of intellect has much to do with the public good, and, therefore, with America's class, race, ethnic, and gender troubles. (Chapter 4 considers issues of poverty, racism, and sexism particularly as they pertain to the schooling of bright working-class and minority students.)

For us, intellect is a social construct rather than an individual one. Culture is the source that feeds the intellect; meanings constructed across generations are the root of culture. Consequently, if the bonds between the generations weaken dramatically, intellect and culture will fail.

Yet intellect and culture are matters critical — if nearly invisible — to the public interest. We take a "constructivist" view of culture, acknowledging that people can and do make meaning wherever they are and in much of their work and labor (and this is our fifth premise). Intellect can meet with environments hostile, benign, or nurturant to it. Schooling seems to constitute a hostile environment for intellect and for culture. (Chapter 5 considers the intellectual potential of schooling in the context of culture generally and the culture of the United States in particular.) One warning is in order here: Though a small minority of intellectuals construct luminous meanings, we also recognize, with Jacques Barzun, that intellectuals are among the chief enemies of intellect.

Finally, we believe in imagination. That is where we can find alternatives to the present troubles. No one can be sure of the actions that would lead predictably to the realization of imagined alternatives, though convention requires discussions like ours to frame specific recommendations directed toward the immediate improvement of practice. But our recommendations tell no one what to do. The practice of pedagogy is action, and, as the philosopher Hannah Arendt reminds us, the results of action are indeterminate.

Most official schemes for the reform of schools, with few exceptions, are myopic about action. The proposals do, however, make quite clear what politicians and bureaucrats want from schooling. But what they generally want, schooling constructed to support economic dominion, is undemocratic, anti-intellectual, and an affront to human potential. (Chapter 6 presents the ideas that we think could serve as a basis for more thoughtful and more democratic education, in which the institutions of schooling guide and support a true education.)

What of our method? What view do we take of research? Probably we come closest to the view of the philosopher Michel Foucault in that we acknowledge a variety of "games of truth" (ways of knowing according to certain conventions). We are, however, convinced that positivist, empirical research is not the certain path to truth its proponents have claimed during most of this century. Such research fragments study into such small parts that sense can no longer be made of the objects of study.

The intellectual woes of our era, we think, can in large measure be ascribed to the combination of "reductionism" and arrogance characteristic of the overwhelming bulk of research studies. We have conducted such studies ourselves, playing by the applicable rules. Such studies are amusing — even interesting — to conduct and to examine; but too much that *is* true escapes their narrow focus. Virtually *all* quantitative studies of schooling should be regarded as belonging to this way of knowing. Ultimately, the way is inadequate, in itself, for constructing meaning.

Something more is called for, we think, if the construction of meaningfulness is what we aim for, something along the lines of cultural critique. Our method, like Barzun's "cultural criticism," is one without an official "methodology," but it is understood to be part of the extended conversation that considers meaning. We *are* cleaving to a tradition, then, but it is one that defies an ordinary sense of "method" on the terms of social science. We think of this tradition as "interpretation" — an extended explication of our understanding of the meanings of the writings (including research studies, when applicable) and issues we think important. Of course, interpretation of this sort constructs meaning in terms of what we find to be important; it obviously reflects our commitments.

Nonetheless, there is warrant in our discussion, though it is not a t- or an F-test, an effect size, or a beta weight; nor is it any particular "hermeneutic methodology." The warrant lies in the meanings approached, the sense made out of the discourse and substance of the circumstances of schooling we uncover. Some readers will not find this warrant adequate, and others will not find the interpretation compelling. This eventuality is in the nature of conversation. We do not intend to establish final answers nor to put forth instrumental directives. We merely wish to share our understanding of how schooling might shelter and inspire the intellect of its students and its people. As part of an ongoing conversation, our sharing is, of course, both an invocation of and an invitation to more extended debate.

This work is also the result of our own conversations and shared reflections—shared for nearly 15 years now—about schooling, children, and what sense life might make. It is true that each of us understands these matters differently from the others, and differently now than at times past, and doubtless differently from times to come. To clarify this temporal and intellectual separation, we want to indicate a little bit about who did what in the creation of this work.

Together we outlined the structure of the book, agreeing on topics and ideas to treat, and we assigned lead authorship for each chapter. Craig was lead author for Chapters 1 and 5, Aimee for Chapters 2 and 6, and Eddy for Chapters 3 and 4. With rough drafts in hand, second authors assisted with revision and heavy editing. Craig and Aimee gave the entire manuscript its final edit before it was submitted to Teachers College Press.

Intellect most cogently represents the practices and artifacts that go by the name of "culture." But too many are fearful of intellect, possibly as elitist, amoral, or immaterial. We hope that the consideration that follows will help people understand why the fate of intellect will decide whether or not a true education can arise in the institution of schooling.

Craig B. Howley
Aimee Howley
Edwina D. Pendarvis

Acknowledgments

Thanks to Jim Borland for inviting this manuscript and to Brian Ellerbeck for putting up with us. We also want to thank Linda Spatig and John Covaleskie for their intellectual and moral support for the work on Chapter 2. Thanks also to Carol Ascher for wise counsel at a critical juncture and Gene Glass for his invitation to publish an early version of some of this material with *Education Policy Analysis Archives*.

CHAPTER 1

The Origins of Anti-Intellectualism in U.S. Schools

Craig B. Howley and Aimee Howley

Public elementary and secondary schools in the United States apply the term "intellectually gifted" to their most academically promising students. The practice derives from the conviction that public schooling does not serve able students particularly well, and gifted education is the formal attempt to change that circumstance. The mechanism, in most cases, for determining which students are intellectually gifted is to administer an intelligence test. Although the history of these and similar tests is a record of misconception and misapplication, other methods of assessing intellectual giftedness have not yet produced more reliable or valid measures of intellectual potential. The continuing debate about intelligence tests, however, overlooks the substance of intellectual purpose and worth.

We can bring this substance into view by examining the differences between intelligence and intellect, differences that bear on the potential of schooling as a means of developing talent in the U.S. To consider this issue is to deal more with culture and ideology, however, than with the empirical investigations of the construct of intelligence, the varieties of talent, or the methods proposed for the schooling of gifted students.

THE DISTINCTION BETWEEN INTELLIGENCE AND INTELLECT

Intelligence and intellect represent dramatically different concepts. Because "intellect" is a term seldom considered with respect to K–12 schooling, we wish to highlight the differences before interpreting them in greater detail. *Intelligence* concerns practical performances; it is quantifiable, individualistic, and instrumental. Intelligence has been developed as a concept to suggest inborn qualities of mental superiority or inferiority that can be passed genetically from generation to generation. These latter features of the concept are in the process of reform; whether or not the concept itself will survive is not yet clear. *Intellect* concerns thoughtful (principally literate) understandings; it is a quality, not a quantity; and it is cultural and expressive. Intellect, in sharp contrast to intelligence, requires intensive nurture, in individuals certainly, but, more importantly, throughout a culture. It cannot survive otherwise.

The possibility of an education for intellect occupies hardly any place in discussions of public policy (Berliner, 1992). Even care for literacy seldom figures in policy or classroom practice (Brown, 1993). Moreover, in the U.S., intelligence is valuable only as it is efficiently trained in the possession of facts, skills, and attitudes that will serve an agenda of economically instrumental ends.[1]

Some observers believe that schooling in the United States reflects the presence of a strong anti-intellectual current in all realms of life in this country (e.g., Adler, 1993; Barzun, 1989; Bell, 1976; Hofstadter, 1963; Lasch, 1991). Others have implied that public schools are not especially hospitable places for bright students (e.g., Coleman, 1961; A. Howley, 1986; Wiener, 1950) or for intellectual dispositions generally (e.g., Brown, 1993; Katz, 1993). Such insights have received little attention from people directly concerned with gifted education, however.

Instead, two arguments typically justify the special accommodations schooling extends to those it identifies as most intellectually able. The first argument asserts that schools must meet the special educational "needs" of gifted students. The second asserts that gifted children are the nation's greatest natural resource. Both arguments serve anti-intellectual functions.

In the first argument, the greater the number of needs capable of being specified, the more nearly will schools be in a position to respond to the unique characteristics of each individual. The unfortunate upshot is that any and all "needs" thus specified automatically become worthy of realization. Israel Sheffler (1985, p. 15) identifies the plight into which this unexamined basis of need casts educators and students: "the myth of uniformly valuable potentials." Needs proliferate to the point of excess, and the relationship of instruction to academic interests disappears altogether. Sheffler points out that potentials (i.e., needs) not only vary in worth (some precipitate evil; some are trivial), but that individuals may possess conflicting potentials, compatible in an individual only so long as they are not both realized. Indeed, many supposed needs have nothing at all to do with the intellect (e.g., O'Tuel, 1983); they may even constitute a threat to intellect.

Because the second argument (i.e., that giftedness is a national resource) compels a far more widespread acceptance than the first, its anti-intellectual basis is perhaps more difficult — and more important — to grasp. The national resource argument reflects "human capital theory," which maintains that what people know and are able to do helps account for international differences in productivity and "competitiveness." People, in short, exist to serve the national security interest — whether this is construed in economic or military terms.

This argument is more dangerous than the first. It runs deeper, it is accepted more widely throughout society, it is backed by powerful organizations, and it manipulates the patriotic sentiments of the general public. Its offense is greater. Whereas the logic of the first argument forestalls decisions about value, the logic of the second recasts judgments of value as judgments of utility. It enjoins citizens to regard themselves primarily as producers and consumers, and it prods the state to develop schooling in that image (Apple, 1993).

Nonetheless, the goal of restoring the nation's worldwide economic dominion — even following the collapse of the Soviet state and sphere of influence — is not one that schooling can realize. Politicians, business people, and citizens alike confront a world system in which national sovereignty is increasingly less important (DeYoung, 1989), and one that is dominated economically by transnational firms, markets, and financial mechanisms. Boli, Ramirez, and Meyer (1985) point out that such international forces make mass education look very similar regardless of national identity.

In the U.S., the influence of the human capital ideology is pervasive, and it is supported, albeit in different ways, by both ends of the political spectrum, liberals as well as conservatives (Shea, 1989). The powerful supporters, moreover, strive hard to raise their views to the status of common sense. Hence, the human capital argument appears in public service announcements on radio and television (e.g., "Education *is* the bottom line!") and in official reports by the dozens (e.g., *Nation at Risk, America 2000, America's Choice: High Skills or Low Wages, Time for Results*, and so on). Nonetheless, the position that schooling should be a tool for exploiting students — *any* students — as natural resources rests on questionable ethical and metaphysical assumptions. Indeed, the comparison with natural resources should give us particular pause because we have a long history of squandering such resources.

A curious chain of transformations associated with the development of industrial society and mass schooling has undermined our capacity to care for the intellect. Boli and colleagues (1985) indicate that such transformations are occurring worldwide, but that they are most firmly established in developed countries: Education is understood to be schooling, literacy is understood as "employability," employability is understood as the foundation of human capital accumulation, and human capital is understood as the foundation of national economic security. This ideological chain preserves for education little "higher" purpose, which now figures as private taste and even as sentimentality (Bell, 1973).

As a guide to educational policy and value, human capital arguments intend, we argue, to inflict damage to intellect so that talent can be directed to instrumental ends. In the long term, educational institutions, under the sway of such instrumentalism, will serve both individuals and society badly (Brown, 1993). Our consideration of the origins of anti-intellectualism in U.S. schools and our interpretation of the role of intellect in talent development, therefore, probe this instrumentalism in particular detail.

Intelligence and Intellect

The terms "intelligence" and "intellect" first appeared in written English about the year 1390. Originally synonyms, by 1430 writers had already begun to distinguish usage of the two terms, with "intellect" referring to the faculty of the mind (or soul) that knows *by reason rather than by intuition* (i.e., not by emotion, feeling, or sensing). They used "intelligence," then as now, to mean "degree of understanding," and, especially, *superior quickness of understanding* (Oxford English Dictionary, 1928/1971). The term "intelligence" applied equally to animals and humans, whereas the term "intellect" applied only to humans. No one credits dogs with the possession of intellect, for instance. Intellect represents the complexity of understanding, critique, and imagination of which the human mind is capable. Already in 1430, intellect had to do with what passes between minds and generations of humans, for reason (unlike intuition) concerns explicit, negotiated meaningfulness.

Centuries of use have made the original distinctions sharper still, especially since the advent of science in the modern world (Adler, 1993). To specify "degree of understanding," educators have, for nearly 100 years, measured intelligence as an actual quantity. In this usage, "intelligence" refers to a student's potential for academic work, even if, in specifying educational need, eventual practice sidesteps academics. The observed variation in this quantity is widely, if mistakenly (Sheffler, 1985), presumed to be inborn. And there has even been much heated debate about the extent to which "degree of understanding" can be passed genetically from parent to child. The debate is fueled by the important political and ethical agendas that depend on the question. The rightist position in the debate seems to desire confirmation of a "natural aristocracy" of merit that would justify the unequal distribution of society's goods. The leftist position is inspired largely by abhorrence of such a determination.

As a result of quantifying intelligence, however, psychological expertise originally determined that some students possessed intelligence in very small measure and, also, that most students were not very apt academically. In consequence, we have—according to Barzun, Lasch, and others—run our schools as if most students could not understand very much, and as if we were not sure what to do with the few who supposedly could.

In comparison to intelligence, intellect, as an idea at least, suffered neglect. The demise, Adler points out, began in the 1600s, as the materialist viewpoint began to exercise dominion ("intellectual dominion," in fact) over the realm of thought.

In the modern era, "mind" has obscured meanings that we intend to help rehabilitate in the term "intellect." If you search for contemporary works that discuss intellect, you will most often encounter a discussion of mind. Mind is conceived as an adjunct function of the brain; it represents the mystery (of thinking and thoughts) that remains when scientific knowledge of brain structure and function is withdrawn. This view has reconstituted mind as a feature, albeit an obscure one, of the brain, particularly of an individual brain. (Note that such a treatment of mind conforms to the idea of degree of intelligence as an inborn property of individuals.)

The brain, in this view, is an intriguing clockwork that holds the secrets of a constant human nature; to understand the brain is to see clearly what form of education is proper. Hence, even putative knowledge of the brain serves as the ultimate warrant for well-intentioned pedagogical daredevils (such as those who would construe math instruction differently for girls and boys on the basis of supposed neural differences). Some observers, like Frank Smith, mock the position; Smith (1990) calls on educators to "put the brain in charge of its own affairs." This is just a figure of speech, for Smith draws not at all on brain research. He is simply aware of the fetishism of the brain.

The disappointment in all this fanfare about the brain is that understanding the brain does not help us construct or grasp the *meaning* of our thoughts at all! The brain has become an object to which its legions of devotees irrationally attribute great power. In the meantime intellect has nearly vanished from consideration.

Intellect, like intelligence and mind, might in the course of its history have been understood as a personal attribute. But it is, in fact, not taken as inborn, and, though greater or lesser "intellects" seem to exist, no one troubles too much about measuring the degrees of difference.

Intellect can be distinguished from intelligence in an additional important way. To exist at all, intellect, unlike intelligence, requires nurture. Lots of nurture, and over a long period. Great intelligence, by contrast, is self-disclosing, emerging by virtue of its own force in the behavior of its possessor. This is part of the reason that advocacy of an intellectual education is so difficult in the United States; we have the sense that natural endowment *ought* to be left alone to flourish or founder in its own way. We have no such misconceptions about intellect, even now. It is perhaps too expensive to nurture.

Despite the nurture it requires, intellect is neither "achievement" nor "attainment" as commonly understood. Both achievement (test results) and attainment (credentials) are testimonials. Testimonials of this sort are a proxy for realms of knowledge—skills and meanings—that derive their integrity from the care that a culture accords intellect. One may speak of this care and all that it encompasses as the *institution of intellect*. When the institution of intellect is weak, inferences about knowledge from mere testimonials become particularly unreliable (Barzun, 1959; Bell, 1973).

Evidence of such unreliability came mainly from conservatives throughout the 1980s; they complained that high school and college diplomas verified little that was useful to restoring America's global economic competitiveness—that, in fact, the quality of graduates had declined. Unreliable testimonials, in this way, appear to threaten the instrumental heart of the human capital scheme. Hence, among other things, the reforms of the 1980s and 1990s called repeatedly for greater "rigor": new kinds of testing, more consistent testing, and diplomas that were more difficult to get.

But rigor can no more rehabilitate the institution of intellect than cold showers can eliminate drug addiction. It can characterize good pedagogy and bad; it can be applied for the wrong reasons; and it can, and often does, enforce thoughtlessness and silence critique.

Even as attempts to make schools "accountable" and to "restore" academic rigor proceed, the most common view remains instrumental: The principal role of academic learning should be to serve economic ends. Official commissions and blue-ribbon panels have seldom taken *any* other view (Berliner, 1992). Schooling aims, as it has for a very long time, to inculcate just those habits, attitudes, and skills that legitimate it in the eyes of powerful economic interests (Brown, 1993; Commission on the Reorganization of Secondary Education, 1918).

The distinction between an instrumental and an intellectual view of schooling is captured in a clever passage of dialogue by Frank Moretti (1993, p. 125). It goes like this:

> When forced to put it [i.e., the purpose of education] succinctly to my students, I say that each person under the best circumstances takes up the challenge of learning what he or she has become without having chosen it and in the process sees new worlds and lays claim to a new freedom.

Care of the intellect, in this view, has rather little directly to do with rigor—or its lack—in mass schooling. Part of the reason is that serious educational consideration of intellect pertains almost exclusively to higher education. Intellect is considered esoteric: It is not for children and it is certainly not for everyone. We take a far different view.

Literacy and Intellect

Confining intellect to the university, we think, is part of the problem. All people possess minds capable of an intellectual turn; more, intellectual artifacts — books, music, art, and meaningful creations from all times and places — constitute a world that belongs to people by right of inheritance (Arendt, 1958). People can be separated from this world only through intellectual deprivation. Under the regime of schooling fashioned to accumulate human capital, such deprivation can become commonplace; it can also invade the university (Barrow, 1990).

A true education, by contrast, *must base its actions on respect for the intellect.* And respect for students — at all levels of their schooling — ultimately derives from respect for the intellect.

Such respect for students has several sources. First, it must entail respect for the *interests of intellect*: contemplation, understanding, meaning, interpretation, and critique. Second, it must entail respect for the accumulating *artifacts of intellect*, especially as embodied in meaningful written expression (see the subsequent discussion of literacy and intellect). These two are prerequisite, and they are often lacking in the institutions of mass education (increasingly including the universities). Finally, respect for the *intellectual potential of all students* is a pedagogical necessity that arises from the other two. In the typical circumstance, all three forms of respect are lacking (e.g., Brown, 1993; Smith, 1990).

Winchester (1987, p. 23), in a discussion of literacy and intellect, charts the scope of intellect:

> The notion of intellect maps out both a realm of interest and a set of powers or dispositions. . . . It is on disciplines that intellect is properly exercised, since the object of intellection is the increase in knowledge, both personally and collectively, of a certain kind or kinds.

Barzun puts it more tersely. For him intellect is simply "the form intelligence takes in the artificial products we call learning" (Barzun, 1959, p. 216). Though Barzun's apparent confidence in intelligence (i.e., confidence that it is a phenomenon of nature rather than a social construct) is more difficult to share at the end of the twentieth century, these two accounts show a key feature of intellect missing in accounts of mind and intelligence: Intellect participates in a dialogue among individual minds and the historical community of learning. Intellect covers a domain that the construct of "intelligence" and the notion of "mind" omit entirely. [2]

A person who participates in the historical community of learning reveals intellect as a turn of mind — a disposition — whether that person is an "intellectual" or not. We would argue that cultivation of such a disposition over the long term is what makes an intellectual, however. Most discussions of intellectuals examine, not intellect, but social roles (e.g., Brym, 1980; Gouldner, 1979). Intellectuals are not those with an intellectual disposition, but jobholders whose jobs involve mental labor — information specialists, academics, lawyers, and various species of media personalities and opinion manipulators. Some of the people in these roles may exhibit an intellectual turn of mind; by and large, they do not (Moretti, 1993).

Accounts of anti-intellectualism generally focus on intellectuals as the victims. The paragon intellectual, in this view, is the university scholar, and Hofstadter takes this approach in *Anti-Intellectualism in American Life.* Barzun, on the other hand, counted university scholars ("by choice or impressment pedants") among the three greatest enemies of the intellect. The two views overlap, for the state of the intellect in the university — as Barzun understood — derives from the disregard of intellect prevalent in the culture at large. But, in fact, attacks on researchers' bad language and reductionism (the tendency to fragment scholarship to the point where meaningfulness is lost) have little effect, and not because the accusations are untrue. The bad language and intellectual triviality are more than vanity. They are part of a larger social apparatus that endorses certain views of the world, debases others, and legitimates the deployment of power (Lyotard, 1979/1984; Postman, 1992). Meaningfulness and criticism are not functional features of this apparatus.

Despite the shortcomings of those who occupy the social role of "intellectual," care for the historical community of learning is most evident in the best work of the mind of one who is truly intellectually disposed. This work might take form in writing, or in the building of houses, the manufacture of machinery, in speech, or even in relationships. The intellect is active even when not in view. Still, the intellect that shapes such works would be most accessible to others in writing (or some system of widely understood notation), so that it could enter widely into the historical community of learning (Winchester, 1987).

Thus, in terms of formal learning (which must concern us most immediately in this book), *literacy* is the basis of the historical community of learning. Literacy for this purpose involves the habitual use of, and affection for, text as the chief tool of thought. Literacy is the *favorable disposition toward and habit of engaging the mind with text to construct meaning* (cf. Brym, 1980; Eisner, 1983; Hofstadter, 1963; Storr, 1988; Winchester, 1987). Literacy of this sort is the handmaiden of intellect (much as mathematics is said to be the handmaiden of science). It is the tool through which minds most often work, and the institution of intellect becomes stronger or weaker as a people maintains it through literacy. Whereas a few individuals may become "intellects," many people must develop intellect as a "turn of mind" if the institution of intellect is to flourish.

Intellect can most certainly operate without literacy, but it does so at great disadvantage. One's associates in the real world (like oneself) have a limited view of matters that concern heart, mind, and soul. The perspective of one's own times have similar limits. But with literacy, intellect has a way to struggle beyond the limits of personal and time-bound association. Literacy offers the mind the chance to extend thought into experience, to impose on experience and to represent reality in forms it would not otherwise take. Eisner (1983, p. 50), for example, writes of literacy as "the generic process of securing and expressing meaning within patterned forms of expression." The patterns to which Eisner refers are those of the historical community of learning; they represent meaningful traditions. The responsibility of intellect, and of minds that take an intellectual turn, is to develop and extend those traditions.

Intelligent students and "little literacies." We must point out that the sort of literacy considered above differs dramatically from the variety of little "literacies" in the documents that badger schools to do more on behalf of international competitiveness. Each of these little literacies is a set of skills (useful as human capital) that comprises functional behavior of one kind or another (e.g., from keyboarding data to finding information).[3]

Awareness is the object of little literacies. Beyond them, lie proficiency and mastery. Little literacies are a first step, therefore, in developing the skills of intelligent students. The gifted, in this view, "need" to become proficiently or masterfully skillful, if they are to solve the many problems that confront society. This function is in keeping with their role as natural resource: Fabricating clever solutions to problems is an urgent charge, which, for the sake of efficiency, must fall to intelligent students.

Problem-solving is not a task for the intellect, but for the intelligence. The search for what is practical, and its separation from what *seems* less practical, in the long run also excludes what is most meaningful — including the development of minds with an intellectual turn.

COMPETING VIEWS OF THE POTENTIAL OF SCHOOLING

Neglect of intellect is pervasive in America. This anti-intellectualism is misunderstood, however, if taken principally as disregard of intellectuals. Indeed, the vast literature on intellectuals as a class suggests that they find it very easy to validate the interests of power over those of the intellect (Barrow, 1990; Barzun, 1959; Bell, 1973; Gouldner, 1979; Howley & Hartnett, 1994). Anti-intellectualism consists rather of disregard of the intellect, and the machinery of schooling is a key instrument of this disregard. The machinery of schooling diverts our attention to technical issues: intelligence(s), assessment schemes, and facts and skills (even "thinking skills" and "metacognitive skills").

Thoughtful educators, it is true, have always considered the importance of critique and meaning in schooling. The astute have also recognized the role that K–12 schooling has played in the twentieth century in *subverting* critique and meaning (e.g., Arendt, 1954/1968; Brown, 1993; Goodman, 1964; Greene, 1982; Lasch, 1991; Smith, 1990).

Official reform efforts cannot embrace care of the intellect because such care is profoundly at odds with the instrumental governing spirit of American education: the distribution of qualifications and skills in the service of the economy. The official plans seek to recast the "entire system" along "competitive" lines: standards, privatization, still more economic instrumentality, and heightened intellectual cynicism (Apple, 1993; Moretti, 1993). No chinks (for the intellect) will be left unfilled. Whether the skills are basic or advanced, whether the thinking is critical or creative, the object is to harness the ("most precious") national resource called human capital in the service of economic "competitiveness." The state promotes systemic reform and restructuring (Sashkin & Egermeier, 1993) as the incantations to bring forth the magic. But the only system brought under scrutiny by the state is the system of schooling. The political-economic, social, and cultural systems that created and must continue to sustain the system of schooling are not of critical concern. The aims of systemic reform have been determined from the start (Apple, 1993).

Blame for the poverty of the American school experience is generally misplaced in our view. Blame usually targets such circumstances as the emergence of the Information Age in the twenty-first century (innocuous); lack of rigor (authoritarian); inattention from social engineers (managerial); deterioration of social bonds (communitarian); incompetence of educators (spiteful); meddling from bureaucracies and legislatures (entrepreneurial); insufficient meddling from bureaucracies and legislatures (regulatory); bad curricula and textbooks (artifactual); and racism, sexism, and classism in general (egalitarian). We blame disregard for the intellect.

Schools *should* be the institutions charged with care for the intellect. But the way we run them, the things they do to children and young people and teachers, the voices they silence and the visions they obscure—these constitute prima facie evidence for our case. The lack of regard is not the invention of the schools or of the people who work there, least of all students and teachers. Students are innocent, at least as they enter school. But it seems that schooling, in general, rapidly and thoroughly socializes students to anti-intellectualism and has been doing so now for a very long time (e.g., Coleman, 1961; French, 1993). The literature on teacher socialization (presented in the next chapter) also provides compelling evidence to this effect.

Most Americans, and most educators, forget that local and national cultures surround and infuse the schools. Whatever happens there has its source outside the schools and outside the profession. Moreover, the prerogatives of the political economy, through which class and ethnic rifts are indeed manipulated, fail to explain fully why the poverty of the school experience is so *pervasive*. The children of the affluent, as well as the children of the poor, those identified as gifted and those not identified, all encounter an upbringing that schooling impoverishes along similar lines. On the reasonable presumption that schooling *should* be the institution that cares for the intellect, the failure is evident and it can be characterized as anti-intellectualism. Teachers are not at fault. What we expect of schooling, of one another, and of our children is. We expect them to be good soldiers and good jobholders. Least of all do we want them to question this fate.

If one assumed, and it is a logical assumption, that schooling were indeed the institution charged with care of the intellect, one would be puzzled by the evident anti-intellectual atmosphere pervading the educational system. We *are* puzzled, still, but we have concluded that anti-intellectualism is more than a feature of schooling: It is the principal condition of education in America.

But one cannot dismiss schooling as a lost cause. Care for the intellect depends on care for the organizations that inevitably shape the intellect, even through disregard. As Arendt (1954/1968) points out, a necessary condition of responsibility for children is responsibility for the world, including its institutions.

Public schools are chief among these institutions in the modern and into the postmodern world. For this reason alone we need to examine more closely major views of the potential of schooling put forward in the United States. What are those major views? What issues are important to each? And where is care for the intellect located in each? Our framework for this examination is to look at how each of five views deals with three qualities valued in common by most Americans.

Three American Values

Americans value three qualities that inform visions of what schools in the United States should do: individuality, excellence, and equity (e.g.,

Bell, 1973; Gardner, 1961). Though widely valued by most Americans, these qualities are also contradictory, and differing commitments to each, in combination with one another, form the basis of competing interpretations of what schools are for.

The outcome of the competition yields the principal aims of, and agendas for changing, American schools. We will discover much about how the school establishment approaches intellect by regarding how the three qualities function in competing ideologies of schooling.

Briefly, an "ideology" articulates a coherent set of ideas from a particular vantage point. An ideology usually embodies an agenda more or less clearly linked to its principal ideas, values, and commitments. We distinguish five major ideologies of schooling. These five — conservative, liberal, progressive, libertarian, and critical pedagogy — vary in the degree to which they emphasize one or another of the three values. But, in the North American context, each must, and does, interpret all three qualities.[4] The distinctions among (and also within) ideologies can be quite complex, as the following examples suggest.

For example, from the *conservative* perspective of human capital theory, schools should provide students with the means to make rational decisions about the investment of their time and talents in cultivating marketable skills (e.g., Marland, 1972). The *liberal* ideology of schooling, while valuing skills, takes the view that inequality sets a limit to what many students can achieve in school. According to many *progressive* educators, by contrast, schools should support individuality by designing curricula to meet individual students' needs (e.g., James, 1915); and according to proponents of *critical pedagogy*, schools should nurture the development of individual potential within the context of democratic communities (see, e.g., Goodman, 1989). From a *libertarian* perspective, however, schools should cultivate individuality by enlarging the realm of students' liberties (see, e.g., Spring, 1975).

The Conservative Ideology: Social Darwinism and Human Capital

The conservative view of the potential of education in the United States originally derived from the application of Darwinian principles to the analysis of society. Social Darwinists — like Herbert Spencer and William Graham Sumner — equated social competition (especially the competition of a market economy) with the biological processes of natural selection (Goodman, 1989; Russett, 1976).

From this perspective, individualism affirmed the individual's "natural right" to participate in life's contest. This was a significant reinterpretation of the traditional body of natural (i.e., "inalienable") rights, for example, the rights to life, liberty, and the pursuit of property. In this new view, individuals' innate differences determined the outcome of the contest (i.e., thereby alienating the "inalienable"). According to Russett (1976, p. 98), social Darwinists believed that "all men were created unequal, for inequality was a law of nature. Man vied with man to win the rewards of nature, and victory went to the fit." Among strict social Darwinists, the role of public education was to provide a setting for natural contest, but, if taken too far, schooling could well be socially counterproductive. Spencer, for example, believed that public education, like other social services, would *interfere* with the natural processes of social selection. Schooling might therefore get in the way of naturally unfolding social progress (DeYoung, 1989; Russett, 1976). Social Darwinism was an ideology that accorded well with the realities of nineteenth-century laissez-faire capitalism.

Public educators in the early twentieth century did, however, embrace the premises of social Darwinism (Gould, 1981). For them, public schools were a theater in which the struggle among unequals could be more efficiently managed. Social selection, as a natural process, inevitably wasted some talent that might otherwise be profitably redeemed. Schools could do better, by grading, sorting, and tracking the various kinds of talents into programs best suited to them. Society, after all, needed all sorts of talents. Schools could accomplish the task of adapting talents to society's needs more efficiently—more scientifically—than nature. This perspective was common sense among educators of the early decades of the century (Callahan, 1962).

Scientific management of public schools was, in fact, a fad of this era, but it was an influential fad, responsible for laying down the resilient "factory model" of schooling (Callahan, 1962; Tyack, 1974). The scientific managers carved out a new and enduring role for schools with special reference to students' unequal merits. Schools were henceforth responsible for *distributing* human capital to the most deserving. According to Spring (1986, p. 224), "The schools were to create a society based on merit by objectively selecting and preparing students for their ideal places in the social order."

The improved technology of education (e.g., age-grade placement, psychological testing, ability grouping) helped to establish this new "meritocratic" function for schools. At the same time, conservative educators could argue that technology would make instruction more humane by "individualizing" it.

The legacy. Conservative educators continue to adhere to this view, boosting the value of excellence and interpreting progress toward equity as an aim dependent on excellence. Reform proposals in the 1980s (e.g., National

Commission on Excellence in Education, 1983) equated excellence in education with *economic competitiveness* in the world market (DeYoung, 1989; Howley, 1991; Shea, 1989). The new twist in this interpretation was the call for urgent response to international conditions. The reform proposals devoted scant discussion to the needs of poor and minority students (Passow, 1984; Tippeconnic, 1989).

The new proposals narrowed the mission of schools, even with respect to the education of the elite. In the interest of national security and economic productivity, the conservative reform proposals were intended as a *socially efficient*[5] response to talent. The emphasis is on technical expertise, tempered by the rote knowledge of a finite cultural canon (e.g., Hirsch, 1987).

The Liberal Ideology: Equal Opportunity and Human Potential

Arriving at proposals that are remarkably like those of the conservatives (Shea, 1989), liberals nevertheless conceive the aims of education quite differently from social Darwinists and their counterparts among contemporary human capital theorists. Both conservative (e.g., Bennett, 1987) and liberal (e.g., Adler, 1982) ideologies emphasize the role of the core curriculum in promoting the aims of education. Among conservatives such a curriculum is the arena in which innate merit establishes itself in competition among students. The contest legitimates the unequal distribution of expertise on the basis of students' background characteristics (Aronowitz & Giroux, 1985).

For liberals, however, the curriculum itself promotes equity and the value of democratic ideals (e.g., Conant, 1953). Moreover, liberals believe that society can use schools to *offset the inequalities* of students' backgrounds by affording all students access to the same educational opportunities (Jencks et al., 1979). Two liberal responses to the inequities of schooling characterize this perspective. Curiously, these two responses are often framed as opposing views (e.g., Mace-Matluck, 1987).

A frequently cited — and just as frequently misunderstood — finding derived from the liberal position appears in the famous "Coleman Report" (Coleman, 1966). Coleman's study was among the first to provide conclusive evidence that background (e.g., socioeconomic status, neighborhood) exerted a *dominant influence* on children's school achievement. The finding was widely misinterpreted as a virtual scientific law, and it understandably disturbed many people. Some educators (e.g., Edmonds, 1979) took the findings to mean that schools had *practically no influence* on achievement.

Coleman and his associates (1966/1987) clearly did not intend to make such a judgment, however. In fact, they concluded that the sources of inequality of educational opportunity appear to lie first in the home itself and the cultural influences immediately surrounding the home; then they lie in the schools' ineffectiveness to free achievement from the impact of the home, and in the schools' homogeneity which perpetuates the social influences of the home and its environs.

Coleman used the results of his study to recommend that schools play an *increased* role in promoting equality. He established the following priorities for school reform [emphasis added]:

1. For those children whose family and neighborhood are educationally disadvantaged, it is important to *replace this family environment* as much as possible with an educational environment — by starting school at an earlier age, and by having a school which begins very early in the day and ends very late.
2. It is important to *reduce the social and racial homogeneity* of the school environment, so that those agents of education that do show some effectiveness — teachers and other students — are not mere replicas of the student himself. In the present organization of schools, it is the neighborhood school that most insures such homogeneity.
3. The educational *program of the school should be made more effective* than it is at present. The weakness of this program is apparent in its inability to overcome initial differences. It is hard to believe that we are so inept in educating our young that we can do no more than leave young adults in the same relative competitive positions we found them in as children. (Coleman, 1966/1987, pp. 35–36)

Another statement of the liberal position was that of "school effectiveness researchers" who set out in the early 1970s to *disprove their misinterpretations* of Coleman's findings. These researchers wanted to show that the methods used in some schools did have a positive influence on academic achievement, regardless of students' economic or cultural backgrounds (Orlich, 1989). Coleman's critics looked for things people did inside schools for poor students (so-called "process variables").[6] The schools they studied were those in which student achievement was higher than might normally be expected (e.g., Schneider & Brookover, 1974; Weber, 1971).

School effectiveness researchers discovered that such schools shared a number of common features. Further, they tended to interpret these common features as the *causes* of the schools' success with impoverished students. Although different researchers identified different commonalities, some general features seemed to recur in many studies. According to Stedman (1987, p. 215), one prevalent conclusion was that school effectiveness entailed five factors: strong leadership by the principal, particularly in instructional matters; high expectations for student achievement on the part of teachers; an emphasis on basic skills; an orderly environment; and the frequent, systematic evaluation of students.

The legacy. The shared perspective of Coleman and of the school effectiveness researchers, however, was that excellence and individuality *depended on equity.* Only through achieving equity could schools develop individuality and nurture excellence. Some liberal theorists (e.g., Gardner, 1961), however, gave somewhat greater weight to excellence. For them, equity and excellence were mutually dependent. For others, namely the progressives, individuality was more important than excellence. The progressive agenda had a pronounced effect on the aims and the practices of American education. Hence, we next examine this basically liberal perspective as a separate ideology.

The Progressive Ideology: Individualization as the Route to Equity

Like other educators with liberal commitments, the progressives believed that schooling was the most viable tool with which to extend equality throughout society. Writing predominantly in the 1920s and the 1930s, the liberal progressive educators had a profound influence on the ideology of American education, but a less pronounced effect on its practice (Cremin, 1961; Cuban, 1982).[7]

The progressive educators furthest to the political left, the social reconstructionists, maintained that progressive education would support "a social order committed to an equality of concern for all its members and to faith in human potential" (Burgess & Borrowman, 1969/1980, p. 37). According to Counts (1932/1987, p. 201), for example, "if the schools are to be really effective, they must become centers for the building, and not merely for the contemplation, of our civilization."

In order to accomplish this ambitious goal, the progressives stressed the importance of "liberating" individual children. According to Perkinson (1968, p. 187), progressive educators

> believed that once the schools helped the child realize his own particular talents and abilities, once the school "liberated" him, then he could make a more worthy contribution to the political life of the society, enriching the quality of direct democracy.

This position indicated the need for a thoroughgoing change in instructional practice. First, schools needed to replace teacher-centered (and subject-centered) pedagogy with *child-centered pedagogy.* Second, teachers needed to *encourage students to think* reflectively and critically rather than to memorize large amounts of factual information. Third, schools needed to promote more *active methods of learning and teaching*; and, finally, schools needed to emphasize the value of *manual as well as intellectual work*. This last change was imperative if schools were to treat students of all social classes as if their backgrounds and aspirations were equally important.

The legacy. Although the progressive program has influenced the radical ideology of schooling, the more significant legacy is its reflection in school practices that are prominently in the mainstream. The emphasis on the diversity of curriculum in the comprehensive high school, for example, reflects the dual progressive agenda: egalitarianism and individualization.

Cusick (1983) documents this association in his study of three comprehensive secondary schools. "The dominating element in the schools . . . was their obligation to the egalitarian ideal" (Cusick, 1983, p. 106). In effect, the elective curriculum comprehended equity, with individual students free to take whichever courses appealed to them, and with individual teachers free to interpret the curriculum however they saw fit. According to Cusick (1983, p. 111) such a circumstance was required for the common good. He notes:

> Were the schools to assume a position requiring a uniformity of curriculum, standards of achievement, or consensus among the staff on how to conduct themselves or their classes, it is inevitable that they would have had to make judgments about and take actions against students which might have damaged those students' opportunity for equality.

Cusick's analysis shows how this mainstream version of progressive ideology interpreted equity in such a way that it depended on individualism. If students and teachers were free to do as they pleased, equity, in this view, was the inevitable result.

Critical Pedagogy: Discourse and the Language of Possibility

Incorporating the method of third world educators like Paulo Freire and the critique of representatives of the Frankfort school (such as Jürgen Habermas, Theodor Adorno, and Herbert Marcuse), critical theorists have developed a twofold ideology of schooling. Their view provides (1) a critique that explains the cultural conflicts in which schooling takes place, and (2) an instructional method that claims to promote resistance to the "cultural hegemony" of the ruling class.[8] As with other ideologies of the left, critical pedagogy tends to privilege equality and individuality and to debunk what it claims are largely rhetorical calls for excellence.

In fact, debunking is a favorite tool of "critical discourse," the method by which "transformative intellectuals" (that is, teachers) engage individuals (especially poor and minority school children) in dialogue that opposes cultural hegemony. Critical discourse is supposed to help students understand the ways in which hegemony limits their behavior, so that they can go beyond such limits. Accordingly, children of all social classes should — through critical discourse — gain equal access to the processes of democratic governance. The major question for critical theorists is the extent to which schooling can accommodate critical discourse. The evident answer is this: "Not very far."

According to critical theorists, however, schooling is a most effective tool of hegemonic relations. Schooling plays an important role in developing among future workers the skills and attitudes necessary for their participation in the workforce (Gramsci, 1971). In fact, the conservative ideology *does* promote such skills and attitudes (e.g., National Alliance of Business, 1984; National Center on Education and the Economy, 1990; National Commission on Excellence in Education, 1983). In so doing — and this is the important point for critical pedagogy — schooling systematically helps future workers agree to their own economic exploitation. Critical pedagogy seeks to *undermine* the terms of this agreement through classroom discussion of a certain type ("critical discourse"). Critical pedagogy is a form of pedagogical activism, based on an ethical, rather than instrumental, view of human potential.

Cultural reproduction. From the perspective of these theorists, schools transmit the culture, knowledge, and prerogatives that "contribute to the ideological hegemony of dominant groups" (Apple, 1982, p. 504). This process — cultural reproduction — depends on schools' role in justifying the distribution of so-called "cultural capital." Cultural capital is simply "the different sets of linguistic and cultural competencies that individuals inherit by way of the class-located boundaries of their families" (Giroux, 1983, p. 88). It is thus easy to see why critical pedagogy gives so much weight to discourse: The way students talk and think (without reflecting, uncritically) is at the heart of cultural reproduction.

Not only do schools create and transmit cultural capital, however, they also "legitimate" the political economy in a more general and symbolic way. To justify a *capitalist economy*, schools must devalue some of the most important premises of democracy. To validate a *democratic polity*, however, schools must applaud equity and pluralism and endorse the idea of an informed citizenry. But serious work toward these latter goals can under-mine the development of a compliant workforce (Apple & Weis, 1986).

The ruling class, therefore, must carefully manage its public rhetoric about education. The quality of the rhetoric depends on the needs of the political economy at a given point in time. At one time (e.g., a time of economic crisis), a conservative meaning may be appropriate; at another time (e.g., a time of social unrest), a liberal meaning may serve better. Hence, according to Carnoy and Levin (1985, p. 44),

> In this decade [the 1980s], the pressures for using the schools for reproduction of the workforce have been stronger than those on the side of democratic and egalitarian reforms. Though much is said about the economy, little is said about democracy in pursuing educational change. But the struggle between the two forces is still very much alive.

One limitation of the analysis of schools as mere agents of reproduction and legitimation is the failure to acknowledge the role played by the working class in shaping its own ideology.

Resistance. Given this limitation, critical theorists like Giroux infer an-other role for schools. From their perspective, schools — especially through the work of teachers — can make students aware of the contradictions of the political economy. Were teachers able to accomplish this work, students would gain control over their own lives. In this way, teachers and students could together change the discourse between ruling and working classes, thereby overcoming the hegemony of the dominant (ruling-class) ideology.

This altered discourse — called the "language of possibility" (Aronowitz & Giroux, 1985, p. 154) — can occur only when teachers become transform-ative intellectuals (p. 40). Accordingly,

> Instead of defining teachers as clerks or technicians, we should see them as engaged and transformative intellectuals. . . . Central to this position is the need for reforms that enable teachers to work under conditions in which they have time to reflect critically, conduct collaborative research, engage in dia-logue with their students, and learn about the communities in which their schools are located. (Giroux, 1988, p. 729)

In this way, teachers would become moral craftspersons. They would show concern, not only about the goals of instruction, but also about the ethical implications of their work and the work of the institutions in which they operate (Zeichner & Liston, 1987). Teachers would be better able to encounter students as individuals. Greene (1986, p. 20) imagines a gradual process by which teachers would become aware "that every young person must be encountered as a center of consciousness, even as he or she is understood to be a participant in an identifiable social world."

The legacy. The roots of critical theory can be traced to the American New Left of the 1960s and to its antecedents in Western European socialism of the 1930s. As a new interpretation of schooling, it is still not familiar to many teachers—the audience to which it is most committed. Nonetheless, the role of moral craftsperson is a mainstream legacy to which critical theory contributes. The role gives teachers the authority and the responsibility to analyze educational practices—the ones they use as well as the ones used in the schools in which they work.

This sort of analysis requires teachers to examine the diverse qualities that underlie competing educational practices and to make ethical choices among them (Sirotnik & Clark, 1988). Ultimately, this process engages teachers in critical reflection about their schools. Through this reflection they "begin to challenge the power of the relationships that define [the schools'] structure and function" (Sirotnik & Clark, 1988, p. 663).

According to the critical theorists, teachers who have engaged in these processes are able to give students similar access to the discourse of reflection and critique. Once liberated through this discourse, students can act on their own behalf. Such action entails responsible resistance and the establishment of democratic mechanisms of self-governance. (For an example of similar views in action, see Wigginton, 1985, pp. 261–274.)

The Libertarian Ideology: Individualism As Its Own End

Whereas critical theorists promote self-determination as a way to *assure the success of democratic forms* of government, libertarians promote self-determination as a way to *limit the power* of any government (e.g., Spring, 1975). For libertarians, individualism is its own end, and, hence, the individual must at all costs be protected from the intrusions of any collectivity (Rand, 1965). Libertarians tolerate government only if it actually serves those it claims to serve. According to this view, individuals in all circumstances have the natural right to choose whether or not they will accept the constraints of government in order to enjoy its protections. In general, libertarians believe that the less intrusive a government is, the safer individuals will be.

In the libertarian view, however, individuals must have the rational faculties needed—with or without a government—to make wise choices. Schools can best develop such faculties *only if* they are completely separate from government. To whatever extent they *are* controlled by the government, schools are conveniently placed to serve the government as tools to inculcate predetermined attitudes, commitments, and skills, thereby limiting rational free choice. The more intrusive the government, the more intrusively will schools serve to inculcate students. Spring (1975, p. 16) explains this logic clearly:

> Any mode of government gains its legitimacy from the recognition and acceptance of people. Control of public opinion through education means continued support. Despotism and injustice can therefore continue to exist in any society in which the full development of reason has been denied within the walls of the schoolhouse.

Two libertarian views of schooling. The libertarian view has two responses to public schooling, a radical (leftist) and a reactionary (rightist) response. Although both responses endorse the freedom of individuals and reject the hegemony of the state, the two responses derive from opposing interpretations within the libertarian ideology. These interpretations differ most pointedly with respect to the values they accord equity and excellence.

The radical response entails "deschooling," the process of eliminating all formal arrangements for delivering education (e.g., Illich, 1971). In place of formal schooling, a variety of public utilities would serve as information centers; individuals would freely seek whatever services they required from these centers (Spring, 1975). The arrangement would let individuals choose among routes of learning most beneficial to them. Given such conditions, radical libertarians believe that individuals would develop their rational capacities to the fullest.

This arrangement would not, in itself, assure equity. According to Spring (1975), such dramatic changes as "deschooling" would need to be coupled with revolutionary social changes to reduce the privilege of the ruling class and eliminate the poverty of the underclass. One approach would be to give children economic independence from their parents:

> If the school were eliminated and at the same time children and youth were given economic independence, the problem of poverty would be confronted directly. Poor children would have enough money to explore and enjoy the advantages now reserved for the middle class. (Spring, 1975, p. 140)

Of course, such an arrangement would require the *massive* intrusion of some powerful collectivity into existing social conventions. Whatever the source of this power, the libertarian scheme would require an elaborate system of taxation and transfer payment—not to mention the imposition and enforcement of sanctions to protect the financial integrity of minors.

The reactionary libertarian response requires a similar type of intervention. Rather than doing away altogether with formal schooling, reactionary libertarians recommend that educational options be determined by the "natural" forces of the free market. The provisions for "choice" would presumably allow individual consumers to influence the characteristics of the schools that serve their children. In one long-considered form of choice, parents would get a "voucher," a coupon worth a certain amount of money, to fund the education of their children. Each parent would be free to use the voucher at any school. In this fashion—and under the support of the state—schools would compete with one another for students, a condition that libertarians believe would naturally develop better programs. "Under competitive markets, education 'firms' that are successful in meeting parental preferences and in increasing student achievement immediately enjoy expanded incomes via increased enrollments" (West, 1982, p. 382).

The voucher system, unlike the proposal for "deschooling," makes no claims about equity. Though it features the choice of parents, the agenda is really a Reagan-era "supply-side" program: Parents are not guaranteed choice. Choice would be a privilege controlled by the market, as entrepreneur-educators explored the markets that afforded the best chance of profit. Thus, depending on residence or affluence, parents would access the choices provided by the free market of schooling. Those who have the most choice now would have the most choice under "choice" schemes.

Vouchers, for example, pay for only part of the tuition—a small part—at elite private schools.[9] In fact, liberals who support choice systems based on the use of vouchers—because of the decentralization it promotes—recommend modifications to the system intended to assure equal access (e.g., Glenn, 1989). Desegregation, for example, is an aim that can be reconciled with choice. Such modifications appear in recent efforts to institute school choice (Uchitelle, 1989). Clinchy (1989) reflects the liberal attitude toward school choice: "We should pursue choice, by all means—but never choice that benefits primarily the already advantaged segments of our society and leaves poor and minority parents and students right where they have always been, behind society's eight ball."

The legacy. Regardless of attempts to liberalize the arrangement, however, the reactionary plan for school choice is essentially an effort to make education more efficient and more responsive to the interests of the business community (Pearson, 1989; Shea, 1989). Consequently, like other conservative recommendations, it makes use of rhetoric that stresses "excellence" and "competitive advantage." This rhetoric is particularly evident in school choice plans that establish specialized magnet or "lighthouse" schools with selective enrollment policies. The purpose of such schools is to demonstrate that — with the proper students — public schools in the United States can be as "good" as schools in competitor nations like Japan.

Despite their comparative obscurity, the radical libertarians share a long tradition with early populists such as Orestes Brownson (see Lasch, 1991, pp. 187-194). Some observers of this tradition (e.g., Hofstadter, 1963) consider it to be anti-intellectual, but Illich's notion of deschooling remains a powerful idea because of its relationship to local autonomy (or "decentralization"). Illich did not, after all, advise doing away with *education*; rather, he insisted on the need to do away with the state's centralized apparatus for enslaving minds: the system of *schooling*. Two issues in contemporary educational practice may perpetuate the radical libertarian tradition. First, issues of organizational scale concern many educators, who realize, in particular, that large-scale organizations (large districts and schools) serve poor students and communities badly (e.g., Friedkin & Necochea, 1988; James & Levin, 1970). Second, the electronic revolution leads many observers to believe that decentralization is more likely now than at any time in the industrial past (e.g., Barker, 1992; Bollier, 1991; Cetron, Rocha, & Lucken, 1988; Office of Technology Assessment, 1989).

THE RIGOR OF THE 1980s

During the 1980s, the ideologies that give priority to excellence and individualism — the conservative and the reactionary libertarian ideologies — were able to set the agendas of school reform and dominate public consideration of the aims of education (Apple, 1993). By the end of the decade, the conservative president in league with the incoming liberal president could induce the 50 state governors to impose a short list of clear aims (National Governors' Association, 1990) on a very decentralized system of national education.

These aims *are* reasonable; they stress the importance of learning. They also reflect the traditionally valued qualities of individualism, excellence, and equity. But the goals are fundamentally a political compromise between *powerful* conservative commitments and *still influential* liberal ones. The viewpoints of radical libertarians, critical theorists, and progressive educators are not part of the compromise — as no one who examined the issue would expect them to be, for that matter. In order to seem ideologically neutral, however, the statement of goals avoids any discussion of the commitments that inform them. Any such discussion would disrupt the ceremonial importance of the occasion, which is the political act of creating and disseminating these goals very widely indeed.

The goals are reasonable because nurturing the life of the mind would surely involve better academic preparation for more students. The use of reason requires that students actively consider the "best" texts that humans have accumulated,[10] that they model the methods of those texts in their own work, and that they advance that heritage in their own right. This sort of academic mission, however, has never—least of all in the national goals—been proposed forcefully for public schools in the U.S. Indeed, schools would encounter nearly insurmountable problems if they *were* to adopt this mission. And, as the consensus has it, they already encounter enough insurmountable problems. Lack of "fiscal free-will" prevents most American parents from exercising the choice—private schooling—that more often tries to implement this sort of academic mission.

Under the Surface: Restructuring Values

On the surface of things, the 1980s' press for rigor made sense. International comparisons had suggested that the United States, allegedly with far more resources, seemed to prepare its young people less well academically than many other countries.[11] The reform reports advised government functionaries in the various states to direct schools in their jurisdictions to do better. The performance of high school students was taken to be of most immediate economic interest, and state after state thereupon insisted that students complete more required courses to get their diplomas.

In essence, however, these "higher standards" were not much more than a return to James Conant's common-sensical curriculum for the most academically able quartile of students in post-Sputnik high schools (Conant, 1959; cf. Bennett, 1987). The full gamut of new skills, new curricula, and new methods proposed in the 1980s did not really contain much that was new (Shea, 1989).

At the same time that higher standards appeared in legislated mandates, influential liberal *and* conservative groups began twisting the phrase "at risk" (from the title of the 1983 report of the National Commission on Excellence, *Nation at Risk*) to cover previously unvoiced concern for impoverished students. At no time in the past, have equity and excellence been so evident, side-by-side, in so many reports making such similar recommendations. Some critical observers (e.g., Carnoy & Levin, 1985; Shea, 1989) suggest that the rhetoric about "excellence" was in earnest, whereas the rhetoric about equity—because it entailed so little action—was not. Some observers charged that the complaints about declining standards had been trumped up—the expectations of the business community were what had really changed (e.g., Berliner, 1992; Bracey, 1991).

Still others noted that the rhetoric of risk and reform signaled a substantial restructuring of the discourse about educational aims (DeYoung, 1989). The notion of "risk," in particular, is an apt symbol for this change. Risk of what? Risk from what? And, even more intriguing, risk for what possible purpose?

Rather than defining constructive aims for education, the new reforms strived to use education to inoculate society against certain risks, as defined by those in charge of vested interests (Shea, 1989). The principal risk, always, was lack of international business standing, and the principal aim was to restore American global economic dominance; thoughtful debate about aims was not to be part of the exercise, ever (Howley, 1991). The mission of those who actually were to carry out such reforms (educators, citizens) was restricted to decisions about ways to meet the predetermined aims (Shea, 1989), even in the more liberal conceptions (e.g., Smith & O'Day, 1990).

Restructuring excellence. The business and government functionaries who engineered the reform campaign saw in academic rigor the means to discipline human capital of the sort needed to outwit alien threats in military and economic battle (Shea, 1989). Business organizations began to talk about "investing in our children" (this was the title of a 1985 report issued by the Committee for Economic Development). The investment was to be directed at developing problem-solving skills, creative teamwork, and respectful attitudes toward business and government in young people.

Business leaders also patronized school administrators, offering to help them benefit from the lessons business managers professedly learned about corporate restructuring during the decade of the 1980s (Edelstein & Schoeffe, 1989). In fact, school administrators are used to accepting such guidance. Their training has always drawn heavily on studies of business administration (Hoy & Miskel, 1987).

While promoting academic rigor and forming characters amenable to corporate life, business and government functionaries at the same time sought to impress educators with the *patriotic urgency* of the reform program (Committee for Economic Development, 1985; Elmore & McLaughlin, 1988; Etzioni, 1985; Holzer, 1989; National Commission on Excellence, 1983; Secretary's Commission on Achieving Necessary Skills [SCANS], 1991). Shea (1989) explained that both liberal and conservative reformers believe in the international threat, but differ in their strategies for addressing it. According to her analysis, the conservatives stress character formation and military superiority. The liberals stress skill development and economic superiority.

Each position acknowledges the importance of what the other stresses, and the conservative position accommodates much of the liberal position.

Rather than a true difference of substance, the pure liberal and pure conservative positions represent a difference of emphasis. Both positions seek a global dominion for the U.S. economy and view education as a critical ally in achieving such dominion (Apple, 1993; Howley, 1991; Nystrand & Gamoran, 1991; Shea, 1989).

As the nation's chief economic threat, Japanese capitalism and Japanese education were cited in many reform reports. Japanese management techniques (Ouchi, 1981) and Japanese educational commitments and methods (Dorfman, 1987) were explicitly commended by the state to American educators as possible inspirations for an improved American product (e.g., Ravitch, 1991).

Very few people, however, seemed to understand that the tenor of the whole campaign constituted an acknowledgment by business of its historic complicity in previously discrediting substantive academic knowledge for all students (DeYoung, 1989; Howley, 1991). The rhetoric about "new" reforms, successive "waves" of reforms, and "restructured" schools was really a reform of *business* attitudes toward education, especially with respect to academics. Quite possibly, the incentive for taking such a reformed stance was the development, during the 1980s, of an unanticipated shortage of college graduates, especially in technical and business fields, a shortage projected to worsen during the 1990s (Bishop & Carter, 1991; Murphy & Finis, 1989).

Among the alternatives, improvement of math and science was finally singled out as an important goal in the search for national salvation (National Governors' Association, 1990), even as it had been during the late 1950s when the alien threat was international communism (Tannenbaum, 1981). Those who pushed for academic rigor in the 1980s, although referencing a real problem (the intellectual shortcomings of U.S. schools), addressed short-sighted reforms to another problem (worry about America's declining economic dominance and at-risk standard of living).

Restructuring equity. One of the most curious features of the reform agenda was the way it framed consideration of equity. Whereas education was widely represented as a direct way to restore economic competitiveness, the connections between educational inequity and the economy were minimized. The agenda particularly avoided treating educational inequity as a function of the political economy. The liberal and leftist concepts of racism, sexism, and class struggle *were* represented, however, by the neutral term "risk."

"Risk" is a function that, in principle, can be managed. Risk management, in fact, has a distinguished history in business administration. Restructured schools would learn to manage risk better, just as businesses had learned. Liberal educators, too, seemed to embrace the term, since dialogue (with more conservative colleagues and functionaries) about equity was not welcome otherwise in the political climate of the 1980s.

The evident need to manage risk reflects salient features of the conservative view of equity:

1. Risk is an individual threat (equity is not a social issue).
2. Risk is inevitable (equity is not a right).
3. Risk is related to productivity (equity is negotiable).

Educational equity, in short, is a tool for ensuring desirable economic ends. As such, it constitutes a technical rather than a political question. Inequity requires management, not a commitment to justice (see Brown, 1993, for a relevant discussion of this circumstance).

The management of risk is a defensive strategy intended to maintain vested interests, and is a familiar tactic in educational history. Such risk to vested interests appears in the consciousness of ruling elites whenever momentous historical changes occur. For example, in the middle of the last century, conservatives in Britain (then the preeminent world power) began to support education for the poor as a means to contain social strife (Bowen, 1981). The British ruling elite understood that education could help prepare workers to accept the rigors of the industrial world emerging at that time, just as contemporary American conservatives understand that schooling can be used to bolster a dominant American role in the postindustrial world economy.

Restructuring individualism. The American system of negative rights[12] has defined a successively smaller realm of liberty since at least 1900 (as the need to protect individuals from corporate excess began to come clear). The rise of scientific management in education (Callahan, 1962) and the subsequent development of what Tyack (1974) ironically calls "the one-best-system,"[13] deflected individualism along two parallel paths: the specialization of students and of teachers.

The individualism of students has come to be equated with their career choices. Students are at liberty to select from among available job specializations, performance of which depends on increasingly specialized (predetermined) school programs. The path toward teachers' specialization is also characterized by personal choice, in this case of what and whom to teach. Teachers specialize in order to impart specialized instruction, on the one hand, or on the other, to apply specialized techniques to particular sorts of children (e.g., exceptional children, children with reading problems, children whose native language is not English).

Individualism of this sort is already fully consistent in most respects with the "reforms" of the 1980s. In the conservative view, better preparation of workers and citizens becomes more likely when students receive appropriate guidance that assists them in selecting the jobs for which they are, ostensibly, best suited. Two modifications to the "one best system," however, attend particularly to individualism as specialization. The modifications restructure liberty and equity in such a way as to diminish both.

The most prominent of these modifications is school choice, which promises to restore a measure of individualism to the system, in two forms: parental license to select schools and corporate liberty to develop different kinds of schools. By involving corporate interests, as in the 1991 "America 2000" plan, school choice began to move schools into the arena of greatest liberty in America, that is, into the free market.

Under school-choice plans, government promotes the value of excellence in education (e.g., by setting national goals), but corporate America has the liberty to mold excellence into various material forms. Moreover, in shaping publicly funded private schools, corporate America has the opportunity to magnify the importance of "excellence" by appropriating government rhetoric into its advertising campaigns. Equity, of course, receives little attention under such plans. Corporate interests may well be able to create additional, or different kinds of, very "good" schools (i.e., schools of students who achieve well), but whether or not they can create *enough* of them for everyone is questionable. Moreover, the extent to which such "good" schools might cultivate meaning or care for the intellect is not even an issue for corporate America. Care for the intellect must reside in the public realm because it is a common good, ultimately without instrumental value.

A less extensive modification in the system equates individualism with special risk. This modification applies particularly to students whose individualism under more liberal ideologies has been associated with their needs. Substituting the concept of "risk" for that of "need," however, attenuates schools' responsibility for such students. Special education and other programs of categorical aid have become very expensive (Verstegen & McGuire, 1991). The concept of "risk" allows the expense of educating "needy" children to be balanced against the potential benefit to society of such education. Rather than justifying expensive special education programs by appealing to the just claims of each individual, policymakers can rationalize the decision to dismantle such programs by invoking concern for the economic health of the nation. "Individualized" attention to needy students is reasonably permissible only to the extent that it makes economic common sense.

When some states find that up to 87% of their students receive "special" services (Verstegen & McGuire, 1991), everyone would agree that the time has come to consider changes. New arrangements, therefore, like "total inclusion," are timely. The underlying goad to action, however, is that special programs are inefficient and redundant. A more stringent screen may be applied to determine which children may be considered "exceptional." Rhetorical attention shifts from the liberal discourse of equity and largesse to the conservative discourse of excellence and efficiency.

THE ROOTS OF ANTI-INTELLECTUALISM

The rigor of the 1980s has effectively altered the way politicians and functionaries look at schooling. Schools and the various agencies of institutional power within education now encounter the conservative ideology wherever they turn (Apple, 1993). School funding is contingent on accommodating the points of the ascendent ideology, just as in the 1960s accommodation to liberal tenets was in order. The conservative view of excellence, however, is no more kind to intellect than many of the anti-intellectual fads of the late 1960s.[14] The roots of anti-intellectualism are deep in American culture.

For the historian Richard Hofstadter (1963), evangelism and primitivism were the sources of anti-intellectualism; for the cultural critic, Jacques Barzun (1959), the sources were art, science, and philanthropy; and for the sociologist Daniel Bell (1973, 1976), the source lies in the cultural contradictions of modernism.

These three thinkers actually have much more in common than their differential diagnoses might suggest. They hold to similar views of culture, and each entertains serious doubts about the beneficent influence of technology. The following section, however, is not a treatment of American culture generally; it is an application of cultural interpretation to schooling.

Barzun, Bell, and Hofstadter — despite the differences in their terms — share a disdain for (1) schooling administered in the name of some limited end (e.g., career access), and (2) schooling that regards children as beings whose natural course of development requires only that adults get out of their way. Such educational perspectives, in their view, are intellectually, culturally, politically, and economically counterproductive. As Barzun (1959, 1989) implies, they actively corrupt the historical community of learning.

Instrumentalism and Sentimentality

Above all else, Americans want schools that produce immediate, practical effects "in the real world." Schooling must at the very least appear to be useful. Curiously, disappointment is common. In an earlier time, Hofstadter (1963, p. 305) observed,

> Concerning the central fact of educational failure there is relatively slight dispute; and the failure itself underlies one of the paradoxes of American life: that in a society so passionately intent upon education, the yield of our educational system has been such a *constant* disappointment [emphasis added].

Hofstadter believed that Americans had made "a mystique of practicality" (p. 237). What he observed then is still true today. The practical results achieved by schools are never quite the ones desired; the neverending quest for exactly the right means to the particular end is a sort of search for the holy grail. The mystique of practicality has misguided crusades, and it has served no one well — children least of all.

Each of the ideologies considered above, in fact, intends an education with a particular end. Each takes the stand that schooling should be a tool to accomplish a particular, practical objective, and that failing to progress toward that objective, schooling is either without purpose or it is heir to some evil purpose.

The various ends put forward by the differing ideologies, moreover, do not differ so dramatically as may at first seem. For example, the conservative seeks to use schools to restore global dominion, whereas the critical pedagogue seeks to use schools to disestablish global dominion.[15] Neither strays very far from the usual instrumental purposes articulated for schooling (e.g., productive employment, good citizenship, worthy home membership) though each makes its own interpretation of the qualifiers "productive," "good," and "worthy."

American educational ideologies — all of them — are profoundly shaped by instrumentalism, the philosophical position that ideas are tools for action and that utility determines the truth of ideas. Instrumentalism takes to an extreme the view that if ideas were never applied to things, they would be unworthy objects of attention. As a guiding principle for the major social institution (i.e., education) whose chief concern must be ideas, instrumentalism so restricts the realm of ideas as to subjugate intellect to the service of particular ends; much is lost, including reflectiveness, critique, judgment, and ethical action (cf. Weizenbaum, 1976).

An analogy may help explain matters. Observers have criticized typical educational research as "reductionist." They mean that the researchers so divide and narrow questions as to produce answers that are meaningless. Connections and context are lost, and with them, the meaning of the answer. Instrumentalism has the same effect on the aims of education as typical research methods have on the meaning of research findings. In the process of keeping school, instrumentalism so narrows the purpose of education as to disable a true education. This is the process that produces and constantly renews the disappointment that Hofstadter noted. Eventually the enterprise must collapse; perhaps the collapse has begun.

Sentimentality is another counterproductive legacy of American educational practice. It stifles both intellect and authentic emotion, and it differs from authentic sentiment, affection, and love. Sentimentality is the thoughtless disposition toward emotional indulgence, especially emotional self-indulgence. Emotional self-indulgence is bad enough as a private habit, but as a feature of schooling it serves as an anti-intellectual antidote to the instrumentalism at the functional core of schooling.

The machinery of schooling has consistently exalted "the virtues of the heart . . . over those of the head" (Hofstadter, 1963, p. 306), and the rhetoric of American schooling is sentimental to excess according to many observers (Arendt, 1954/1968; Barzun, 1959, 1989; Lasch, 1979). Katz (1968) recounts the suspicion with which reformers of Horace Mann's generation (ca. 1830) viewed education that concentrated on "head culture." Even as the practical American education was progressing toward its eventual end in the factory model, educators fretted over changing mores and attitudes. The early reformers sought to improve the character and attitudes of children as much as to reform the organization of schooling (Katz, 1968).

Contemporary educators articulate this sentimentality in a variety of positions that entail tampering with the emotional and spiritual condition of children. For example, some believe that before schools can deal with ideas, they must first shape character (Bennett, 1988; Thanksgiving Statement Group, 1984) or that dealing with ideas is a form of character education (Orr & Klein, 1991); that schools must either inculcate values (Deaton & McNamara, 1984; Etzioni, 1985) or clarify them (Vann, 1988); that promoting social and emotional well-being takes precedence over or "balances" academics (Wynne, 1988); or that spiritual needs merit special emphasis (e.g., Beck, 1988; Kolander & Chandler, 1990; Mitchell, 1988).

Such views, though they come in great variety, are pervasively held. Sentimentality in education represents the view that "right attitude" is a prior condition of "right thinking."[16] This position has limited merit. Grant (1982), for example, arguing *against* instrumentalism, makes the point that adults need to act with authority to establish a "provisional morality" in support of meaningful classroom discourse.

The danger of sentimentality per se, however, lies in making the formation of attitudes the main purpose of schooling (Katz, 1971). When the formation of attitudes becomes the central purpose of schooling, educators

relinquish the only authority that makes purposeful instruction possible—
the authority of the intellect. [17]

Instrumentalism and sentimentality each comprehend an intellectually
limited scope for schooling. Their combination militates against the unto-
ward appearance of critique and reflection and the sorts of discourse that
support them in most classrooms most of the time. The combination is fatal
to intellectual nurture. Barzun makes plain the result:

> Modern theory inverts the relation [between the learner and what is taught]
> and makes of subject-matter a device for correcting what the teacher thinks is
> wrong in a child's temperament. . . . The final inversion of purpose character-
> istic of the self-conscious curriculum [is that] it assumes in each pupil the
> supremely gifted mind, which must not be tampered with, and the defective
> personality, which the school must remodel. (1959, pp. 101–103)

> The aim of the school is no longer instruction in subjects, but education in
> attitudes to meet the needs of life. (1959, p. 113)

The criterion of worth in this scheme is the ordinary operation of
the world—competition on (and for) the job, in society; and, in personal
circumstances, functional adjustment ("happiness"). Still, until quite recently, the way this anti-intellectual combination has worked itself out in
the schools has been sufficiently effective to satisfy the needs of industrial-
era business and government (Committee for Economic Development,
1985).

Radically similar ends for schooling. The postindustrial era, however,
calls for a new round of investments, and, in fact, not simply for the old
quest for the right means to well-worn ends, but for a "radically" new
end (Edelstein & Schoeffe, 1989; National Center on Education and the
Economy, 1990). The old schooling no longer suffices—assembly-line
work, like agricultural work before it, is in rapid decline, though no one is
quite sure what will replace it for most people (Leontief, 1982; Schor,
1991; Wiener, 1950). The new instrumental end proposed for schooling,
nevertheless, is to supply business and government with adequate numbers
of employees to whom more complicated tasks can be successfully delegated (Bishop & Carter, 1991; Committee for Economic Development,
1985; Secretary's Commission on Achieving Necessary Skills [SCANS],
1991).

This new end is every bit as intellectually narrow as the old end of basic
skills and life adjustment. Indeed, it is more of the same, but the realities
have shifted a bit; schooling must accommodate the shifts to give "work"
what it "requires" (SCANS, 1991). Schooling restructured along these lines

will, in fact, be *radically similar*—that is, identical in its anti-intellectual roots—to its predecessor.

At present, the simultaneous valuation of basic skills, problem-solving skills, and good job attitudes (SCANS, 1991) illustrates the limited scope of schooling well. Business groups expect the combination, implanted in every worker, to restore America's global dominion. Most likely, this expectation is not warranted (DeYoung, 1989). Moreover, even if it were, this sort of schooling disregards the issues of meaning, reflection, interpretation, and critique, thereby disregarding the aims of a true education.

The Dilemma of Gifted Education

Despite what one might otherwise expect, effective provisions for the education of unusually able students have not flourished in this context. So-called "excellence" is the acquisition of human capital: math, science, functional language skills, and cooperative attitudes. Intellect is not part of "excellence," as justice is not part of equity, nor liberty a realm of action for individuals (cf. Brown, 1993). The impediment to meaningful programs seems to be utility: What do such provisions usefully contribute to the restoration of America's international economic dominion?

Comparative education provides a reasonable response: very little. For example, official studies of Japanese education (Dorfman, 1987) suggested to some observers that U.S. schools must train more students to higher levels of skill in math and science. The national goals subsequently adopted just this position. According to James Fallows (1987, p. 20), a thoughtful journalist,

> The highest levels of just about everything, from physical comfort to highly refined academic skill, are higher in America than in Japan. But our lowest levels of just about everything are *much* lower than Japan's, and the difference is beginning to tell. One American reporter told me not long ago, "Japan's secret is that it has the best bottom fifty percent in the world."

In fact, if the purpose of education really is national economic security, then it follows that gifted education is *not* a very efficient means to the end. The contrary position—that the gifted are the nation's most important national resource (e.g., Hoyt & Hebler, 1974)—is merely an illusion of the old ideology. In their restructured forms, both excellence and equity work together against intellect in public education. Risk is construed as an individual's failure to access sufficient human capital, whereas excellence is success in accumulating it.

Nonetheless, in a conservative analysis, gifted education might be compared to giving tax breaks to the wealthiest citizens. Conservatives provide tax breaks for the wealthy in order to put money in the hands of those most likely to invest it, rather than spend it. Citizens of more modest means cannot afford to invest their tax savings and, in this view, contribute less to the national economy — principally through consumption rather than investment.

The analogy would proceed as follows: Very intelligent students are more likely to translate scarce resources into the skills and knowledge that comprise human capital of the highest value. Other citizens, less likely to develop a high quality of human capital even with similar training, would nonetheless contribute their share to economic development by applying ("consuming") this best knowledge, which comes from the work of the most accomplished, highly skilled intelligent citizens.

The appeal of this argument is diminished, however, by research into gifted students and evaluations of gifted education. Because gifted students possess a comparatively rare degree of ability, one expects that their adult contributions — in culture or in the political economy — will be outstanding. The expectation, however, is *not* supported by available evidence. Follow-up studies of the 1500 gifted students identified by Lewis Terman in the early 1920s showed that none became renowned cultural figures or transformational leaders. They simply became rather typical professionals — doctors, lawyers, professors, and writers — though at a much higher rate within their own cohort than among the cohort of students not identified as gifted.

Other research on the relationship between intelligence and adult earnings (a common measure of human capital) suggests that educational attainment — years in school — exerts the greatest unique influence on earnings, not tested intelligence (Bowles & Gintis, 1976; Jencks et al., 1979). Such findings tend to support the view that cultivating giftedness, as now defined, is largely *irrelevant* to the pursuit of "excellence." The Commission on Excellence, for example, though it received testimony about the relevance of gifted education and the importance of gifted students, apparently understood the contentious nature of the testimony it had received. *A Nation at Risk* gives about the same amount of attention to the gifted as Conant (1959) did — virtually none. A more important effort, reflected in the national goals, would be to retain more students in school for longer periods of time.

Evaluations of gifted programs are hardly more encouraging. Whether or not gifted programs in themselves contribute much to the subsequent economic utility of the gifted is anyone's guess. Because most gifted programs are part-time activities that lack even an instrumental academic focus (Stanley, 1986), the hypothesis that gifted programs are useful for developing human capital cannot reasonably be entertained. In any case, it has not been tested. Part of the difficulty, as Rogers (1986b) notes, is that part-time enrichment programs without an academic focus cover such a variety of activities that they are virtually impossible to evaluate in any meaningful way.

Another proposed utility of gifted programs is related to the issue of focus. This utility reconciles risk and excellence: By serving talented working-class and minority students, special programs liberate these students from risks to their talents. Available evidence, however, suggests that such students are *not* typically served in this way by existing programs (Howley & Howley, 1989; Pendarvis, Howley, & Howley, 1990). Considering the previously mentioned weaknesses in program focus and evaluation, the argument is specious at best.

The most serious trouble with the argument about mitigating risk, however, is that it applies equally well to children from middle- and upper-middle-class backgrounds. Gifted programs try to protect *all able students* from the unproductive boredom and regimentation of regular classrooms. It may be true that existing gifted programs give very able students a break from pointless drudgery (Howley, Howley, & Pendarvis, 1986); whether this benefit, absent substantive academic work, has any real effect on the long-term occupational performance or intellectual development of the gifted is *extremely* doubtful, as noted above. Further, it is difficult to deny that very similar programs could protect all students, whether gifted or not, from the rigors of the one-best-system. The argument based on risk, therefore, ends with the dilemma of all categorical programs: Most students could benefit from intense help.

Concern for at-risk gifted students (i.e., talented students from working-class and minority backgrounds), however, combines the qualities of equity and excellence deftly enough, if quite illogically, to win modest political support. Establishment of the National Center for Gifted and Talented Research, for example, received sufficient congressional support to overcome objections from the administration. Key features in the award of the contract concerned research about programs for poor and minority students and explorations of new conceptions of giftedness. Absent understanding of the structural relationships between poverty and intelligence, such exploration, like earlier investigation of working-class and underprivileged children, is misguided.

SCHOOLING FOR CONTINUITY IN THE
SHARED COMMUNITY OF LEARNING

Seeking to teach and to preserve only what is immediately useful, educators must divine precisely which knowledge will be more or less immediately useful ("instrumental"). This task is more arduous than it might seem for two reasons.

First, the basis of intuition about utility is common sense, that is, a normative sense of what knowledge seems to be more or less useful in present circumstances. For over 100 years, that knowledge—the "knowledge of most worth"—has been *practical* science. Herbert Spencer, for example, in the middle of the nineteenth century, proposed science as a general method that could be straightforwardly applied to all realms of life down to the most mundane, including housework.

Science is still commonly believed to be the most useful tool for guiding virtually any sort of work. In this view, the value of research consists principally in its results—its applications as technology (Bell, 1976). The manifest importance of science and mathematics to the restoration of America's global dominance is evident in the National Education Goals: American schools are to produce students who will become the world leaders in mathematics and science (National Governors' Association, 1990). As a result, the nation will, once again, securely corner the market on world-class expertise.

Knowledge, as the heritage of literacy and as the process of coming to know with reason, is demeaned by the instrumental interpretation (Weizenbaum, 1976; Postman, 1992). The full heritage of literacy and reason requires continuity in the historical community of intellect. Already our corporate practice and legal mechanisms seek to guard knowledge as a proprietary holding. The export of technological "secrets" can be a crime, depending on who the recipient is. To the extent that this anti-intellectual climate influences teaching practice, it works against the only ethos under which formal learning on a wide scale is possible: the concerted effort of teacher and student to share knowledge.

Instrumentalism as a general principle of schooling subverts this community. Much of what contemporary schooling attempts is, in fact, based on the presumption that learning becomes the property of the one who learns. Further, the objects of such learning (particular skills and particular kinds of knowledge) function to narrow the realm open to the consideration of reason and to provide a basis for differentiating which students should acquire which particular skills and kinds of knowledge (e.g., Apple, 1982; Eisner, 1983).

The second difficulty with instrumental schooling does not lie in the *particular* ends it seeks but rather in its narrow, instrumental conception of what is, in a general sense, useful. As a relative standard, instrumental utility is a poor arbiter of merit: Its application depends on the time frame used to encompass judgment. Ideas that at first seem useless can after a time produce substantial effects, but an instrumental view imposes a very narrow standard of utility—that which produces a given result from a given resource at a given time.

The root of this difficulty concerns the interpretation of work: Schooling approaches the task of learning in accord with unexamined assumptions about the nature of work. Common usage equates work with a particular job, and most people are bound to accept the reality that work—in this common construction—must be drudgery (Arendt, 1958). The chief purpose of schooling is, at least in the most influential ideologies, preparation for jobs. And, as noted previously, the ends of schooling have changed principally because the job market is believed to be changing. Engagement, commitment, passion, and meaning most commonly take place *off the job*.

Moreover, school is understood to be the "job" of both teachers and students. The shared perception that schooling itself is merely drudgery is the inevitable result. But this result cannot be reversed by a switch to right attitudes, because the underlying reality of work—in the experience of most people—*is* drudgery.

A different understanding of the *idea of work* would change matters. If work were understood to transcend particular jobs, if people widely understood their work as comprising a larger scope than labor for pay, both students and teachers could engage learning as something other than drudgery. Barzun (1959, p. 125) shows how the separation of work and its opposite (play) subverts learning:

> The question resolves itself again into that of work. . . . Of all the deprivations modern life . . . imposes on intellectual man, the abandonment of work is the cruelest, for all other occupations kill time and drain the spirit, whereas [true] work fills both, and in the doing satisfies at once love and aggression. That is the sense in which work is "fun" . . . a pleasure altogether different from that for which educators have turned school subjects into activities and play. Under the habit of play, drudgery, when it comes, remains drudgery, instead of an accepted purgatory close to the heaven of work. No [one] who works in the sense I mean can despise himself, even if the work is below his deserts, or its perfection short of his ideal.

What might this different idea of work be? The old notion of a "calling"—a vocation—provides some clues. A calling involves a person heeding a higher purpose, traditionally a purpose in accord with ethical principles (quite variously interpreted). The reference to intellectual constructs outside those that particular jobs impose is the key feature of a "calling." This idea of work sometimes does emerge from experience (natural education), but it should also be nurtured by formal education. If the institution of education, however, fails to care for ideas as something other than tools— that is, if it fails to care for the intellectual constructs that embody various "higher purposes"—only a stunted idea of work (work as drudgery) will emerge. At present, the instrumental purposes of school and of work are immune to such a treatment of ideas and to such an understanding of purpose (Berry, 1990). This oversight is a major tragedy of modern education (e.g., Barzun, 1989; Bell, 1973, 1976; Berry, 1990; Keizer, 1988; Lasch, 1991; Wigginton, 1985).

Perhaps misconstruction of the idea of work is partly responsible for the failure of the National Education Goals to mention the humanities. The politicians who framed these goals apparently believed that the enduring dilemmas of the human condition are merely problems that can be delegated to properly trained technocrats. In the case of justice and identity, the technocrats can devise risk management and life adjustment schemes. But the public is certain to be disappointed: No matter how skilled, technocrats will be jobholders trained to construe even the most baffling dilemmas as discrete tasks—part of the *job*. In reality, however, the enduring dilemmas of the human condition require more meaningful *work* and more public *action* (Arendt, 1958).

Ideology and Teaching

Bell (1976) distinguishes two roles for ideology, an instrumental one (which legitimates the domination of existing groups, and is often illogical), and an intellectual one. In the latter role,

> it is in the character of ideologies not only to reflect or justify an underlying reality but, once launched, to take on a life of their own. A truly powerful ideology opens up a new vision of life to the imagination; once formulated, it remains part of the moral repertoire to be drawn upon . . . as part of the range of possibilities open to mankind. . . . They can be called upon and reformulated throughout the history of a civilization. Thus an ideology gnawed at, worried to the bone, argued about, dissected, and restated . . . becomes a force in its own right. (Bell, 1976, pp. 60-61)

Bell is wrong that ideologies *require* discussion in order to become forces in their own right—ideologies are by their nature compelling. But his main point makes sense. Though they should not found instruction on dogma, teachers *must* found it on a meaningful worldview—an ideology that has intellectual merit. They should approach the historical community of learning from some vantage that helps them make sense of it. Such an approach constitutes an intellectually productive treatment of ideology in which students ought to be coached, and that teachers ought to model. Education that advances intellect helps students examine the assumptions on which ideologies are based; the habit of so doing is the basis of literacy (writ large). Using dogma to inculcate students with particular attitudes and commitments, however, disrespects students and offends intellect.

Classroom discourse and intellect. How, then, ought teachers to nurture the habit of literacy in their classrooms? Among the ideologies considered in this chapter, one provides a clue. Critical theory, though as instrumental in its aims as the others, emphasizes the importance of *discourse.*

The nature and quality of classroom discourse has also received attention in the past. Reflective, philosophical, and empirical treatments of the topic have appeared over the years (e.g., Bellack, Kliebard, Hyman, & Smith, 1966; Brown, 1993; Bruner, 1966; Edwards & Furlong, 1978; Erickson, 1982; Martin, 1970). Each of these interpretations, in its way, considers the importance of "exact speech." And each emphasizes the overarching intellectual worth of discourse that employs such speech. Jerome Bruner (1966, p. 102) puts it this way:

> I have often thought that I would do more for my students by teaching them to write and think in English than teaching them my own subject. It is not so much that I value discourse to others that is right and clear and graceful . . . as that practice in such discourse is the only way of assuring that one says things right and courteously and powerfully *to oneself.* For it is extraordinarily difficult to say foolishness clearly without exposing it for what it is.

Discourse — spoken and written argument, explanation, analysis, and inquiry — is the vehicle of literacy and the strength of intellect. The quality of discourse in the classroom represents the historical community of learning, but, as Bruner so clearly points out, it is also the reflection of the influence of that community in the community of the classroom and in students' own minds. Instructional discourse maintains, or subverts, *continuity* in the historical community of learning. It is the only vehicle, at least in schools, for helping students understand violations of that community, both inside and outside the classroom. One should also note that students who can distinguish between clear and obscure expression are much better placed to discriminate wise and unwise political action. As Arendt (1958) notes, clearheaded speech and clearheaded action occupy common ground.

Growing concern for the quality of classroom discourse is no longer just a worry, however. For some time, research about teachers' questioning practices has examined this characteristic of classroom discourse in considerable detail (Gall, 1984). This literature treats the kinds of questions most frequently asked, the proper mix of factual and conceptual questions that should be asked, teachers' behavior in posing questions to various types of students, techniques to elicit more extended and elaborate responses from students, and the style of questioning necessary to sustain and focus mean-ingful interchange among students. Moreover, application of this research has yielded a variety of materials for helping practicing teachers to improve their "questioning behavior."

Ways to improve questioning in classrooms are but one part of the complexity of classroom discourse. Carlsen (1991) points out that research about questioning — because its main object is the behavior of teachers — tends to overlook the way the meaning of questions depends on the general climate of discourse in classrooms.

A more intellectually comprehensive, but still very practical, approach to the issue of classroom discourse has been articulated by the National Council of Teachers of Mathematics (NCTM). The Council's *Professional Standards for Teaching Mathematics* (NCTM, 1991) is a remarkable docu-ment in many respects. First, if poor quality of discourse is a predicament in many classrooms, mathematics classrooms are, according to the Council, not an exception. Indeed, the Council reports that in many mathematics classrooms virtually *no meaningful discourse* occurs: Students work out practice problems with little assistance, explanation, or inquiry. Second, the Council's *Standards* are not a typical accountability device; the document is really a handbook for teachers. Finally, throughout the document the role of intellect and understanding receive consistent emphasis. According to the Council (NCTM, 1991, p. 1), elementary and secondary mathematics teachers must, for instance, become more proficient in:

- Selecting mathematical tasks to engage students' interests and intel-lect
- Providing opportunities to deepen [students'] understanding of the mathematics being studied and its applications
- Orchestrating classroom discourse in ways that promote the investi-gation and growth of mathematical understanding.

The *Standards* model this approach for teachers. Every point is clearly elaborated and warranted, and "vignettes" illustrate application of the point in classrooms. Three of the six standards for teaching deal explicitly with discourse: the teacher's role in discourse, the student's role in discourse, and tools for enhancing discourse (NCTM, 1991, pp. 25–56).

Rexford Brown (1993, p. 234) vividly describes the typical discourse of the classroom.

> We came to call this language "talkinbout," because we saw so many people talking about reading but not actually reading, talking about writing but not actually writing, and so on. "Talkinbout" is an abstract language, an adult

reconstruction after the fact of an experience that the student is not allowed to have firsthand. It is a rumor about learning.

Is "talkinbout" a universal accident? We think not. Perhaps it has an instrumental purpose, perhaps to frustrate learning where authentic learning might be dangerous.

THE UTILITY OF CARE FOR THE INTELLECT

Ordinary Americans have historically demonstrated a remarkable concern for schooling and for a progressive extension of the right of all citizens to as much of it as they could stand (Counts, 1930; Curti, 1943). In fact, that concern was a *popular* cause, exercised against the increasingly remarkable silence of the U.S. Constitution on the educational franchise (Zinn, 1980).

Because the right to an adequate education has never been recognized as an issue of sufficiently high purpose to deserve explicit protection in the federal Constitution, the struggle for educational rights has taken shape under the rubric of states' rights. Over the centuries, in response to popular pressure, state courts have tended, in piecemeal fashion, to construe education as a "fundamental right" under successive drafts of the various state constitutions (Stephens, 1991).

But neither the recently enlightened self-interest of the business community nor the traditional popular struggle to extend the educational franchise represents a commitment to nurturing the life of the mind among ordinary students. That life is the pursuit and application of reason, based on the conviction that constructing meaning and taking wise action in the world constitute the fundamental purpose of human existence.

Reason takes its proper shape in many ways, of course, and humans misdirect it in equally many ways. Many people, for instance, equate "technical rationality," instrumental reason, with reason, and so believe that emotional life is separate from the intellect. Instrumental reason helps discredit intellect. The tragedy is that as care for the intellect, the life of the mind, diminishes, our ability to perceive the misapplications of reason also declines. The impediments that reason raises to greed, injustice, exploitation, and other evils, can be more easily sidestepped, lacking concern for the life of the mind (Arendt, 1981).

Weizenbaum (1976, pp. 273–276), in a discussion of advice provided by concerned consultants (university scientists) to the Department of Defense during the Vietnam War, shows how technical rationality narrows the issues. The scientists opposed the bombing of Hanoi. Their approach was to demonstrate the bombing's ineffectiveness. The tactic worked, for a time. But the scientists failed to raise the most fundamental issues, according to Weizenbaum. They gave the impression of cooperation, and, despite their convictions, colluded in development of a "more effective" substitute.

One might well ask what, if not reason, is to order the lives of individuals and institutions (Richards, 1942). Many answers might be possible: established religious groups, civil authority, existing social institutions, or the license of the marketplace. These alternatives can, indeed, serve the purpose of order. But the order they most commonly serve is the order of existing power arrangements, which often entail relations of domination. Lacking care for the life of the mind, such vested interests are more likely to determine matters among us than they would otherwise be.

Escape from such a determinism lies principally in the life of the mind, and that is why its nurture is so important (Adler, 1993; Arendt, 1981; Richards, 1942). Without it, schooling corrupts individuals, democratic institutions, and the very learning in whose service good teachers attempt to act. At least from Aristotle onward, the capacity to reason has been construed as the one characteristic that separates humans from other creatures. The capacity to reason is the human approach to good and evil—not that humans are endowed with more good than evil, but that they are capable of inventing, discerning, and *choosing* good or evil (Arendt, 1981). Further, the ground of such decisions and actions must, with humans, lie in the exercise of reason; that is what humans are for. The cultivation of reason, especially through literacy, is intellect. Only intellect possesses the authority to examine, critique, and judge the conditions of existence in an articulate fashion. Such discourse elaborates discussions that the commitments of vested interests would sooner suppress.

American ideologies prize freedom as the basis of individualism, but American schooling avoids the virtue that realizes freedom. Intellect, however, is not a life that provides an abstract solace or a refuge from everyday venality:

> Intellect needs to be understood not as some kind of a claim against the other human excellences for which a fatally high price must be paid, but rather as a complement to them *without which they cannot be fully consummated.* (Hofstadter, 1963, p. 46)

That is, other human virtues—those of the heart and spirit—are limited by stunted intellect. Intellect can, as noted previously, develop outside formal schooling. But Hofstadter makes the key point: Failing to nurture intellect inevitably diminishes the power of all human faculties. Adler (1993) goes further. For him, intellect encompasses spiritual and emotional qualities that technical rationality has denied the world, for centuries, and to the detriment of humankind.

Perhaps schools fail to address intellect because it is dangerous. Through reason, intellect considers the world and strives to judge it coherently. Logic, internally consistent expression, and clear language are the standards of reason. Reason has just cause to ignore vested interests, to form questions that may yield inconvenient answers, and to give offense to unfounded advantage. Reason in its proper form is fearless, and that is its strength; the life of the mind is the perilous struggle to realize that strength in the world.

CHAPTER 2

The Mechanisms of Anti-Intellectualism in the Schools

Aimee Howley and Craig B. Howley

In the past educators sometimes articulated anti-intellectual perspectives overtly (Callahan, 1962; Katz, 1968). Now anti-intellectualism, which on the surface seems incongruous with the prevailing rhetoric of "educational excellence," is primarily a covert aim of schooling. This covert aim is accomplished largely through socialization, which derives from and influences the people who are most deeply involved in the school enterprise — teachers and students. More fundamentally, however, the way schooling socializes teachers and students, so that they come to subordinate intellect to practical know-how, reflects and perpetuates a peculiarly American ethos.

Although the specific features of a school's culture reflect the local context, the general character of schooling is shaped by the ethos that links teaching and learning to political and economic ends. This ethos underwrites educational practices that emphasize the instrumental rather than the intellectual worth of academic learning (Brown, 1993; Gibboney, 1991).

In the previous chapter we examined the ideological sources and ramifications of anti-intellectualism. In this chapter we consider the specific ways in which an anti-intellectual school culture is built. To do so, we look at the anti-intellectualism of teachers, particularly in terms of the forces that limit the scope of their work. But we also examine the controversial literature on teachers' characteristics that declares them indifferent to intellectual concerns and weak academically.

Then, by considering how peers and parents shape views about academic learning, we look at the anti-intellectualism of students. Finally, we bring to light literature about university education in the U.S. that points out the conflict between its intellectual and instrumental functions. This conflict not only affects the culture of the university classroom by influencing the content and delivery of the curriculum, it also affects the university's culture of research, which, in turn, has a significant impact on how American culture regards knowledge generally.

THE INTELLECTUALISM OF TEACHERS

Can teachers act as intellectuals as some commentators (e.g., Giroux, 1988) suggest they ought? What evidence bears on such a determination?

The Nature of Teachers' Work

One important source of evidence concerns the nature of teachers' work. Literature on the professionalization of teaching points to workplace conditions that limit teachers' power and, consequently, their willingness and ability to shape any, including an intellectual, school mission. Even educational reforms that claim to empower teachers seem to limit the scope of their decision making, narrowing the focus of their deliberations to technical matters (Metropolitan Life, 1985; Smyth, 1992).

According to literature on the working conditions of teachers, teaching has become such a "deskilled" job that talented teachers either leave teaching or learn how to treat it mechanistically (see e.g., Apple, 1987; Glickman, 1990). Guttmann (1987, p. 77) summarizes this interpretation: "Most teachers who begin with a sense of intellectual mission lose it after several years of teaching, and either continue to teach in an uninspired routinized way or leave the profession to avoid intellectual stultification and emotional despair."

This response on the part of teachers occurs because most schools treat learning as consumption of information and teaching as delivery of information (Devaney & Sykes, 1988). Depicting a limited prospect for learning and teaching, this approach narrowly circumscribes the teacher's role. Teachers meet the expectations of this role by using the most popular techniques to deliver the information that makes up the curriculum. Most teachers neither choose the curriculum nor invent the techniques of instruction. Rather, they follow the curriculum that the state or district mandates and mimic the techniques that educational research validates. According to Prawat (1991, p. 749),

> teachers typically have little voice in workplace issues, such as the choice of curriculum material, the types of tests used to evaluate instruction, the scheduling of classes, and the allocation of instructional resources. Nor do teachers exert much control over their profession as a whole. They lack the structures and processes present in other professions, like law and medicine, that control entry into the profession and weed out those deemed unqualified to practice.

Several features of schooling reinforce this conception of the teacher's role. Devaney and Sykes (1988, pp. 16–19) identify these features as: (1) the large numbers of students with whom teachers must work, (2) the need for teachers to maintain order, (3) the schools' requirement that teachers use adopted textbooks, (4) the prevalence of accountability systems that rely on standardized tests, and (5) the overarching concern that students learn basic skills (see also McLaughlin, Pfeifer, Swanson-Owens, & Yee, 1986).

Schools with these features reflect a custodial orientation (see e.g., Cusick, 1973; Rosenholtz, 1989). According to Hoy and Woolfolk (1990, p. 281), such schools provide "an inflexible and highly regimented setting concerned primarily with maintaining order." These schools suppress teachers' intellectual curiosity and inventiveness as characteristics that disrupt the orderly routine (Casey, 1992). Teachers become socialized to a school culture that promotes isolated work, discourages interaction among colleagues, and resists change (see e.g., Liston & Zeichner 1990; Rosenholtz, 1989; Sarason, 1971). In custodial schools, teachers come to believe in the necessity for order, and they lose their optimism about the efficacy of schooling (Hoy & Woolfolk, 1990). Moreover, teachers themselves perpetuate the custodial culture by socializing newcomers to what seem to be the necessary conditions of teachers' work (e.g., National Center for Research on Teacher Education, 1991; Tabachnick & Zeichner, 1984).

Teachers as Intellectual Crusaders

But are these conditions really necessary? Some educators believe not. They believe teachers, through their commitment to an intellectual mission, can transform the culture of schooling. Such educators, however, hold somewhat diverse, if not incompatible, conceptions of intellectual work (cf. Prawat, 1991; Valli, 1990). Some commentators (e.g., Duckworth, 1986; Glickman, 1990; Schaefer, 1967) construe intellectual work as any form of active inquiry. In their view, teachers become intellectuals when they engage in research or reflection about teaching and learning. This approach enlarges the scope of teachers' work and, as a consequence, increases their feelings of efficacy. Moreover, it alters the way that teachers view students' learning, so it contributes to better teaching.

Critical educators (e.g., Aronowitz & Giroux, 1985; Giroux, 1988), in contrast, maintain that teachers' work, which is, by nature, intellectual, invariably has political ramifications. They claim that the intellectual work of teachers either perpetuates, supports, critiques, or counters the status quo. According to Aronowitz and Giroux (1985), for example, teachers' intellectual work reflects one of four possible orientations. On the one hand, teachers who are *hegemonic* intellectuals actively perpetuate the dominant culture; and those who are *accommodating* intellectuals accept the dominant culture uncritically and, consequently, serve it. On the other hand, teachers who act as *critical* intellectuals unmask the power relations of the dominant culture from a disinterested vantage; and those who serve as *transformative* intellectuals resist the dominant culture by sponsoring a dialogue that both unmasks and refocuses power relations. From the perspective of critical educators, this last orientation is, of course, the most desirable.

Whereas critical educators (i.e., those who promote the role of "transformative intellectual" for teachers) acknowledge the constraints that currently limit teachers' activity as transformative intellectuals, they nevertheless believe that teachers can acquire power and counter such constraints (Smyth, 1992). Advocates of this position claim that committed teachers can empower themselves by joining forces with like-minded colleagues in the project of reformulating curriculum, altering the nature of classroom discourse, and establishing alliances between schools and oppositional political movements (Aronowitz & Giroux, 1985; Smyth, 1992). Through these practices, teachers will be able to redefine their role, establishing credibility as teacher-scholars and also as political activists. Like the best among their university peers, such teacher-scholars will assume responsibility for stimulating and supporting the inquiry, critique, and political praxis of both students and colleagues.

Critical educators suggest that schools will regard knowledge differently when sufficient numbers of teachers become transformative intellectuals. Furthermore, they claim that this change has the power to transform schools' fundamental mission. Instead of emphasizing the technical distribution of information, schools under the stewardship of reflective, politically engaged teachers will cultivate personal and collective practices for making meaning and taking ethical action (Aronowitz & Giroux, 1985; Britzman, 1986; Liston & Zeichner, 1991; Smyth, 1992).

Despite the benefits that may result from teachers' active engagement as intellectuals, many teachers will find it difficult to sustain the effort of "teaching against the grain" (Cochran-Smith, 1991). Few structures support such a conception of teachers' work: In general, teacher education programs reproduce rather than challenge the conventions of practice, and the culture of schooling tends to promote conformity rather than to stimulate critique. Furthermore, in some cases, teachers may actively resist critique because such a stance conflicts with their fundamental values and their professional ambitions.

The Reproductive Role of Teacher Education

Even though there are some quite notable counterexamples, most teacher education programs reinforce rather than confront prevailing prac-

tice (Eubanks & Parish, 1990; Goodlad, 1991). This circumstance may
show the limited influence that teacher education programs have on prospective teachers, or it may show the concordance of such programs with
conventional educational beliefs and practices. Findings from the National
Center for Research on Teacher Education tend to favor the first explanation.

> Compared with other influences on learning to teach, teacher education is
> generally regarded as a weak intervention. At the preservice level this often
> means that programs do not challenge the "apprenticeship of observation" —
> the years of teacher-watching that shape prospective teachers' views of teach-
> ing. As a result, teachers often leave preservice preparation with their initial
> view intact. They tend to teach as they were taught rather than as they were
> enjoined to teach by teacher educators. At the inservice level, the argument
> often focuses on the socializing impact of the school culture. Left to sink or
> swim on their own, novices understandably fall back on early models or do
> what they see others around them doing. Experienced teachers, cynical about
> most inservice programs and isolated from their colleagues, also tend to main-
> tain rather than question conventional practice. (NCRTE, 1991, p. 67)

Another explanation treats teacher education less favorably, noting its
attention to technical skills and the surface features of instructional practice
(Spatig, 1995). This view faults teacher education for its narrow focus on
skill training and its reliance on public school apprenticeships. Lawson
discusses the limitations of teacher education programs (specifically induction programs) that rely on this approach:

> During this era of hope for the simultaneous reform and improvement of
> both teacher education and schools — with talk about teachers as reflective
> practitioners or transformative intellectuals engaged in personal and collective
> renewal as well as social change — designated induction programs often embody
> the ideology, logic, and protocols associated with training regimens. Although
> training per se is not necessarily detrimental, educators should question the
> ends it serves amidst conflicting images about teachers, schools, teacher educa-
> tion programs, and society. (Lawson, 1992, p. 168)

From this perspective, teacher education programs that fail to take a critical
stance and to cultivate teachers' attention to the covert aims of schooling
perpetuate practices that deny teachers both an intellectual and a political
voice.

Questioning the effects of their programs, many contemporary teacher
educators are struggling to recast the mission and practices of teacher education. This work, however, is taking place in an environment — both in
academe and in society generally — that puts forth messages about teaching

and teacher education that are contradictory at best (Clifford & Guthrie, 1988; Katz & Raths, 1992). At worst, the messages are distinctly hostile, purporting, on the one hand, to demean the role of teacher education and, on the other, to usurp it (see e.g., Goodlad, Soder, & Sirotnik, 1990). Under such circumstances, the fate of teacher education is uncertain. It does, however, seem unjustifiably optimistic to imagine that teacher education, with its contradictory history and current dilemmas, will assume leadership in redefining schools' mission or even in substantially altering instructional practice.

The dangers of teaching "against the grain." Whenever teachers adopt the reflective stance of intellectuals, either as impartial inquirers or critical pedagogues, they defy the norms of classroom practice (see McDonald, 1986, for an example). Taking a reflective stance, they are likely to question the conventional wisdom about students, teaching, classroom discipline, and the school context. This propensity to challenge convention, if applied to instructional practice, may actually jeopardize their effectiveness in performing routine classroom functions (Britzman, 1986). When such teachers fail to behave predictably in accordance with school norms, their colleagues may perceive them as dangerous, incompetent, or both (Cochran-Smith, 1991). Moreover, outspoken and unconventional teachers often provoke the ire of principals and supervisors, many of whom still subscribe to an authoritarian view of administration (Casey, 1992).

As a result of these conditions, few teachers examine, critique, modify, or challenge the traditions of schooling (Cochran-Smith, 1991). And because of the strength of traditional school culture, beginning teachers rarely employ critical reflection even when their teacher education programs explicitly set out to cultivate such inquiry (Feiman-Nemser, 1990; Goodlad, 1991; Zeichner, Tabachnick, & Densmore, 1987). Nor are prospective teachers well served by presenting themselves as intellectuals: School boards are reluctant to hire teachers, especially those who are intelligent, outspoken, and inventive—whom they believe will be hard to control (Imig & Imig, 1987).

These observations suggest the tenuousness of hopeful claims that large numbers of teachers will act reflectively, as intellectuals or as political activists in the school setting. Findings about teachers' beliefs and values, professional aspirations, and class interests also cast doubt on the prospect that teachers will work collectively to transform the culture of schooling, either by altering its intellectual focus or by reframing its social and political function.

Teachers' values and beliefs. Despite the obvious influence of teachers' values and beliefs on their actions, little research has examined this relationship (Pajares, 1992). The few studies of the beliefs and value orientations of preservice and practicing teachers do, however, illustrate teachers' tendency to support the status quo (Lortie, 1975; Pajares, 1992). Furthermore, such studies show that teachers view their work as predominantly affective rather than intellectual in character (Porter & Freeman, 1986; Weinstein, 1989; Wilson, 1990).

Data from *A Study of Schooling*, for example, provide an illuminating if inconclusive picture of teachers' educational commitments. Among the secondary teachers in the sample, fewer than half took the intellectual function of schooling to be the most important (Tye, 1985). To many teachers the personal, social, and vocational functions of schooling take precedence over its function in cultivating even basic academic skills. Because this study defined schools' intellectual mission in terms of basic academic instruction, however, it ignored the possibility that some teachers might conceive of this mission in different terms. Some teachers might, for example, associate basic academic instruction with vocational rather than intellectual aims. Given the nature of the survey instruments used in the study, such teachers would have been unable to express the view that other intellectual aims (e.g., cultivating critical reasoning) were most important.

A recent study that examined the values of teachers in West Virginia found intellectual values to be the most salient in the sense that intellectual concerns explained the greatest variance in teachers' value orientations (Howley, Ferrell, Bickel, & Leary, 1994). This finding indicated considerable disagreement among teachers about the relative importance of schools' intellectual function. Further, the study showed that male teachers tended to value intellectual and instrumental concerns more strongly than female teachers did. These results appear to challenge the common assumption that intellectual and instrumental values are incompatible. In fact, for many of the male teachers in this study, intellectual and instrumental values seemed to be mutually reinforcing. Perhaps this alignment reflects the practical decision that many teachers make to pursue academic studies as a way to become upwardly mobile. This interpretation is consistent with most analyses of teachers' class backgrounds and professional aspirations.

Teachers' Professional Aspirations and Class Interests

Public school teachers, particularly the men, come from working-class backgrounds (Betz & Garland, 1974; Ducharme & Agne, 1989; Gardner, 1982; Sedlak & Schlossman, 1986), and they see teaching as a route to social betterment (Lortie, 1975). As a result of their aspirations for upward mobility, most such teachers tend to support the values of the upper classes. The majority describe their political and social orientation as right of center

(Gardner, 1982; Massialas, 1969); and more than three-quarters report involvement with a religious organization (Gardner, 1982). These findings have led several analysts (e.g., DeYoung, 1986; Ozga & Lawn, 1981) to conclude that teachers would be unlikely to form alliances with workers for the purpose of engaging in social transformation. Moreover, recent calls for the "professionalization" of teaching may limit teachers' attention to popular concerns, securing their allegiance to upper class interests through inducements of high salary and enhanced prestige (Howley & Covaleskie, 1993; Strike, 1993).

Intellectuals among the university professoriate, by contrast, tend to come from advantaged backgrounds and continue throughout their lives to enjoy the privilege, in income and status, of the upper middle class (Ladd & Lipset, 1975). Despite their class location or perhaps because of it, such intellectuals tend to regard sympathetically the plight of working-class and oppressed groups (Halsey & Trow, 1971; Ladd & Lipset, 1975). The majority of university professors, for example, describe their political orientation as liberal or radical and their religious views as atheistic (Hamilton & Hargens, 1993; Ladd & Lipset, 1975; but cf. Faia, 1974).[1]

This comparison, though merely illustrative, does point to some of the difficulties with proposals that view teachers as the group most likely to generate and sustain serious critique and political resistance. Like certain other workers, whose class location has been called "contradictory" (Wright, 1979, 1985), teachers share certain economic interests of workers but also certain interests of owners. Managers, for example, do not own the means of production, but they share the aspirations and often the worldviews of those who employ them. Nevertheless, such workers are in a pivotal position by virtue of the fact that their class location is contradictory. Their contradictory relationship to the means of production provides a kind of creative tension, opening up the possibility that under different circumstances they will ally themselves with either the ruling or the working classes.

Whereas teachers' contradictory class location does offer the promise that under certain unusual circumstances teachers might serve in a transformative role, it also makes it unlikely that teachers will routinely assume such a role. Teachers, like most workers in the United States, will continue to view their interests in personal rather than political terms, focusing their attention on advancement, defined conventionally as improvement in salary and status, rather than on social reconstruction. For example, the deskilling and underpayment of teachers (Apple, 1987; Filson, 1988) has not contributed to their radical consciousness-raising, although it has increased the frequency with which they engage in militant work actions. While improving teachers' tangible benefits, militancy has narrowed rather than enlarged their conception of the scope and potential of their work (Kerchner & Mitchell, 1988).

Problematic also are the recent claims made on behalf of teacher empowerment, teacher professionalism, and site-based management. These claims may, for example, be more rhetorical than substantive (Burbules & Densmore, 1991; Howley & Covaleskie, 1993; Soder, 1991). But even if these trends do have the effect of giving teachers a greater voice in decision making, they may fail to alter in meaningful ways the discourse and practice or the underlying power relations of schooling. Given voice, teachers may still construe education in technical and instrumental terms. Empowered to engage in reflective practice, teachers may, nevertheless, use the opportunity to affirm unexamined assumptions.

These possibilities, unsettling though they be, gain credibility in light of evidence about the characteristics of teachers themselves. Whereas teachers' characteristics obviously do not exist apart from the context of schooling that conditions them, they are of more than rhetorical concern. The pertinent literature about teachers' aptitudes and interests may be controversial, even discomfiting, but it nevertheless bears on our analysis of teachers' potential to serve as an intellectual vanguard.

The Characteristics of Teachers

Our consideration of teachers' characteristics ought not to be construed as "teacher bashing" simply because it concludes that most teachers are not now intellectuals, nor are they likely to become intellectuals until the purposes of schooling change. We are not writing about some character flaw universally shared by teachers, but of cultural and ideological influences that repress intellect among teachers. Teaching is among the most difficult work that anyone can undertake. Yet schooling has been designed for something other than to support good teaching. We conclude that the culture of schooling — the gestalt of the enterprise — militates against intellectualism, even among those teachers who most clearly understand the significance of an intellectual mission. As subsequent discussion (in Chapters 5 and 6) will show, the kind of schooling we imagine can only come into being with the help of and under the authority of teachers who reconceive this mission of schooling.

The cognitive aptitudes of teachers. Even though some scholars exhort practicing teachers to engage in active processes of inquiry (e.g., Glickman, 1990), teachers do not often undertake challenging intellectual work for its own sake. One indication of this characteristic of teachers is their relatively low performance on measures of academic aptitude and achievement (in comparison to other college graduates). Another indication is their limited interest in scholarly activities.

Several studies (e.g., Schlechty & Vance, 1981; Vance & Schlechty, 1982; Weaver, 1978, 1979) document the low standardized test scores of prospective teachers. These studies suggest that high school seniors and college students who intend to major in education show less academic promise than those who intend to major in other subjects. Additionally, these studies demonstrate that the recent rate of decline in the scores of prospective teachers exceeds the rate of decline in the scores of other college students. By comparison with the scores of students majoring in other fields, the Graduate Record Examination (GRE) scores of prospective teachers are quite low and continue to drop. Prospective teachers' scores rank lower than those of prospective nurses, biologists, chemists, aeronautical engineers, sociologists, political scientists, and public administrators.

In addition, there appears to be a negative correlation between teachers' academic ability and their tenure as teachers. Research comparing teachers who stay in teaching and those who leave (see e.g., Schlechty & Vance, 1981; Vance & Schlechty, 1982) indicates that academically talented teachers are much more likely than less talented ones to leave the classroom. According to Levin (1970), many academically capable individuals give up teaching in order to pursue careers that more generously reward their talents.

Levin's interpretation blames the poor economic rewards of teaching for the exodus of talented individuals. This interpretation, however, seems to ignore the finding that individuals really do choose teaching because of its intrinsic, not its extrinsic, rewards (Lortie, 1975). Despite the appeal of such rewards, however, graduates of two elite liberal arts colleges reported that they would select teaching only on an interim basis, for several years between undergraduate and graduate education (Kane, 1990). While recognizing the satisfactions that accompany teaching, these graduates found the disincentives — noncompetitive salary and low status — too potent to ignore.

Whereas findings about teachers' academic aptitude seem compelling on the surface, we need to be cautious in equating academic competence with intellectualism. Academic performance is, after all, not the only condition for the exercise of intellect. We know, for example, that many academically talented individuals use their talents to pursue practical rather than scholarly occupations (see e.g., Hofstadter, 1963; Katchadourian & Boli, 1985). It might then be the case that somewhat less talented individuals choose to engage in scholarship rather than in other sorts of work. Public school teaching might, according to this logic, provide such individuals with the opportunity to pursue their academic interests.

The academic interests of teachers. Considering this possibility, it makes sense to examine research that describes the academic interests of teachers. There is, however, no body of research that directly addresses this question; related research of two types nonetheless allows us to make some reasonable inferences. One type of related research evaluates the course-taking of prospective teachers, and another type considers teachers' reading habits and preferences.

Research that evaluates the types of college courses that prospective teachers complete provides an imperfect reflection of the academic interests of such individuals. Most college programs include particular sequences of required courses, and many programs leave little room for students to choose electives. In spite of these circumstances, however, we suspect that individuals who have compelling academic interests would be likely to promote those interests by taking higher level courses in areas of interest; and we also suspect that individuals who complete few higher level courses in *any* field probably have limited interest in academic scholarship.

A content analysis of college transcripts provides the basis for comparing the course-taking of prospective teachers with that of other college students (Galambos, Cornett, & Spitler, 1985). This study found that prospective teachers took fewer liberal arts courses than did their counterparts in other arts and sciences majors. In addition, the teachers took fewer upper division courses in subjects other than pedagogy. According to the authors, "Teachers, as compared to arts and sciences graduates, take fewer hours in mathematics, English, physics, chemistry, economics, history, political sciences, sociology, other social sciences, foreign languages, philosophy, and other humanities" (Galambos et al., 1985, p. 79). These patterns suggest that, in general, prospective teachers do not make a special effort during their college years to pursue advanced study in fields other than pedagogy.

Qualitative studies (e.g., Goodlad, 1991) of how prospective teachers view their training provide similar insights. These studies suggest that most such individuals resent the portion of their training that provides academic knowledge and value the portion that provides practice teaching. Moreover, prospective teachers dislike and fail to see the relevance of professional studies (e.g., foundations courses) that examine educational practices from a scholarly vantage.

These findings address the question of teachers' academic interests indirectly, and, perhaps, they reflect the nature and quality of curricula in teacher education programs rather than the interests of prospective teachers. Another body of related research, however, provides somewhat less tenuous evidence about teachers' interests. This research considers the reading habits and preferences of teachers.

For several reasons, measures of teachers' reading are appropriate (if proximate) measures of their scholarly interests. First, reading is, by its nature, an intellectual act, requiring the reader to reflect on what is written and construct meaning from it (e.g., Freire & Macedo, 1987). Readers tend, in general, to be more reflective and more critical than nonreaders. Second, reading provides access to content that is available nowhere else; text is a means of recording ideas in great detail. People, therefore, who are concerned with ideas (i.e., those with intellectual interests) must frequently encounter text in order to compare and contrast their ideas with those of others who make use of the literate tradition. Finally, reading provides entry to the intellectual forum in which scholarly dialogue takes place. As a consequence, those who read widely in a field are more likely than others to make a significant contribution to that field.

Taking these features of reading into account, we believe we are justified in considering the frequent reading of literature in an academic field as a necessary (if not sufficient) condition for scholarship. Moreover, we find that the types of books and periodicals that a person reads provide evidence of the nature and intensity of that person's academic interests. With these premises in mind, we turn to the research on teachers' reading habits and preferences.

Studies of teachers' reading show two consistent patterns. First, they show that teachers do not read very much. Duffey (1973), for example, found that, on average, teachers read 3.2 books during the year preceding his study. He also found that approximately 11% of the teachers that he surveyed had not read a single book during that year (Duffey, 1973). In another study, however, teachers seemed to read a bit more: 8.5 books per year (Roeder, 1968 cited in Ilika, 1974). This amount of reading was not much greater than the amount done by other middle-class individuals, who read, on average, 8 books per year. Using a different method of measuring the quantity of teachers' reading, Vieth (1981) found that 34% of the teachers in her sample spent less than an hour per day reading.

The second pattern that this research reveals is teachers' overwhelming preference for popular rather than scholarly or professional literature. According to Duffey (1974), nearly 69% of the teachers in his sample who were reading a book at the time of the survey were reading a popular book. Of those who were reading about education, most were reading books intended for the general public.

Teachers' journal reading reflects similar trends. Cogan and Anderson (1977), for example, concluded that teachers spent very little time reading professional journals. A survey conducted by Koballa (1987) showed that middle school teachers of life science most often selected practical rather than theoretical journals about science or science teaching. In fact, many of these teachers ranked *Science World* as one of the two journals they found most helpful. This finding disturbed the researcher: *Science World* is a journal targeted for middle school students, not for middle school teachers (Koballa, 1987). By contrast, only 4% of the teachers ranked *Scientific American* as one of the two journals they found most useful.

The research about teachers' reading is illustrative, if not definitive. It seems to suggest that, on average, teachers do not have well-developed academic interests. This general picture contrasts sharply with descriptions of outstanding teachers, whose compulsion to study subject matter appears to precede their choice to teach it (e.g., Cohen, 1991).

Teachers' Contribution to Schools' Anti-Intellectualism

The discussion thus far shows how the characteristics of teachers and the conditions of their work conspire to perpetuate an anti-intellectual culture of schooling. This culture reproduces itself, as veteran teachers socialize beginners to adapt to what appear to be the inevitable conditions of classroom teaching. Furthermore, this socialization process tends to offset the efforts of teacher educators who advocate and sometimes model a more reflective or critical stance. We suspect, however, that new teachers ignore the alternative view that their training sometimes attempts to inculcate because such a view is incompatible with their own experiences and values.

But teachers are not alone in supporting a school culture that values personal, social, and vocational aims over intellectual ones. Students and their parents also pressure schools to hold low expectations for academic performance while providing ample opportunities for other types of experience. We will examine the dynamics of this "bargain" in the next section.

STUDENTS, PARENTS, AND THE ANTI-INTELLECTUAL SCHOOL CULTURE

Like teachers, most students and many parents seem to value noncognitive over cognitive school aims. Lucas (1979), for example, found that teachers' and students' value rankings were similar. In her study, both groups ranked character and psychological values more highly than they ranked either intellectual or aesthetic values. Whereas these findings were consistent with those of most such studies, other of Lucas' findings were not. Notably, Lucas' subjects rated intellectual values above social, physical, economic, and political values. By contrast, most other studies find that teachers and especially students rank social and economic values more highly than intellectual values.

Coleman's (1961) classic study, *Adolescent Society*, examined high school students' values in depth and concluded that social values were predominant. He found, for example, that the popularity of top-athlete boys and socially active, well-dressed girls far exceeded that of top scholars of either gender. Moreover, students in the social elites of the high schools were more likely to discredit the value of intellectual activity than were their less popular peers. This anti-intellectual bias was evident among the social elites in all of the schools but was especially striking in the school that served upper-middle-class students.

Coleman found these results troubling: Anti-intellectual values along with other values established in adolescence are likely to persist into adulthood. Given the attitudes of the most popular adolescents in the most affluent schools, Coleman noted the distinct possibility that "society's social elite" would become "oriented away from anything with a strong stamp of intellectual activity upon it" (Coleman, 1961, p. 245).

Within the subculture of the high schools studied, the anti-intellectual climate was so pervasive that the brightest students tended to minimize their brilliance and to exhibit low levels of academic effort. The students who did make the effort to excel academically were the most compliant, not the brightest. This situation led Coleman (1961, p. 266) to conclude:

> The implications for American society as a whole are clear. Because high schools allow adolescent societies to divert energies into athletics, social activities, and the like, they recruit into adult intellectual activities many people with a rather mediocre level of ability, and fail to attract many with high levels of ability.

Curiously, Coleman found that, though anti-intellectual values were prevalent among high school students, these values did not originate in the adolescent subculture. Instead, students' priorities derived from more diffuse socializing experiences within their communities. According to Coleman, adults in the community inculcated anti-intellectual values by placing special importance on certain high school activities, notably interscholastic sports and the other extracurricular activities (e.g., cheerleading and band) that support athletic programs.

Tye's (1985) more recent analysis using data from *A Study of Schooling* provided a similar portrait of high school culture. She found, for example, that only 27% of the high school respondents claimed that they attended school primarily to learn basic skills in reading, writing, arithmetic, and other subjects. Thirty-one percent indicated that they attended school primarily so that they could get better jobs. Tye (1985, pp. 337–338) was distressed by the instrumental way in which so many students viewed their education:

> The belief that the reason a person goes to school is to get a good job and earn more money as an adult has robbed our society of two important values. First of all, it deprives young people of the feeling that what they are doing *now* is important. All the rewards are seen to be somewhere in the future. Secondly, it deprives society of the understanding that learning has value in itself and not just as a saleable commodity. This greatly reduces the range of knowledge that is considered worth having, and creates a population of narrowly-educated citizens.

Tye discovered, however, that in schools that hired considerably more teachers of academic than of nonacademic subjects, students more strongly supported schools' intellectual function. Students from racial and ethnic minorities also seemed more likely than their white counterparts to expect schools to accomplish intellectual aims. Tye (1985, p. 140) hypothesized, "ethnic minority students still value the traditional function of schooling [i.e., that academics prepare students for good jobs] noticeably more than white students do." Given the academic disengagement of many minority students, this interpretation may be unwarranted. Whereas students from ethnic minorities may provide answers that match the expectations of white researchers, their behavior appears to reflect genuine cynicism about the benefits of schooling (Ogbu, 1978). [2] Part of the difficulty in Tye's findings may also pertain to the failure of *A Study of Schooling* to distinguish basic academic instruction from intellectual purpose.

Yet even when the students in Tye's sample placed a high value on schools' academic aims, they did not appear to enjoy the academic experience of high school. Fewer than 6% of these students identified coursework as the one best feature of their school experience. More than one-third, however, considered "friends" to be the "one best thing" about school (Tye, 1985, p. 160). Like the students in Coleman's study, these high school students ranked athletes as the most popular group and "good-looking" students as the second most popular group. Only 7% identified smart students as the most popular in the school. Surprisingly, the two lowest rankings were of student government leaders (4.6% of respondents identified these students as the most popular) and wealthy students (2.8% identified these students as most popular).

Like Coleman, Tye also found that parents appeared to support the academic aims of schools more than either students or teachers did (see Table 2.1). Coleman (1961, p. 32), however, treated his similar finding with some skepticism: "The disparity between professed parental values, on the one hand, and the values expressed by their actions, on the other,

Table 2.1 *Comparison of Students', Teachers', and Parents' Expectations for Schooling, by Category (in percents)*

	Intellectual	Personal	Vocational	Social	N
Teachers	25.6	29.7	14.8	9.9	656
Parents	46.5	19.3	25.5	8.7	4065
Students	27.3	25.6	31.1	15.9	6670

Source: B.B. Tye (1985), *Multiple Realities*. Lanham, MD: University Press of America. Reprinted by permission.

may be very great." Coleman's caution seemed well advised particularly considering the claims of students that their parents would feel greater pride over their athletic than their academic accomplishments.

Despite the pervasive culture of high schools, certain groups of students do hold atypical values. One would suspect that gifted students, who have the demonstrated propensity for intellectual work, would be one such group. A study, done at the same time as Coleman's, examined the value orientations of gifted students and found that even this group of students downplayed intellectual values (Drews, 1964). Among the students in the sample, for instance, only 20% identified themselves as creative intellectuals. Sixty percent considered themselves to be studious, and the other 20% identified themselves as social leaders.

The greatest contrasts in values and academic performance were between the creative intellectuals and the social leaders. When asked, for example, to choose one of four terms to describe how they would most like to be remembered ("student with highest grades," "star athlete," "most popular," or "brilliant"), 70% of creative intellectuals chose "brilliant." By contrast, 90% of the social leaders chose either "star athlete" or "most popular." Whereas the creative intellectuals had the highest IQs (136.5, on average), they had the *lowest* grades (an average GPA of 3.16). Nevertheless, the creative intellectuals expected to attain higher graduate degrees and to enter more prestigious occupations than the social leaders did.

These patterns appear to reflect two general trends. First, most gifted adolescents seem to hold values that are similar to those of less academically capable students. Such students, regardless of their aptitude, appear to conform to the norms of the school culture. Second, a minority of gifted students holds values that differ from those of other adolescents. These students assert their intellectual identity in defiance of the school norms that surround them. They tend, therefore, to be "quiet, introverted, and bookish" (Drews, 1964, p. 30). Furthermore, as evidence of their defiance, these students seem to pay less attention to the academic expectations of their teachers than do other gifted students (e.g., as reflected in their comparatively low grades).

The discussion above suggests that teachers, students, and, perhaps, parents place a relatively low value on the intellectual mission of schools. One obvious explanation for this circumstance is the anti-intellectualism of society in general. This explanation seems to rely on circular reasoning, however, since society comprises the beliefs and actions of adults (teachers and parents) and children. Other explanations that examine the ideological sources of anti-intellectualism in schools may be more persuasive.

The Implicit Bargain

According to several authors (e.g., Cusick, 1983; Sedlak, Wheeler, Pullin, & Cusick, 1986), the high school culture, in particular, encourages students, teachers, and sometimes even parents to bargain in order to minimize the academic focus of the classroom. Cusick attributes this phenomenon to the egalitarian ideal of the comprehensive high school.

His argument goes like this: (1) comprehensive public high schools are required to enroll all students, many of whom are uninterested in the formal curriculum; (2) uninterested students are typically unwilling or unable to engage in difficult academic work; (3) such students are potentially disruptive; (4) schools cannot operate with many disruptions; therefore, (5) schools offer a curriculum that minimizes disruptions. According to Cusick, the type of curriculum that accomplishes this purpose is one based on students' choice of subject matter. Such a curriculum allows students to enroll in courses that require the least effort, and it encourages teachers to accept students' compliance in lieu of academic engagement.

Of course, student choice often reinforces social stereotypes, a phenomenon that Cusick views as a self-induced form of tracking.

> While formal tracking was prohibited, only the better students took Mrs. P.'s ethics class, where they read and discussed literary classics, and only the poorer took "Girl Talk," where they learned to spell and practice writing simple sentences around the themes of their personal lives. Only the brighter took calculus or math functions and only the slower took foundations of math, where they struggled to learn to add and subtract, multiply and divide. (Cusick, 1983, p. 46)

Because of the system of student choice, however, Cusick found that schools can transfer responsibility for tracking to the students themselves.

> By creating such an open system wherein . . . students were free to elect what they wanted, the staff could demonstrate that they were not only trying to

satisfy the needs of every student, but they were not preventing anyone from fulfilling himself. What could not be tolerated was the accusation that they were forcing the black students into the lower classes. (Cusick, 1983, p. 46)

Cusick also noted that the elective system encouraged even the brightest students to enroll in easy courses. These students determined the minimum requirements for high school graduation and tended to meet those requirements only. Moreover, because courses were scheduled on the basis of enrollment, teachers were inclined to offer only those courses that students would take. To maintain a clientele of students and to make their jobs less tedious, teachers usually developed specialty courses, which they justified on the basis of students' needs. "The curriculum was opened to all the variations that the teachers added. . . . One had only to argue plausibly that the students 'needed' this or that material or approach" (Cusick, 1983, p. 111).

Whereas Cusick (1983) blames high schools' decline in academic focus on the egalitarian ideal, Sedlak and associates (1986) attribute it to a more complex set of conditions. According to these authors,

Responsibility for this decline is complicated. The achievement of adolescents depends upon their engagement in, and commitment to, rigorous academic work. The level of adolescents' commitment and particularly their opportunity and ability to be engaged in academic learning are shaped by individuals and institutions largely beyond their control. Prior educational experiences, the skill of their teachers, options that compete for their time and effort, their assessment of the eventual payoffs for sustaining engagement, and parental pressure, together determine the level of a high school student's commitment to concentrated academic learning. (Sedlak et al., 1986, p. 4)

These researchers, however, do not believe that adolescents' lack of academic engagement is a problem of recent origin. Instead, they report evidence suggesting that, as early as the 1920s, high school students in general demonstrated little commitment to academic learning: "Like their counterparts in the late 1960s and early 1970s, students earlier in the century were preoccupied with social activities, romantic involvements, personal appearance, and sports" (Sedlak et al., 1986, p. 16).

Sedlak and associates, nevertheless, conclude that the problem of academic disengagement has worsened in recent years. They attribute the decline in large part to the reduced value (economic, social, and personal) of the high school diploma. Moreover, they claim that, even when students value the diploma for its economic benefit (as a credential), they do not see it as representing a certain level of competence. According to these authors, students have learned that acquiring the diploma depends more on attendance and compliance than on skill mastery. This realization makes it possible for students to stay in school, performing at minimal levels, for the sole purpose of acquiring the credential. When, under such circumstances, the diploma loses its power as a credential, many students cease to have any reason to stay in school (Wingspread Group, 1993).

The effects of elementary schools and colleges. Students are not born cynics, however. In fact, much research supports the common-sense observation that young children are natural learners (e.g., Hudson-Ross, 1989). Nevertheless, these same children seem to acquire, often by middle childhood, a jaded attitude toward both learning and schooling. Perhaps, as Sedlak and associates suggest, this change results from students' experiences in the elementary grades.

There, students learn that compliance, rather than academic performance, is the most desirable behavior. According to Nystrand and Gamoran (1989) students become engaged with the procedural routine of school rather than with its substance. The routine of the elementary classroom requires students to work independently, completing seatwork that often has little academic merit (Anderson, 1981); teachers rarely assign unstructured problems or ask thought-provoking questions (Daines, 1982; Lucking, 1977); and discussion most frequently consists of recitation in which the teacher asks factual recall questions at a rapid pace and students repeat answers directly from the book (Gall, 1984; Nystrand & Gamoran, 1989). Under such conditions, students are sometimes penalized for asking relevant but challenging questions, for attempting to collaborate on work assignments, and for pursuing divergent lines of inquiry (Sedlak et al., 1986). Furthermore, the most repressive expectations of the elementary classroom dominate in schools for working-class students, making it quite unlikely that such children will ever achieve much academic success or take much pleasure in learning (e.g., Anyon, 1980).

Sedlak's analysis of anti-intellectualism in the high school implicates colleges and universities as well as the elementary school. He and his associates claim that "few institutions of higher education in a position to do so exert pressure on high schools to demand more of their students. Neither colleges and universities nor accrediting agencies provide incentives for high school students to exert themselves academically" (Sedlak et al., 1986, p. 78). The declining college-age population has encouraged many colleges and universities to lower admission standards as a way to attract students. Furthermore, because the undergraduate curriculum has been responsive to faculties' demand for increased specialization, it has become fragmented and incoherent (Sedlak et al., 1986). As a result, higher education faculties and administrators find it difficult to identify the prerequisite knowledge that students must possess in order to succeed in college coursework.

Whereas the effect of such trends on high schools' academic expectations and programs may be oblique, their influence on the academic climate of college and university classrooms is quite direct. These influences are among the anti-intellectual mechanisms at work in higher education, and we will treat them with considerably more detail in the concluding section of this chapter. Here, however, we want to emphasize the way in which the expectations of both elementary schools and college contribute to adolescents' limited appreciation of their intellectual options.

Parents' role. There is little evidence about parents' level of support for the intellectual mission of schools. Moreover, the evidence that does exist provides an incomplete picture of parents' attitudes toward and active promotion of the value of intellect. Neither does it provide a clear indication of the effects of such attitudes and activities on children's attitudes and performance. In the Tye study discussed above, for example, parents seemed to be more supportive of an academic mission than were either teachers or students. Research by Sedlak and colleagues (1986), however, indicated that some parents valued academic performance primarily because of its positive bearing on their children's potential to do well economically in a competitive job market. Therefore, they encouraged their children to get high grades, even when doing so necessitated the children's enrollment in low-level, repetitive courses.

Interpreting findings about parents' support of the intellectual mission of schools poses difficulties because that mission is so variously construed. For example, as the Sedlak study suggested, some parents may claim to support academics not because they want their children to be knowledgeable or to be careful thinkers, but because they believe academic success will increase their children's job prospects (cf. Barzun, 1991). Other parents may value academics because they consider that the schools' role should be to uphold certain traditions of discipline and academic rigor. Seldom, if ever, have research studies defined "intellectual mission" as we define it.

Despite their different reasons for supporting the academic performance of their children, parents' academic expectations do seem to influence how well their children succeed in school. Findings from the research on parental expectations suggest three sources of influence: (1) parents' modeling of academic performance and attainment, (2) parents' verbalization of support for such performance, and (3) parents' structuring of conditions for children's academic success. Studies of highly gifted individuals (e.g., Bloom, 1985) confirm that talent development benefits from all three sources of influence. Many talented athletes, musicians, and artists have parents who themselves are talented, who explicitly urge their children to achieve, and who consistently monitor their children's learning.

Moreover, the research literature implies that children's success in school is increased incrementally by each of these types of parent involvement. For example, studies consistently find that parents' academic attainment (i.e., years in school) affects children's academic performance and attainment. The association between parents' and children's attainment is so strong that parental educational level is frequently included in research studies as "a crude indicator of family influence on the educational aspirations of . . . students" (McDill & Coleman, 1965, p. 119). In addition to this influence, however, parents' explicitly stated expectations contribute separately to children's achievement and attainment. When fathers' education is held constant, for example, the strength of parents' encouragement of children's academic progress, nevertheless, remains a potent predictor of actual performance (Cohen, 1987). Despite parents' modeling of high attainment and their espoused expectations, children may fail to perform if parents do not monitor actual performance and provide stimulating experiences outside of school (e.g., Pringle, 1970; Raph, Goldberg, & Passow, 1966).

The way in which parents monitor their children's performance is an important consideration, however, because only certain types of parental structuring have predictably positive effects. For example, parents who give their children extrinsic rewards (like money or privileges) for high performance actually discourage their children's intrinsic motivation and consequent academic achievement (Deci & Ryan, 1985; Gottfried & Gottfried, 1991).

Similarly, parents' assistance of their children with homework assignments may depress rather than improve achievement. Epstein (1988) attributes this apparently counterintuitive finding to the fact that, at least in elementary schools, the students who need the most help with homework are the ones whose achievement is apt to be the lowest. This finding is distressing, however, because it casts doubt on the benefits of two seemingly productive sources of help for low-achieving students. Neither the extra time-on-task that homework provides nor the assistance of concerned parents seems to off-set the effect of children's initial difficulties with school work. Furthermore, the persistent practices of assigning homework to low-achieving children and of asking their parents to provide assistance may, in fact, keep parents from providing the types of structure and support that would condition higher achievement. For instance, parents may become so preoccupied with remediation that they fail to read to their children or provide other "enriching" cultural experiences.

Among high school students, the correlation between time spent on homework and achievement appears as the more intuitive, positive association. This finding, however, may demonstrate the effects of tracking in secondary school more than it shows the improved efficacy of homework at this level (Epstein, 1988). By the time low achievers are in high school, they have elected, or their guidance counselors have assigned them to, classes with low expectations for performance and few requirements like homework.

The typical effects of tracking do not, however, fully determine the achievement of low-ability students. In a large-sample study relating homework time to school performance, Keith (1982) found that homework had an effect on high school grades even when such variables as race, family background, ability, and school program were controlled. By completing 10 hours of homework per week, low ability students were able to earn equivalent grades to those earned by high-ability students who did no homework.

Parents of high school students do not typically help their children with homework. Nevertheless, their involvement in their children's schooling — including nonacademic involvement such as attendance at athletic events — contributes positively to children's achievement (Brown & Steinberg, 1991). Interestingly, fathers' monitoring of their adolescents' school performance had a more significant influence on students' grades than did mothers' similar involvement.

Parenting style also appears to affect adolescents' school performance. Using Baumrind's (1971) typology of parenting style, Brown and Steinberg (1991) found *positive* associations between the "authoritative style" and children's achievement, and *negative* associations between both the "authoritarian" and "permissive" styles and achievement. Apparently, the high expectations, firm structuring, open communication, and mutual respect associated with authoritative parenting contribute to children's academic success. Parents who are overly demanding as well as those who are undemanding seem to be less effective in eliciting high academic performance from their children.

These general associations, however, do not obtain with respect to parenting among ethnic subgroups (Brown & Steinberg, 1991; Dornbusch, Ritter, Leiderman, Roberts, & Fraleigh, 1987). For example, among Asians, the authoritarian style seems to be more productive of high performance (Dornbusch et al., 1987), whereas among African Americans and Hispanics, no particular style seems better than another in conditioning the academic success of youth (Brown & Steinberg, 1991).

Student and Parent Contributions to Anti-Intellectualism

As numerous researchers have suggested, students contribute to as well as respond to the anti-intellectual culture of schools. Conditioned to focus on the instrumental purposes of learning, students view education as a means to an end. Students become inattentive to academics when they find that exciting and lucrative jobs, the purported result of their academic effort, fail to materialize. If they discover that the diploma—a credential with an ostensible economic value—has little bearing on their likelihood of getting a job, they are justified in dropping out altogether.

Parents, while probably contributing to this instrumental view of education, nevertheless can play a role in supporting children's involvement with academic work. Their own inclination to engage in such work and their active monitoring of children's school performance contribute positively to their children's academic engagement. Nevertheless, parents often predispose their children to expect immediate economic rewards in return for the investment of time and effort in academic pursuits. To the extent that parents and students see academics in this contingent way, they discredit a view of education that would support an intellectual climate in schools, better suited to the cultivation of talent.

THE ANTI-INTELLECTUAL UNIVERSITY

A society that does not particularly value intellectual work would be unlikely to sponsor organizations with the expressed goal of nurturing such work. Yet, this goal is espoused in two of the three conventional representations of the university's mission. The teaching mission engages students in the work of acquiring more than rudimentary knowledge, and the research mission engages scholars in the process of extending knowledge. In recent decades, moreover, the resources devoted to university education and research have increased substantially.

Despite their espoused goals, universities by no means give free reign to intellectual endeavor. Barzun (1991, p. 151) notes,

> The college—and the university around it—have been transformed into a motley social organism dedicated to the full life. It does include the mental life, but certainly makes no fetish of it. Rather, intellect weaves in and out of the main business, which is socialization, entertainment, political activism, and the struggle to get high grades so as to qualify for future employment.

Often, in fact, the intellectual work of the university—both the transmission and production of knowledge—gets narrowly construed so as to coincide with the immediate concerns of business and government (Atwell, 1993). Such narrow instrumentalism has not always characterized higher education in America, however. When colleges and universities served a small, elite clientele, their concern for utility was restricted to the general notion that good education would help citizens take action in the world (e.g., Barzun, 1991). This view of higher education supported a "traditional" curriculum, rooted in the liberal arts. As industrialization progressed throughout the late nineteenth and into the twentieth century, however, this rationale for higher education diminished in importance. A brief review of the history of colleges and universities in the United States elaborates these changes.

The Useless College

Beginning in the colonial period, colleges prepared an elite group of young men for service in the institutionalized church. To the extent possible, such colleges resembled their European counterparts, cultivating a guild of scholars who nurtured, extended, and promulgated the ecclesiastical tradition (Nisbet, 1971). According to Hofstadter (1955), however, these colleges differed from those in Europe in their emphasis on sectarian dogma to the detriment of intellectual inquiry. Despite some concern for practical training (Gallagher, 1993), these early colleges did provide sufficient nurture of intellect to produce a cadre of educators who became vocal advocates of rigorous scholarship (Veysey, 1965). These intellectuals maintained the view that liberal studies would condition both mental and moral discipline.

For these educators, however, scholarship and inquiry were not fully compatible. They considered scholarship to be the means of fostering the reasoning skills of students and, thereby, strengthening students' appreciation and understanding of religious truths. By contrast, they viewed inquiry—particularly scientific inquiry—as a threat to such truths. Veysey (1965, p. 41) characterized this view as follows:

> Science . . . was to be mistrusted on a variety of levels. It conveyed a tone which these men did not like, one which the older phrase "natural philosophy" had comfortably muffled. Science paraded nakedly, seemed vulgar; it appeared to denigrate the position of man in the universe. Its subject matter was also believed too easy and undemanding to deserve a major place in the classroom. In theory, science might reluctantly be given a realm of its own, comparable to that of religion in providing an understanding of the universe. In practice, science was chastised for abandoning its humble subservience.

Despite the efforts of such educators to preserve tradition, scientific and practical studies became prominent features of the antebellum college (Gallagher, 1993). Interest in the German model of higher education furthered this trend, resulting in the transformation of some of the nation's elite liberal arts colleges into major, multipurpose universities.

The Useful University

The multipurpose institution that developed after the Civil War attempted to accomplish a variety of possibly conflicting aims: cultivation of intellect, production of new and useful knowledge, and inculcation of vocational skills (Gallagher, 1993; Veysey, 1965). This institution combined elements of the British, German, and American traditions into an amalgam that some educators found workable and others did not.

Kerr (1963, p. 18), for example, saw considerable value in the emerging institution, which he termed, "the multiversity":

> The . . . combination does not seem plausible but it has given America a remarkably effective educational institution. A university anywhere can aim no higher than to be as British as possible for the sake of the undergraduates, as German as possible for the sake of the graduates and the research personnel, as American as possible for the sake of the public at large — and as confused as possible for the sake of the preservation of the whole uneasy balance.

Dungan (1970, p. 143), however, questioned the extent to which universities actually managed to perform the different, perhaps incompatible, functions expected of them:

> The university in the United States has long been described as multi-functional, but a candid examination of the distribution of resources within the collectivity of institutions would show that there is a concentration in activities of interest to relatively few. Despite our protestations about pluralism and multi-functionality, we tend on the whole in higher education to do essentially the same thing with quite divergent degrees of quality.

Kurtz (1974, p. 187) disputed the value of assigning multiple functions to the university and, instead, claimed:

> The university ought to be the institution of society preeminently concerned with the cultivation of learning and inquiry. It ought to be the repository of the best insights of past civilizations, and it ought to push the frontiers of knowledge in the future.

Regardless of the role for which it was best suited, however, the antebellum university tried to assume as wide a variety of roles as its clientele demanded. In fact, some universities attempted to be so responsive that they developed academic programs constructed solely of elective courses. Charles Eliot, president of Harvard from 1869 to 1909, was perhaps the most notable advocate of this system. Eliot believed that an elective system would allow students to select the most appropriate courses to prepare them for their chosen occupations. Furthermore, he believed that individual choice would advance the interests of society by sponsoring progress of all sorts—social, economic, and scientific (Miller, 1988).

Although many faculty and administrators in higher education subsequently argued against this system, most did not disagree with its intent. Only a small group of these dissenters insisted that the purpose of the university was to preserve and transmit a cultural canon, rather than to prepare *useful* citizens. Most dissenters, by contrast, condemned the elective system, not for its ultimate goal of social utility, but rather for its inefficiency in meeting that goal.

At Columbia, for example, President Nicholas Murray Butler argued that a *required* core curriculum grounded in the liberal arts would be the type of program most likely to cultivate in students a willingness to align personal interests with the interests of the larger society (Howley & Hartnett, 1994). Butler and many other educators of the time believed that this outcome was particularly important, since increasing numbers of students—from diverse backgrounds and with different aspirations—had begun to enroll in colleges and universities.

These students saw higher education as the route to specialized and lucrative jobs in an economy in which social progress seemed contingent on evident economic growth. Furthermore, such students, and their families, began to see the college degree as a symbol of status (Levine, 1986). As a consequence, educators responded to the market demand and founded new colleges to accommodate the vocational interests and socioeconomic aspirations of an increasingly large minority of young people. Moreover, established colleges expanded and modified their offerings to address the needs of this more diverse clientele. According to Levine (1986, p. 21), these changes resulted in stratification among institutions of higher education:

> The culture of aspiration stimulated an unprecedented demand for higher education of any kind as a symbol of economic and social mobility; it also created the demand for status that enabled some colleges to select their students for the first time. Ethnic and poor students often surpassed their more affluent peers in academic ability and drive, but more often than not they were channeled into less acclaimed schools and less prestigious occupations. Urban and public institutions offered new courses and new hope to those who clamored for an opportunity to move up the economic and social ladder, while at the same time the now-selective liberal arts college provided a check against undesired democratization to those who wished to preserve the hegemony of the white Anglo-Saxon Protestant upper middle class.

Levine's analysis, however, simplifies what seems to have been a more complicated response on the part of institutions of higher education. There is considerable evidence that changes took place even at elite schools like Harvard and Columbia (e.g., Howley & Hartnett, 1994; Miller, 1988; Rudolph, 1977). These institutions made significant efforts to democratize their curricula and to establish mechanisms for working with promising students from diverse backgrounds. For example, such schools began to offer essential types of courses, such as English and mathematics, at varying levels of difficulty. They set up advising systems to help students match their aptitudes to their vocational goals; they established articulated sequences of courses in particular subject areas to correspond to the presumed needs of students at various stages in their academic careers; and they adopted tests to determine students' initial placement in these curricular sequences.

To institutionalize these changes, universities saw the value of organizing their faculties into specialized divisions and departments. This organizational structure, in turn, encouraged further specialization of faculty and promoted competition among departments (Rudolph, 1977). In addition, it supported the development of graduate programs—some to educate aspiring professionals and others to nurture new generations of scholars (Miller, 1988).

In the 1900s institutions of higher education became increasingly vocational in both their undergraduate and graduate programs (Gallagher, 1993). Interestingly, this vocationalism did not result from the concern of business for a technically educated work force. Rather, it derived from educators' interest in demonstrating the practicality of higher education. Whereas many businessmen of that era doubted the association between academic and real-world success (Callahan, 1962), educators anticipated the benefits, both humanitarian and material, of promoting such an association (Miller, 1988). As they saw it, an expanded system of higher education, while providing business with necessary expertise, would also, and probably more importantly, provide the nation with the human resources required to solve technical and social problems. In an era characterized by its infatuation with progress, the university seemed like the logical place to bridge the gap between theoretical knowledge—particularly in the sciences—and practical utility.

The U.S. involvement in World War I provided colleges and universities with the opportunity to follow through on the claim that their principal role was to serve the nation. Not only did such institutions incorporate military training into their curricula, many of them also—at the behest of the government—adopted courses in history and economics that illuminated war issues in particular ways (Howley & Hartnett, 1994). These courses consisted of propaganda disseminated by the National Historical Service Board (NHSB), whose task, according to Barrow (1990, p. 128), involved "rewriting social science and humanities curricula and . . . developing interdisciplinary 'war issues' courses at colleges to help institutions meet their responsibility for interpreting the war correctly."

The Army believed that the "war issues" course was so important ideologically that the Student Army Training Corps appointed a faculty member from the Massachusetts Institute of Technology to serve as the national director of the course. According to its director, the course served the following purposes:

> This is a war of ideas, and . . . the course should give to the members of the Corps some understanding of the view of life and of society which they are called upon to defend and of that view against which we are fighting. (Aydelotte, 1919, cited in Allardyce, 1982, p. 706)

The chauvinism that prompted such efforts did not end, however, once the war was over. Many colleges and universities, for example, incorporated the ideological tenets of the war issues courses into new curricular offerings. These courses, required at some colleges, reconfigured the history curriculum to address political, social, and economic problems of the day. At Columbia, social science and humanities professors worked collaboratively to develop such a "peace issues" course, which, soon after, became the cornerstone of an interdisciplinary core curriculum (Allardyce, 1982).

Another consequence of the war was the expansion of the research mission of American universities. Institutions of higher education responded to the government's call for scientific research to advance the war effort. The National Academy of Sciences (NAS), for example, passed a preparedness resolution in 1916 that advocated increased cooperation among "governmental, educational, industrial, and other research organizations to facilitate national preparedness" (Barrow, 1990, p. 131). Moreover, the NAS, in league with the government, established the National Research Council, whose goals were to formulate national research priorities, to assign teams of researchers to carry out high-priority research projects, and to funnel money to the organizations that employed these researchers.

Applied natural science had an obvious military utility, but social science also had a place. The Army, for example, hired university psychologists to design mental tests of various sorts to assist in the assignment of personnel. Furthermore, social science offered the promise of controlling social problems at home, a promise particularly encouraging to dispirited progressives who encountered with some alarm the social and cultural dislocations resulting from the war (Miller, 1988).

In a number of ways, World War I attuned university administrators and faculty to the needs of the nation. Attention to such needs was not, however, incompatible with the aims that such institutions had already started to formulate for themselves: (1) the education of technical experts, (2) the production of knowledge with immediate social utility, and (3) the direct application of such knowledge in service to society. Following the war, however, these practical, and possibly anti-intellectual, aims came increasingly to form the character of the contemporary university. Furthermore, they permanently altered the university's conception of intellectual work, rendering academic scholarship valuable primarily by virtue of its usefulness.

Educating technical experts. As the twentieth century progressed, more and more Americans acquired respectability and a modicum of prosperity by moving into the middle class. Their upward mobility was supported by structural changes in the economy that shifted the focus from agrarian to industrial production. These changes resulted in the unprecedented growth of cities, with a consequent increase in social problems. Further, the expansion of factories and their potential to generate profit led industrialists to seek ways to rationalize the production process. Thus, the management of factory work and the amelioration of social problems became important new roles for aspiring professionals. The modern university, with its authority to confer credentials, provided legitimacy to a new class of social and managerial "engineers" (Bledstein, 1976).

The increasing vocationalism of the university manifested itself differently in elite as contrasted with more accessible institutions (Rudolph, 1977). Elite schools tended to preserve the traditional B.A. degree but to confer it to students regardless of whether their studies were academic or vocational. According to Rudolph (1977, p. 247), "specialization and a professional orientation . . . came to dominate the undergraduate experience at the very colleges and universities that had been the most trustworthy guardians of the humanist tradition." The land-grant colleges and state universities, which had always had a more vocational focus, abandoned the B.A. in favor of more practical degrees. Both types of institutions, however, began to expand the duration of professional training beyond the baccalaureate level.

Moreover, vocational education, such as the training of teachers and nurses (which had previously taken place outside of higher education), gained in stature by finding a place for itself within the higher education community. Teacher education programs, for example, acquired credibility by means of their transformation from 2-year normal school to 4-year degree programs at teachers' colleges. These programs further enhanced their professional status when teachers' colleges became state colleges and, later, state universities (Goodlad, 1991).

According to some authors (e.g., Reisman, 1981), the vocationalism of higher education has been a response to the consumerism of students. In this view, competition for student enrollment has caused colleges and universities to become increasingly sensitive to students' demands for practical, relevant programs (Veysey, 1965). Another perspective, however, suggests that colleges and universities have been responsible for shaping public demand for vocational programs and services.

> The university and its sources of livelihood reflect the structural organization of our society itself. This has generated the entrepreneurial system of the American university, in which the policy-initiating bodies—both administrations and faculties—acting in the manner of capitalist entrepreneurs have become actively and competitively involved in seeking out what kinds of intellectual pursuits society could use (and therefore be willing to support) and in developing the corresponding programs of research, education, and service. (Luria & Luria, 1970, p. 76)

Regardless of which view is correct, contemporary colleges and universities, even the most elite, place greater emphasis on the training of technical experts than on the cultivation of liberal learning or the elaboration of reflective thought (Bellah et al., 1985; Bloom, 1987; Wilshire, 1990). Students, too, seem to be more interested than ever before in the immediate utility of what they learn (e.g., Barzun, 1991). Despite the fact that some college students seem to value intellectual pursuits, many others view such pursuits skeptically. Many students claim to value academic scholarship simply as the means to acquire credentials that provide access to lucrative professional jobs; they take no intellectual pleasure in their studies (Katchadourian & Boli, 1985).

Producing useful knowledge. An essential focus of the contemporary university—one derived from the German model—is the production of scientific knowledge. This knowledge (the knowledge of research per se) provides, in the modern conception of reality, a totalizing view of the material and social world (Best & Kellner, 1991; Wilshire, 1990). According to Wilshire, this view discredits personal experience and alienates individuals from a sense of community. As a consequence, people come to substitute their socially defined and narrowly circumscribed technical roles for more legitimate forms of self-definition; they accept the seeming necessity of the linkage between expertise and power. This view of social reality compels people to cede considerable power to experts, a default that advances the economic and political interests of the dominant classes of society (e.g., Habermas, 1975; Lyotard, 1979/1984; Windmiller, 1967).

The transfer of power to specialists obviously implicates the university, whose role in the production of expertise is twofold (Bledstein, 1976). The university takes a primary role in training each new cadre of experts. Its other role in promoting expertise, however, is more direct and, as a consequence, even more significant. This role involves the employment and protection of professors who build small but potent empires for soliciting, conducting, and marketing research (Barzun, 1991; Lyotard, 1979/1984; Nisbet, 1971).

Such research became important to business, the government, and the military during World War I. It increased in volume considerably during World War II; and, by the 1950s had eclipsed teaching as the major function at many prominent universities. Moreover, it altered power relationships in institutions of higher education in ways that degraded the authority of academic scholarship. Nisbet (1971, pp. 99–100) describes this process:

> No one who was on the American university campus when the large research institutes began to flourish is likely to forget the shifts which took place in authority, in influence, in wealth, and in status. Overnight, it seemed, two nations came into being: the haves and the have nots; the first possessed of a form of wealth and power that owed little if anything to the university; the second identified increasingly by their lack of research money, their dependence upon the university, their largely local identities, and their ever-diminishing status in the eyes of not only administration and faculty but, in due time, of the students.

The university's shift in focus from pure to marketable research not only altered its relationship to the larger society, it also, and more importantly, changed the way that Americans viewed knowledge (Kerr, 1991). In the earlier view, knowledge consisted of the collective wisdom of past and present thinkers. *Any person* could decipher such wisdom through rigorous study and could contribute to it by following systematic procedures of inquiry. In the revised and now prevailing view, knowledge is impersonal, timely, and transitory. It is available only to those who have *privileged access*, and it can be expanded only by those with certain prerogatives through systematic, heuristic, and certainly adventitious production (cf. Barzun, 1991).

This revised view of knowledge construes practical applicability as the primary warrant of truth claims, rendering truth at once both temporary and commercial. The result is that knowledge has become a stratified array, with certain information accessible to everyone to the extent that he or she needs it to fulfill a social destiny, and other information highly proprietary, accessible only to those with great wealth and power. In this view, the most significant knowledge is ephemeral (Barzun 1991) — insider information that enlarges the dominion of the ruling class (Howley, 1993).

Serving society. Closely allied with the university's role in producing practical knowledge is its role in using that knowledge to solve pressing social and technical problems. Because these problems are defined by the established order and because work to solve them is funded by that order, their solution usually falls within ideologically prescribed limits (Atwell, 1993; Luria & Luria, 1970). Nevertheless, the claim that such solutions are value free (as an outgrowth of objective, positive science) most often disguises their ideological basis (e.g., Aronowitz, 1988; Engler, 1967).

Producing such solutions, however, provides considerable economic benefits to those professors who accept the work (Gallagher, 1993). Catering to their corporate or government employers, these professors in fact distance themselves from the clients whom, ostensibly, they are hired to serve (Engler, 1967). As a consequence, even the most forward-looking efforts to solve social problems usually become feats of social engineering that require clients to adapt to the expectations, however inappropriate, of the prevailing power structure (Luria & Luria, 1970). Moreover, technological problem solving conducted by university scientists typically has military and industrial ramifications that contribute to the machinations of political and economic empire-building.

Can Knowledge be Anti-Intellectual?

The three-pronged mission of higher education clearly concerns work that involves knowledge, and common sense holds that work with knowledge is, almost by definition, intellectual. In our view, however, the extent to which work with knowledge can contribute to the development of intellect depends largely on the way knowing and knowledge are construed.

When knowledge is atomized as information with a particular temporary utility, its role in cultivating intellect becomes suspect. Under such circumstances, knowledge functions as a commodity rather than as a tool of reason. Professors and students come to appreciate it for the price it fetches rather than for the insights it permits. Its logic becomes the logic of the marketplace rather than any logic of internally consistent warrant; and its seemingly value-free status allows the "scholar" to disregard the ethical necessity of thoughtful reflection (Habermas, 1971; Postman, 1992). In our view much of what is taking place in the contemporary American university contributes to making knowledge anti-intellectual in just this way (cf. Barzun, 1991).

ANTI-INTELLECTUALISM AND THE LIFE OF THE MIND

Whereas the pursuit of knowledge forms the substance of education, its role in U.S. schools from the elementary through the graduate level is to cultivate useful performance rather than to provide the basis for informed discourse and ethical action. As a consequence, the mechanisms of schooling have come to embody features that limit inquiry, narrowly circumscribe literacy, and substitute grant mongering for scholarship.

We have, for example, seen the way in which teachers' backgrounds and beliefs contribute to a limited vision of the intellectual possibilities of schooling. More importantly, the culture of schools conditions responses from teachers, students, and parents that constrain learning to quite specific instrumental purposes. Even institutions of higher education, the historical bastions of a purely intellectual mission, have in large measure abandoned intellect.

Given the mechanisms of schooling that routinely ignore or work against the life of the mind, we find warrant to conclude that intellect must be, in some fundamental way, irrelevant or threatening to the national purpose. Further support for this judgment follows from an analysis of how students who are defined by their schools as the most academically able typically fare within both regular classrooms and those expressly designated for their "special education." It is to this analysis that we turn next.

CHAPTER 3

How Gifted Education
Devalues Intellect

Edwina D. Pendarvis and Craig B. Howley

The most common rationale for gifted education is that the children it serves have such superior aptitudes for scholarship or art that they cannot be adequately educated through *ordinary* methods. This rationale implies that schools should use *extraordinary* means to develop these students' unusual aptitudes. Special programs established for gifted students, however, often devalue and inhibit intellectual development. Rather than giving these students appropriately challenging instruction, public schools typically identify such students as superior, separate them from other students for part of the school day or week, and socialize them — through the content and form of the gifted program — to regard themselves as especially deserving of privilege.

As a consequence, most intellectually precocious students, like others in the public schools, remain largely unprepared to engage in scholarly or artistic work that requires concentrated study and dedication to ideas. Their special preparation, however, does successfully differentiate them from other students: They are prepared for high-status jobholding in careers that support the interests of the wealthy and powerful. In this role, gifted individuals are expected to respond efficiently and pragmatically, as technicians and managers, to job-related problems while overlooking the broad social, economic, and political context in which the problems are set. Schooling cultivates in bright students the disposition to view their talents narrowly and to respond uncritically to what society asks of them. Both the content of gifted programs and the unchallenging context of regular school programs contribute to this outcome.

It is important to recognize that neither talent nor talented children should be blamed (or punished) for the mistaken notions that guide schooling. And in many cases, teachers, with their students, are equal victims of such mistaken notions, as we suggested in the previous chapter.

ENTITLEMENT REPLACES SCHOLARSHIP

Gifted programs often adopt goals that are irrelevant to students' abilities. Many gifted programs emphasize counseling or adopt exclusively social goals, such as development of "leadership skills." In the name of improving gifted students' creativity, programs typically eschew substantial academic content and instead teach generic "problem-solving skills" that are easily mimicked, but lack much relevance to academic or artistic disciplines. At the same time, educators, including many in gifted education, exaggerate the emotional and social risks of acceleration and other intellectually appropriate provisions for able students. Parents are often discouraged from seeking such provisions for their children.

In short, the most valid rationale for gifted programs (i.e., the development of exceptional talent) is not much addressed in practice. As discussed in Chapter 1, another rationale informs actual practice more strongly.

Leadership Training and the Reproduction
of the Managerial Class

The anti-intellectual character of gifted programs is sometimes justified by the rationale that such programs offer specialized instruction to students who will become leaders in their "chosen" fields. In this view, gifted children as a group are presumed to be more essential than other children to the nation's economic well-being (Sapon-Shevin, 1993). The leadership rationale for gifted education is sometimes used alone, and sometimes in conjunction with the rationale that gifted programs are part of a more widespread, democratic effort to meet the needs of all children. Through the use of the "greatest resource" rationale, the special preparation of students from privileged backgrounds for a life of continued privilege is made to appear just.

There is little support, however, for the hypothesis that high levels of academic ability in children predict adult leadership. In contrast, ample evidence does support the rationale of talent development: Some children *are* capable of benefiting from advanced academic work, and their talents develop when instruction is accelerated to match more nearly their evident learning rates (Daurio, 1979; Kulik & Kulik, 1984; Stanley, 1981). The talent development rationale requires no inference about the relationship between childhood ability and adult occupational destiny, a relationship that has been questioned by many researchers in the field of gifted education (e.g., Jarrell & Borland, 1990; Feldman, 1984; Csikszentmihalyi & Robinson, 1986; Sternberg, 1986). It assumes that providing instruction commensurate with children's capability, whatever the achievement level, constitutes good pedagogy. And there is considerable support for the claim that regular classroom instruction fails to match the achievement level of students who are intellectually or artistically talented (e.g., Clark & Zimmerman, 1984; Stanley, 1976).

The attempt to develop leadership, however, derives from no valid developmental construct by which to judge children's progress toward becoming better leaders. It offers no pedagogical ground on which to base special provisions for some students and not others. Schools generally encourage compliance, however, and they seem to create habits and attitudes more conducive to following than leading (Gearing & Epstein, 1982). Thus, removing some children, particularly children from relatively privileged backgrounds, from a program (i.e., the regular classroom) that habituates docility, and instead grooming them to expect the prerogatives of leadership, is not only pedagogically indefensible, but ethically suspect.

Leadership training may be warranted for some adults who occupy or are being prepared for administrative positions. For children and youth, whose life choices are unformed, however, such training is at best premature. Further, because the majority of children included in programs to develop leaders are white children from affluent families, the practice makes unfair distinctions. It segregates children by class and race without compelling reason.

The class interests of gifted programs. Because of the circumstantial nature of leadership, reliable identification of leadership potential is very much in doubt (Pendarvis, Howley, & Howley, 1990). Research about available instruments and procedures, at any rate, suggests that we cannot identify which children possess unusual leadership potential or the sort of leadership potential they might possess (Shore, Cornell, Robinson, & Ward, 1991; cf. Stogdill, 1974).

The prevalence of leadership training for able students absent adequate empirical support for the practice stems, in our opinion, from the imperative to create a professional and managerial stratum that advances the material interests of the wealthy and powerful. Of course, such identification, and especially such training, also advances the material interests of the majority of the "graduates" of gifted programs (Margolin, 1994). Some evidence suggests that their material advancement comes, however, at the expense of their intellectual and moral development (Trumpbour, 1989). Moreover, the damage to society and the environment that accompanies the shortsighted opportunism that characterizes so much of our political economy—including this cooptation of bright children—may well damage everyone's material interests in the long term (Foster, 1993).

Democracy requires an educated citizenry. But mass education can also institutionalize undemocratic or anti-democratic functions, though the processes of such institutionalization are not well understood (Cheney, 1990). Clearly, however, in any *imperfectly* democratic nation, institutionalizing the educative function inevitably entails reproduction of prevailing injustices because public schools can be no more just than the society that sponsors them. In democracies generally, the institutionalized warrants for injustice (e.g., institutional racism) perform the same service in support of the status quo that coercion does in totalitarian regimes (Foucault, 1979; Poulantzas, 1980).

Workable democracies, of course, protect the rights of citizens to articulate visions of a just society. Such articulation requires development of the mind's critical faculty, the intellect, so a schooling that deflects or deforms the development of the intellect strikes at the core of democratic intent.

If students support the prevailing relations of power in their society, they will try to justify the imperatives contingent on such relations. If, on the other hand, they question the wisdom or justice of these imperatives, they may sponsor informed resistance. Because bright students are regarded as uniquely powerful in terms of potential influence (perhaps properly so, in the case of their ability to articulate opposition to injustice), they are perceived as at once more useful and more dangerous than other students. Society's love-hate relationship with gifted students has been explained in this way by Gallagher (1985).

In a society with nothing to hide, gifted students' education could focus on developing their intellectual powers. But intellect asks questions about causes and ends. When injustice becomes institutionalized in a democracy, the state-sponsored schools have reason to limit students' ability and propensity to engage critique. Hence, public schools develop attitudes and skills associated primarily with technique, and discourage critique and debate about why things are as they are, how they might change, and how students might direct their energies and talents to such ends. Gifted education, in these circumstances, abets a system that undereducates some students and miseducates others, while devaluing intellect widely.

Gifted programs are estimated to identify only 50% of all highly capable students (Fetterman, 1988). The unidentified half (and those who are identified but not actually served) are *undereducated*, in that they spend all of their time in the regular classroom, where instruction is usually slow paced. Among the identified half, however, just one-third are included in special programs to develop their talents (Fetterman, 1988). We estimate, therefore, that less than 20% of gifted children receive any sort of special education. Those who do receive special education are typically *miseducated* in that they are provided enrichment pull-out programs that socialize them to accept their privileged status without question. Reports that corroborate this analysis are by no means uncommon (e.g., Margolin, 1994; Sapon-Shevin, 1993; Stanley, 1986; Weiler, 1978).

Most gifted children in the U.S. who do participate in special programs come from privileged families whose interests are clearly aligned with those of the economic and political elite (Margolin, 1994). A large proportion of the neglected gifted children (the unidentified 50%) come from backgrounds whose material interests conflict with the interests of the privileged classes. As competition for well-paying jobs gets more intense, this proportion is likely to *increase*. If implemented, reform efforts such as vouchers and other means of "educational choice" may contribute to this result (Lowe, 1992).

The contradictory functions of gifted programs. According to Gintis and Bowles (1988), schools help to reproduce the status quo, but, at the same time—though to a much lesser extent—they help to promote resistance to it. U.S. schools, as a branch of the state, constitute a contradictory site in the political economy. As a government institution, they participate in a tradition of liberal democracy even though they also are part of a mechanism of oppression (Carnoy & Levin, 1985; Gintis & Bowles, 1988).

Tied closely to the general aims of schooling, gifted programs participate in these contradictory functions. Admittedly, some programs for the gifted, often under unsupportive conditions, have made positive differences in the lives of students, not only the privileged but the underprivileged as well. To the extent that gifted programs develop intellectual habits of mind among students who represent proportionately the different genders, ethnic groups, and social classes, they serve democratic ends.

In general, however, programs cater primarily to students from affluent backgrounds, and they often fail to address intellectual aims. Like other school programs, gifted programs simultaneously promote and undermine the development of their students' intellectual potential. By restricting talent development to narrowly instrumental ends, programs help select and groom intelligent careerists—administrative or professional experts who manage, rationalize, and promote the interests of the politically and economically powerful. This is a generally *unacknowledged* outcome of gifted programs (Margolin, 1994).

Of course, neither gifted programs in specific nor schooling in general can effectively suppress all resistance to the social, economic, and political status quo, but they systematically weaken such resistance (cf. Foucault, 1979). Most educators do subscribe to the principles—if not always the practices—of democracy and due process. And they believe that they generally act in the best interests of all of their students. Often they do. The odds, however, are institutionally stacked against them: The political economy seems to require certain injustices. The civil rights movement of the mid-twentieth century, for example, was historic and heroic, but the persistence of racism and recent increases in poverty rates attest to the difficulty of real change.

Differentiation Between Gifted and Regular Programs

Regular classroom teachers tend to regard gifted programs without enthusiasm, and at times with open hostility. In many cases, their hostility is warranted. Many complain, legitimately, that the gifted students are enjoying entertaining instruction that is no better suited to them than to other students, who are excluded from the program. Some also claim that the gifted program is easier than the program in the regular classroom, and they are often right.

Many regular classroom teachers resent the inference that they cannot effectively teach bright students, and most doubt that the gifted program is necessary for even their brightest students. In general, classroom teachers see gifted programs as having little merit for gifted students and as causing considerable harm to other students. In this view, gifted programs usurp resources that schools could use in more productive ways (cf. Margolin, 1994).

According to Fetterman (1988), however, gifted-program teachers themselves judge the instruction they provide to be educational as well as entertaining. They see themselves as dedicated to their students, often working beyond the regular school day to counsel and coach them. These teachers report that they often help their students deal with conflicts with other students and with teachers. They spend time outside of school developing activities to address students' interests. And it is true that they do such work in largely hostile contexts of resentment and envy.

Many parents say their child is happiest in the gifted classroom and is best served by the teacher of the gifted. When gifted programs are threatened with funding cuts or reductions in personnel, parents almost always offer informed and energetic resistance. Although most parents are extremely supportive of the programs, many also say they would prefer a clearer academic emphasis. Parents have often confided to us that school personnel (including teachers of the gifted) see them as "pushy" — cherishing unreasonable expectations of academic accomplishment for their children.

Like their parents, most gifted children have generally positive things to say about gifted programs. They enjoy enrichment activities, interchanges with other able children, and the more informal climate of the gifted classroom. As Fetterman (1988) notes, however, some feel cut off from other students in the school, and some feel unfairly put upon when the gifted-program teacher exhorts them to try harder in their studies. Apparently, the competitive, albeit anti-intellectual, environment of the schools creates resentment of and hostility toward academically able children, and identification and placement in the gifted program may well compound this effect.

Most children who are *not* identified as gifted report few definite perceptions about gifted programs. Sapon-Shevin (1993, p. 37) found that teachers discourage discussions about why some children are selected and some are not: "Some teachers said that the children simply 'never ask,' and many of the teachers seemed quite relieved that there was limited discussion about the issue and added parenthetic comments such as 'They're good about it, they don't ask' or 'I don't have any problems with them—they don't ask.'"

Lack of discussion, whatever the motive, ensures that children who remain in the classroom accept as natural the assumptions that govern identification and instruction for able students. Circumstances are so structured as to convince children not identified as gifted that their relative shortcomings keep them from the privileges that others ("the gifted") enjoy (Margolin, 1994; Weiler, 1978). Identification procedures select preponderantly middle- and upper-class children to enjoy experiences from which anyone might profit (i.e., privileges), and the discourse of the classroom and the general procedures of schooling put discussion of this unfair circumstance not only off limits, but quite literally "out of mind."

Qualitatively different programs. Gifted programs are often said to be qualitatively different from other school programs. The instructional philosophy behind such programs is humanistic and predominantly student centered. The regular education program, by contrast, is generally more authoritarian and more attentive to the curricular goals established by the state or district.

Enrichment pull-out programs exemplify "qualitative differences." Class sizes are generally smaller than in the regular classroom, and instructional formats are more varied. Instructional objectives usually focus on cognitive processes such as inquiry, divergent thinking, problem solving, and on metacognitive processes such as planning and organizing complex tasks. Many, if not most, enrichment programs include the development of social and leadership skills among their objectives (e.g., Maker, 1987). Enrichment teachers generally view the nurture of complex disciplinary knowledge to be outside their scope.

The rationale for providing qualitatively different programs is that gifted students are different in kind from other children (e.g., Kanevsky,

1990; Rogers, 1986a). Support for this widely endorsed misconception is drawn from the research literature that ascribes to giftedness such qualities as creativity, a sense of humor, independence, and the ability to transfer or generalize concepts. Such qualities are universally human, not restricted to the class of individuals singled out by virtue of superior academic aptitude. The conclusion that differences in kind distinguish gifted children from other children is totally unwarranted. IQ, aptitude, and achievement test scores, for instance, most certainly measure differences in degree, not in kind.

Establishing and maintaining qualitatively different classes has also been a matter of expediency. In some instances, gifted programs were set up with the understanding that they would sidestep any academic content that was treated in the regular education program. The rationale behind this restriction was usually that providing academic content would (1) intrude on the domain of the regular classroom program, and (2) contradict the ostensible basis for *special* education of the gifted. If gifted students need academic instruction, which classroom teachers are qualified to teach, why would special programs and specially trained teachers be required?

Many gifted-program teachers have lived with this dilemma for years. If they avoid teaching academic content, then other teachers regard the gifted program as a program of entertainment. If they do teach academic content, then they may duplicate some of what regular classroom teachers offer.

When schools have limited resources, gifted programs, like most "add-on" programs such as speech therapy and other remedial programs, suffer; administrators in impoverished schools are understandably reluctant to allocate scarce resources to programs that are tangential to the basic education of the majority of students. In extremely underfunded schools, resources expended on special programs may reduce the effectiveness of regular classroom programs in that the special programs expropriate needed classroom materials, equipment, and even teachers. Because funds are so limited in many communities, the benefits to students must be carefully considered in pedagogical and ethical terms. Given the dilemmas of providing appropriate instruction for able students in our society, impoverished schools are likely to regard qualitatively different gifted programs as a waste of money.

Whereas qualitatively different classes predominate at the elementary level, secondary school programming for gifted students tends to consist of advanced classes (generally in the regular program) augmented by enrichment experiences (provided by the gifted-program teacher) such as seminars or mentorships (Cox et al., 1985). These latter provisions vary greatly in the amount of academic learning they offer. To the extent that students who could benefit are excluded, such experiences are indefensible as provisions solely for the gifted. If, for example, a high-IQ student is given special instruction on computers from an out-of-school mentor, but other students — possibly more capable as programmers — could benefit as much or more from the mentorship, then providing the experience to the gifted student and denying it to the others is elitist and pedagogically unsound.

Continued insistence that gifted children are different in kind from other children and that they therefore require instruction in different sorts of things (leadership, creative problem solving, and "enrichment" generally) institutes a host of evils, the worst of which are the lessons we teach to children. We teach children identified as gifted that their potential is an entitlement to a privileged life, and we teach other children that this allocation of privilege is perfectly natural.

Quantitatively different programs. Acceleration and, sometimes, advanced classes are considered quantitatively different programs for gifted students. The rationale for these provisions reflects the defining characteristic of intellectually gifted children: They learn verbal and mathematical concepts more rapidly than other children. Such children, therefore, should have the chance to encounter academic content at a pace that matches their rate of learning. Because they have achieved early mastery of some of the skills taught in school, gifted students are unable to progress academically without being exposed to content that is more advanced than that presented in the typical classroom for children their age.

Acceleration includes early admission to school, grade-skipping, placement in higher grades for particular subjects, and early admission to college. It also can be accomplished through rapid-paced classes that combine two or more terms of instruction into one term. Such classes, however, are relatively rare although research, such as Stanley's Study of Mathematically Precocious Youth (SMPY), indicates that, to develop talent, they should be common (Stanley, 1976, 1981). Such courses, however, are almost always limited to mathematics.

Although quantitatively different programs are appropriate options for most gifted students, the use of acceleration as the primary means of meeting gifted students' needs is often disparaged. It is criticized as merely moving gifted children through an inadequate curriculum more rapidly or as simply getting the accelerated students out of school a year or two earlier. These criticisms seem to disregard the fact that, in general, more advanced levels of curriculum present students with more complex problems that are more likely to be interesting to gifted students, even though the teachers' techniques may be similar to those in lower grades.

Accelerative placement in the regular classroom avoids many of the inequities associated with enrichment pull-out programs without inhibiting gifted children's academic achievement. Although some advocates for gifted students argue that acceleration within the regular classroom leaves these students at the mercy of the routine instruction associated with the regular curriculum, most children who are identified as gifted spend most of their time there anyway—without the benefits of acceleration.

If acceleration were used more often, it is possible that parents and other advocates for gifted children might put their energies into changing the regular curriculum, rather than trying to get their children away from it. If changes in the regular curriculum are not forthcoming, however, we expect that eliminating pull-out programs is likely to result in many gifted children's parents joining the fight for voucher systems and the privatization of schooling.

Although not always regarded as acceleration, another quantitatively different option is advanced course work. Students who take Advanced Placement courses, for example, are accelerated to college-level work even though Advanced Placement is usually offered on high school campuses by high school teachers. Advanced classes are the most common means of providing acceleration to high school age gifted students and high achievers (Cox, Daniel, & Boston, 1985). Unfortunately, many advanced classes are not advanced enough to provide a sufficient challenge to exceptionally able students.

Whereas acceleration is often understood as the antithesis of enrichment, acceleration and academically relevant enrichment are necessarily related, as Stanley (1981) suggests. As academic concepts and skills become more advanced, they become more complex and abstract, and ought, therefore, to be taught in ways commonly associated with enrichment (e.g., induction, extended discourse, complex projects). Understood in this light, enrichment should be part of the regular school program, available to all students.

Accelerative options, *quantitatively* different from the regular program, are viewed with disfavor by so many educators and parents because they appear to ignore the allegedly unique, *qualitative* differences of gifted students. Educators and parents also fear that rapid-paced instruction will cause maladjustment and unhappiness in gifted students. Research strongly suggests that these fears are unfounded (Howley et al., 1986; Rogers, 1986b).

In the following sections, we claim that, in the name of addressing students' qualitative differences, gifted programs often undermine gifted students' real differences from other students—those differences associated with their levels of academic performance. We do not see this circumstance as merely an unfortunate outcome of educators' and parents' misunderstanding of the nature of gifted students. Rather, we argue that the misunderstandings take shape, at least in part, in response to society's tendency to reproduce existing power relations. Such misunderstandings tend to foster knowledge, skills, and especially the attitudes needed by the white-collar elite — professionals and managers who serve as apologists and functionaries for wealth and power. The undereducation and miseducation of gifted students in public schools is merely a necessary part of how our political economy does business.

Identifying Gifted Students: Entitling the Elite

To some extent, different groups at different times have different ideas about what constitutes giftedness (Csikszentmihalyi & Robinson, 1986). Some groups offer unitary definitions and some offer multifaceted definitions. The practical importance of the issue is that the way giftedness is defined, especially its operational definition, determines who is and who is not eligible for gifted programs. To date, whether schools adopt unitary definitions, multifaceted definitions, or process-oriented definitions of giftedness, their operational definitions — the procedures and cut-off scores by which definitions are enacted — have generally ensured that gifted programs serve a largely privileged clientele (Margolin, 1994).

Defining giftedness. In principle, students must demonstrate that they are significantly different from the norm on some trait or behavior regarded positively by society in order to be considered "gifted." One of the earliest and most common definitions of giftedness is Terman's (1925) operational definition based on a single-factor theory of intelligence: a high score on the Stanford-Binet Intelligence Scale.

Terman believed that high IQ scores indicated children's inherited ability and superior potential for eminence in adulthood. Terman's test, the Stanford-Binet, however, was based on the work of Alfred Binet, whose prototype intelligence test had actually been designed to predict *scholastic achievement*. Binet believed that intelligence as he had construed it for purposes of the test was not inborn and fixed, but was acquired and amenable to environmental influences (Gould, 1981).

Terman and others' (e.g., Jensen, 1973; Seligman, 1992) reification of what intelligence tests measure misconceives the nature of IQ scores and how they can legitimately be used. As Gould (1981) shows, these misconceptions preposterously misrepresent both nature and intellect; they also possess an interesting lineage to virulent forms of nineteenth century racism (consult Gould, 1981, for this history).

Apparent challenges to Terman's definition are usually based on multifactor theories of intelligence, such as Guilford's (1959) 120-factor model, Renzulli's triadic model (1978), Sternberg's (1985) triarchic model, and Gardner's (1983) seven-factor model. One of the problems with *both* unitary and multifactor models, however, is that they define intelligence in terms of factors (one or many) that are derived arbitrarily from tests constructed for that purpose. In a fundamental way, these factors are artifacts of the tests and the statistical procedures used to analyze test performance.

> It has been recognized for a long time that the reduction of giftedness to a unitary dimension is completely arbitrary. Some writers have also taken the next step by admitting that the number of distinct talents we wish to recognize (like the level at which we wish to set the threshold of giftedness) is purely a matter of convention and convenience. (Csikszentmihalyi & Robinson, 1986, p. 268)

Although there is no logical connection between a unitary intelligence and heredity, the concept of a single, general factor, *g*, has historically been associated with the view that giftedness is inherited. With equal disregard for logic, the concept of multifactored intelligence has been associated with efforts to include in gifted programs children who would be excluded by a single-factor definition. However, the multifactored construct of intelligence has also been used to justify inequities in the schools *by allocating particular innate specialties to different groups* (Lehman, 1992).

When Taylor and Richards (1991), for example, discuss patterns of IQ scores in black, Hispanic, and white children, they dismiss the likely possibility that the subtests on which minority-group students do best are those in which differences between mainstream and minority *culture* are smallest. This observation suggests that apparent "strengths" and "weaknesses" reflect nothing more than the degrees to which the cultures of different minority groups converge or diverge from the mainstream culture. On the basis of their investigation, the authors conclude that education should be differentiated on the basis of ethnicity. Implementation of this view could well isolate minority groups even further from the prerogatives reserved for the ruling class.

To criticize interpretations such as that of Taylor and Richards is not to say that differences in ability do not exist, or that different cultural milieus may not value one or another sort of ability more strongly than others. There *is* empirical evidence that particular groups show characteristic "strengths" and "weaknesses," but such evidence hardly warrants the conclusion that these strengths (and weaknesses) represent innate abilities.

Neither the unitary nor the multifactor approach to intelligence seems adequately to explain the plasticity of cognitive characteristics, that is the way human abilities interact with environmental factors (Csikszentmihalyi & Robinson, 1986; Gould, 1981; Lewontin et al., 1984). To acknowledge such plasticity would undermine the ideological basis of meritocracy. If material success and outstanding achievement of all kinds are understood to result substantially from the influence of environmental differences, rather than from inherited superiority, and if environmental differences are seen to reflect, to a considerable degree, unequal access to resources based on discrimination against some groups, extreme disparities in wealth are much less justifiable.

Difficulties in selecting gifted students. Methods of selecting gifted students vary in their particulars, but whatever the definition of giftedness, they tend to combine teacher nomination with standardized testing. As commonly used, both methods favor privileged students. Although some states' regulations include language about taking economic disadvantage and cultural difference into consideration, the regulations often fail to specify what procedures such consideration might entail, and local school districts have considerable leeway in how they operationalize these mandates.

In fact, gifted programs do fail to identify students from minority ethnic and racial groups and from the working class. This failure has been acknowledged as a problem for nearly half a century. The Gifted and Talented Children and Youth Education Act of 1985 reported that economically disadvantaged children were still underserved, and it established the identification of underserved students as one of the highest priorities for the use of federal funds under that act. The effects of the projects that this act supports are unknown at this time. But they are not likely to be robust because mere legislation cannot hope to address the economic and cultural structures that limit the attainment of these groups in society (cf. Gintis & Bowles, 1988).

A federal mandate to provide special education to all gifted students would probably improve the fairness of selection procedures; however, there would be considerable opposition to such a mandate. This opposition would likely be expressed through a single-issue coalition encompassing contradictory beliefs about schooling in America (e.g., that schooling ought to be under local control, that gifted education is elitist, that the underprivileged already receive too many benefits). Without a clear mandate to serve *all* gifted students nationwide, however, even the best extant projects will have few long-term effects.

Though most educators probably support efforts to identify students with superior potential, they disagree about the effectiveness and fairness of various identification methods. The most popular methods, however, employ eccentric statistical procedures, unreliable techniques, or a combination of the two.[1] Among such techniques are teacher referrals and checklists.

The use of teacher referrals contributes to the practice of placing students in gifted programs on the basis of background characteristics other than ability. Few schools *systematically* refer *all* children with test scores or grade point averages above a given threshold. Instead, teachers' referrals are common. Such referrals represent children in whom teachers have taken a special interest, sometimes as a result of the intervention of parents. Children thus referred are disproportionately white and privileged.

Referrals of this sort often determine which children will proceed to a second stage in the identification process, where more objective measures (e.g., IQ or achievement tests) may be used to assess children's eligibility for the special program. Relying on teacher referrals, in this case, means that as many as half the children who would otherwise score in the gifted range on such tests are overlooked (e.g., Denton & Postlethwaite, 1982; Pegnato & Birch, 1959). Teacher referrals may well miss many more children in the early grades and kindergarten (Jacobs, 1971) and even more minority students (Reid, 1992; cf. Sharp & Watson, 1981).

Based on subjective judgments of classroom behavior or hunches about particular children's hidden talents, teacher referral overlooks certain gifted students. Even when teachers try to overcome their personal biases by using "behavior" checklists, their referrals are likely to be unreliable. Many such checklists (rather than describing observable behaviors) merely implement a system for recording subjective judgments about undefined personal characteristics (cf. Hagen, 1980). Research suggests that teachers' effectiveness in identifying gifted students can be improved through inservice training (Borland, 1978), but teachers rarely receive inservice training for this purpose.

There are checklists specifically designed to identify children from underserved groups, but many of these checklists reflect similar difficulties. Assuming that giftedness is mostly inherited, though disguised by circumstance, such checklists function to identify children whose giftedness is *discernible*. The discernible quality, however, is likely to constitute an upbringing more similar to the mainstream than that of other underachieving students in the class or school.

This shortcoming is compounded by the fact that, although some of these checklists do identify traits associated with giftedness in a particular subculture, many others merely adapt items based on research about mainstream gifted children. The items on these lists may not match the manifestations of giftedness among poor or minority students (Reid, 1992).

Although some schools use teacher referral as the sole method of identifying gifted students, most do not. One common alternative to this practice is to combine teachers' judgments with test scores using a "matrix" that incorporates several ratings of performance into one composite rating. This approach is intended to allow multiple means of entry into gifted programs. Instead, it often excludes some of the very students it purports to identify — underachieving minority, underprivileged, and working-class students. Combining a number of different types of measures by adding or averaging them, as a matrix approach typically requires, is statistically indefensible; and it usually favors the well-rounded high achiever, even over the *brilliant* underachiever (Dirks & Quarfoth, 1981).

The multifactor matrix approach in general, we think, constitutes a well-intentioned, but failed, effort to use multiple criteria to improve the chances of eligibility for poor and minority students. The rationale for using multiple criteria is that one measure used alone may fail to identify some gifted students. According to this view, if students are allowed to qualify on the basis of any one of several measures, fewer gifted students will be excluded from programs.

Unfortunately, the principle on which multiple criteria could support eligibility — by allowing children to qualify on the basis of one of several criteria — is negated by the matrix approach. The effect of the matrix, which usually compiles scores to arrive at a single score, is to require children to do well on *more* than one criterion. Shore and colleagues (1991, p. 49) note pointedly, "Where multiple criteria exist, they are used as cumulative hurdles, rather than alternatives." The observation applies even when matrix formats are not used. The recommendation to use multiple criteria to discover more talent implies an "either/or" format, for example, either outstanding grades *or* a high achievement test score; in actual practice many schools, wishing to avoid placing children on a single criterion, continue to require both good grades *and* high test scores.

Educators are, with good reason, skeptical of identification procedures that rely solely on standardized IQ tests. The most commonly used of these tests show systematic bias against children from underprivileged and minority backgrounds. Consequently, some educators seek more culture-fair tests to identify gifted students from racial or ethnic minorities. Torrance (1974), for example, applied Guilford's (1959) Structure of Intellect model as a foundation for assessing creativity on a culture-fair test. The Torrance Tests of Creative Thinking, in fact, seem to be more culture-fair than IQ tests because they do identify a larger proportion of underprivileged and minority students (Torrance, 1971). Unfortunately, though these tests may identify a more diverse group of high scorers, it is not certain what high scores on these tests mean (Wallach, 1970).

The nearly inescapable problem with *any* culture-fair test is its diminished predictive power, since tests reflect to some extent the prevailing allocation of success (affluence, occupational status, and so forth) in our society. Tests are constructed out of the ethos of the dominant culture in order to predict success in the dominant culture. Tests that attempt to break this vicious circle, by altering the content of items, consciously destroy this linkage. It is unclear, therefore, just what such tests can predict.

Recently, Sternberg (1985), whose work on intelligence emphasizes cognitive and metacognitive processes, has argued for a type of testing that allows children to show that they *can* learn rapidly or well rather than requiring them to show only that they *have* learned rapidly or well. Processes, however, may be just as susceptible to environment as "products," like vocabulary or information. In fact, some research suggests that complex analytical processes may be even more subject to environmental influence than ordinary cognitive processes. Some researchers (e.g. Taylor & Richards, 1991) report, for example, that African-American students score higher on vocabulary tests than on tests that require the *analysis* of verbal or nonverbal materials.

Using standardized measures with an eye to fairness. Objections to IQ tests most often concern their misuse (Haney, 1993). One of the greatest misuses of IQ tests is to attribute school failure to characteristics of individual children. If these tests were more clearly understood for what they are, educators and parents would not look to them for explanations about why children are doing well or poorly in school.

The tests merely sample a wide range of — mostly verbal — knowledge. The scores derived from this sampling technique estimate children's comparative academic performance to date. The inference that children do well *because* they are gifted (high IQ score) or badly because they are retarded (low IQ score) is not an explanation, but a tautology. It presents the phenomenon for which explanation is sought as the explanation, though it disguises the redundancy in jargon. It does not — it cannot — "explain" why a child does poorly in school. IQ tests are technically adequate *only* for making inferences about *demonstrated learning rate*. Most achievement tests (with the exception of high-ceilinged group tests of achievement and some individually administered wide-range achievement tests) are not adequate for this purpose.[2]

We also misuse IQ tests if we infer that students will inevitably continue to perform in accord with the rate indicated by the test score. In this case, we forget that past circumstances created the impression given by the test score, but that future circumstances can undo the impression. The point is to support the academic ability of all students. A complex set of circumstances provides such support, with educators assuming primary responsibility for what schooling might provide.

Nothing guarantees that a rapid rate of learning will continue; in fact, we have frequently observed the effects of decreased rates of learning among gifted children. We believe these losses stem from instruction that lacks intellectual and academic substance. Similarly, under decent circumstances (estimated to entail additional costs of about $1,000 per student), slow rates of learning can be accelerated schoolwide (Levin, 1991).

We conclude that comprehensive, individually administered intelligence tests and high-ceilinged achievement tests *can* serve selection procedures fairly (see also Ortiz & Gonzalez, 1989). Individualized intelligence, aptitude, and achievement test scores represent children's mastery of certain school-related skills at a certain time in life. Extremely high scores on any of these standardized measures should qualify children for dramatic modifications in their schooling. In contrast to teacher referrals and checklists, biases of objective instruments are rather easily identifiable. A preponderance of research, in fact, shows that the IQ- and achievement-test point penalty imposed as a result of minority group membership is generally about one standard deviation (Haney, 1993).

In using standardized tests, however, educators need to understand that scores most certainly reflect social biases. These biases consist precisely in their accord with the biases that determine success in our society. We *must* acknowledge that standardized test scores violate one of the assumptions of valid assessment, namely that children who took a test had *approximately equal opportunities to learn what the test measures* (Salvia & Ysseldyke, 1991).

Certain defensible and academically relevant practices enable educators to circumvent the biases inherent in standardized tests. By establishing local norms, by using tests normed on minority groups, and by implementing quotas, schools can ensure that gifted programs serve poor and oppressed groups much more equitably than they now do. This strategy is no more difficult than using matrix methods or multifactor criteria.[3]

We acknowledge that the use of separate norms or lower score cut-offs for poor and minority students is unpopular; conservatives, for instance, view quotas as "reverse discrimination." This objection conveniently obscures the point that "reverse discrimination" is *not* unfair discrimination. Quotas are a just and efficient way to accommodate the reality that minority students have often been denied a fair "opportunity to learn." Kozol's (1991) *Savage Inequalities* and many studies of school finance and socioeconomic status attest again and again to this fact.

Discrimination, in fact, is necessary; it takes place when students are identified for special treatment of any kind; it takes place whenever the intellect makes fine distinctions. When the aim of discrimination is injustice, of course, the issue is an ethical one. And what cynical critics call "reverse discrimination" is merely a necessary, and hopefully temporary, measure to reverse *unfair* discrimination. Sincere efforts to identify *all* gifted children will have to confront resistance to the use of quotas, as does any effort to reverse unfair discrimination.

PROCESS REPLACES CONTENT

We think that instructional arrangements for precocious students ought to consist in advanced academic curriculum, taught well. Most gifted students will fail to progress without receiving advanced academic instruction. Nonetheless, gifted programs typically "teach" cognitive and affective processes disconnected from real intellectual substance. The applicability of these processes to academic problems or to problems in the "real world" is questionable (Rogers, 1986b). But we do know, for example, that one cannot be an accomplished physicist without knowing a lot about physics, without being able to read difficult scientific material, and without understanding difficult mathematical concepts.

Higher Order Thinking: Deskilling Knowledge

As used in gifted programs, the process-oriented approach is intended to develop students' higher level thinking. Curriculum and materials for this approach are usually unrelated to academic content, and mere facts, such as historical dates, names, and events, are treated with contempt. But Bruner (1960), one of the earliest advocates of process-oriented instruction, considered factual knowledge *necessary* for the development of problem-solving skills (see Taba, 1965, for a similar discussion). McPeck (1986, p. 8) describes the relationship between factual knowledge and higher order thinking:

> Facts are complex things which have connections and logical implications which reach beyond themselves. And the mental weaving of these connections is what education and critical thinking is fundamentally about. Indeed, so-called "higher order" learning is itself predicated on having this broad understanding of how certain facts and information are connected or related to something else.

Despite the sensible view of these educators, other advocates tend to focus on the processes alone, detached from the presumably inessential academic content. As Bloom's (1956) taxonomy came into widespread use (with its hierarchy of cognitive functions), many educators began to emphasize the verbs associated with different levels of the hierarchy over the nouns to which the verbs might apply. For example, in gifted education, *analysis* is often considered as pedagogically valuable when it is directed toward solving a hypothetical but trivial problem (e.g., determining what one might need to take on an imaginary trip to the Australian outback), as it is when it is directed toward understanding a literary work.

Recently, this assumption has been more generally questioned. Analyzing a literary work requires skills quite different from those for analyzing the reasons for the success of the student bookstore. Putting aside for the moment the question of value, the influence of the subject on the process seems evident. Among the many differences, analyzing a work of literature may require comprehension of much more subtle ideas than analyzing a business venture (simply because of the sorts of distinctions literary analysis makes). It may also require reasoning with complex verbal concepts embodied in a sophisticated vocabulary. Guilford's (1959) Structure of Intellect model does set some precedent for the emerging recognition of these distinctions by at least considering broad categories of content as important elements in defining its 120 independent factors.[4]

Keating (1988) questions the validity of the concept of content-free thinking skills as well. He summarizes the status of research about the effectiveness of programs that purport to teach critical thinking skills, as follows:

> Convincing evidence . . . has not been forthcoming. In many cases, there is little formal evaluation of any sort. Where careful evaluations have been done, the criteria of success are typically the students' performance on materials exactly the same as, or very much like, the training materials. Though this may be a necessary first step in the evaluation process, it is weak evidence of a strong claim (the general enhancement of thinking). The next and crucial step of transfer to quite different kinds of content has apparently not been undertaken in any systematic way. Of course, the criteria may be hard to specify, but without this information the issue is reduced to how effectively particular programs "teach to their own test." (p. 15)

Problem-Solving: Applications of Deskilled Knowledge

"Yankee ingenuity" — an ingenious approach to getting things done — is a traditional American virtue. In the early years of the nation, this peculiarly American sense of practicality was not an object of special training. It was an approach not only accessible to every citizen regardless of station in life, but a new spirit; it was simply part of the American outlook. Americans were eager to discard the old ways of viewing the world and doing its work. Yankee ingenuity was more a spirit than a skill, more an attitude than a technique. Being an American, among other things, indicated that one had adopted the American attitude. And the freshness of this attitude would permit an American to refashion traditional ways of doing things in virtually any field of activity, but most particularly in agriculture and manufacture – the production of food and goods.

Though Americans did prove to be wildly and productively inventive, the heroes of nineteenth and early twentieth century industrial and agricultural ingenuity – Cyrus McCormick, Thomas Edison, Henry Ford – owed remarkably little to their formal training (Zinn, 1980). The sort of schooling practiced on the frontier and in the wards of young cities might have helped propagate the American attitude among immigrants, but it did not ever aim to teach "problem-solving skills." The requisite ingenuity rather emerged mysteriously on American soil as the result of some synergy of character and circumstance relevant to manifest destiny.

Hofstadter long ago noted that American society valued the inventor-entrepreneur over the theoretical scientist or the scholar (Hofstadter, 1963). And today, corporate interests have become so powerful that, even in the universities, researchers are prized more for their ability to translate research into something marketable, or to secure grant monies, than for the explanatory power of their theories (Trumpbour, 1989). Furthermore, the fulfillment of "manifest" destiny and the construction of mass schooling put an end to the *mystique* of Yankee ingenuity. And Yankees have relinquished any unique claim on ingenuity – Japanese, Germans, Koreans, and Swedes are as likely as Americans to devise ingenious solutions to managerial and technical problems.

This history, in the context of America's quest for global economic dominion, helps explain why gifted programs inculcate the importance of solving managerial or technical problems with ingenuity. A concern with how to do things – sentimentally reflective of the American spirit – lies at the core of process-oriented instruction.

Yet such instruction is no better able to help students learn how to solve narrowly instrumental problems than it is to help them think well. As noted previously, process-oriented instruction, advocated by Bruner (1960), was intended to *teach* academic content. Development of the intellect and its habits was the aim. The new math, the new biology, and the new physics developed under Bruner's influence integrated intellectual processes with substantial academic content. Bruner's social studies program, "Man, A Course of Study" (MACOS), for example, used films, readings, and artifacts to help students understand basic anthropological concepts.

The sort of instruction Bruner imagined and helped to design is not widely practiced today (Gallagher, 1985). Inductive lessons (like the innovative curricula of the 1960s) *are* difficult to teach. But reassessments of the 1960s' curricula do indicate the general superiority of those conceptions over conventional instruction (Sealey, 1985), particularly in terms of achievement gains for a gamut of bright students (e.g., Gallagher, 1985).

Gifted programs continue to endorse process-oriented instruction, but such instruction is unlikely to cultivate the kind of thinking Bruner envisioned. Inquiry-training, brainstorming, synectics, and many other game-like methods predominate. To the extent that the process-oriented approach has been routinized and trivialized, it ignores the ends for which it was originally intended. The rote application of problem-solving skills may, in fact, be more meaningless, in terms of intellectual development, than the rote memorization of facts. Bloom's (1956) hierarchy, for example, implicitly acknowledges this circumstance because memory and comprehension of concepts support the "higher order" processes of application, analysis, synthesis, and evaluation. Higher order processes cannot take place in an intellectual vacuum.

Child Development as the Curriculum

Partly a legacy of the whole-child movement and partly a legacy of the process-education method, the *curriculum* of many special education programs derives almost as much from child development as from a conception of pertinent academic goals. In essence, views of child development rather than knowledge or learning constitute the curriculum. As a form of special education, gifted education is highly susceptible to the influence of this peculiar view of the nature of curriculum. For instance, goals for individual gifted children often come from the children's performance on measures of cognitive or affective domains such as visual-motor perception, vocabulary, reasoning, divergent thinking, and interest in abstract ideas and aesthetic activities. Efforts to cultivate these abilities or attitudes frequently displace knowledge and ideas as the focus of special programs.

Gallagher and Courtright (1986) explain the need to distinguish between educational and theoretical approaches in defining giftedness. The practical upshot of making such a distinction is the realization that psychological constructs reflected by test scores do not automatically warrant development of curriculum in domains sampled by the tests.

Perhaps one of the most extreme, and misguided, examples of combining process-oriented education with child development applies Guilford's (1959) Structure of Intellect model to inform educational planning for individual gifted students. The intermediary for translating the Structure of Intellect (SOI) model to the individual child's development is Meeker's (1969) SOI *test*, designed to measure children's performance on many of the 120 factors Guilford identified. The test measures students' performance on items that sample such putative "abilities" as cognition of figural units, which requires students to identify an object (such as a safety pin) represented by incomplete line drawings. SOI test results are used to form a test profile depicting individual students' relative "strengths" and "weaknesses" on many factors, which then form the basis of the educational plans drawn up for each student. The relationship of any such plans to substantive intellectual matters is doubtful indeed. In this case, Guilford's conception of development has replaced the academic curriculum.

Gifted programs that subordinate the academic curriculum to one that implements child development *as* the curriculum ironically serve to stunt development, rather than to promote it. Certainly, the value of an academic curriculum can be disputed, complaints against the nature of instruction in the liberal arts are common (e.g., that they rely too much on lecture, that they are too remote from experience to interest students, and that they are merely elitist), and scholarship *can* be construed as pointless quibbling (cf. Barzun, 1959). But the academic tradition, no matter how poorly taught, contains substantial value to which students might connect, if they manage to see beyond the immediate features of classroom life. The value of good books persists; the community of intellect such books represent reaches into the past and into the future. But the value of such "factors" as cognition of figural units is difficult to determine. Some educators may find it appealing, certainly. This warrant, though, hardly suffices to commend it as a source of curriculum.

FEELING REPLACES THOUGHT

Affective education, like process-oriented instruction, avoids dealing with intellectual development. For the most part, it aims to teach gifted children how to get along with others. Given the limited resources available for teaching gifted children, the emphasis on affective education is offered at considerable cost to the development of students' intellect. The justification for this sacrifice is, in essence, that exceptional intellectual potential constitutes an exceptional threat to the emotional well-being of the gifted.

Emotional Risks of Exceptional Talent

Whereas concern over emotional difficulties is appropriate for children who are emotionally disturbed, such concern seems irrational with respect to gifted children. Substantial evidence confirms the fact that gifted children are generally better off emotionally and socially than other children

(Margolin, 1994). Gifted programs are, nonetheless, valued as emotional "safe harbors" for gifted children (Fetterman, 1988).

The particular emotional risks thought to afflict the gifted are those supposedly associated with the challenges of rigorous academic work. Fetterman (1988), for example, regards parental, teacher, and peer pressure for academic performance as threatening to the well-being of gifted students.

But we must distinguish between *debilitating* and *challenging* expectations. Challenging expectations can be met. If they are not successfully met, however, the attempt to meet them still has value: Lessons are learned that pose new challenges; the effort of making the attempt provides satisfaction. But debilitating expectations are designed as prescriptions for failure. What is worse, the failures are conclusive. If a debilitating expectation is not met, the result is necessarily damaging; failure, after all, constituted the de facto expectation.

This distinction may sometimes be subtle, but it is the sort of distinction that the development of talent and the nurture of intellect requires. From the pedagogical perspective that constructs challenging expectations, instructional events are an opportunity to elicit the best from students, in a variety of ways, some of which may be surprising. From the pedagogical perspective that constructs debilitating expectations, however, such events are tests which must elicit failure — usually from a predictable portion of students. The most debilitating expectation of all, of course, is that this predictable portion of students will fail repeatedly, until such time as they finally realize that their cumulating failures are, indeed, final.

In our experience educators and parents generally err by confusing debilitating expectations and challenging expectations. Relatively few seem to understand the distinction, which is not in any case evident in how schooling is usually practiced. Many students are, after all, doomed to final failure by a climate of debilitating expectations in schools. In one sense, then, the concerns of parents and gifted-program teachers are justified. The proper course of action, however, is not to shield a privileged few from this theater of humiliating trial and error, but to implement an intellectual program in which challenging expectations shape curriculum and instruction for all students, including the gifted.

Even if such an eventuality is unlikely, however, research about the social and emotional development of the gifted ought to reassure parents and educators. The preponderance of studies shows that, in general, children identified as gifted are at least as well-adjusted and mature as other students. Recently, for example, the communication skills, socialization skills, and daily living skills of gifted children were compared with those of other children. Douthitt (1992) found a significant positive relationship between children's IQ scores and their adaptive behavior scores. Douthitt's study confirmed an earlier study by Childs (1981), which also found gifted children superior to other children in adaptive behavior skills. As Shore and colleagues (1991) note, gifted students identified on the basis of high scores on IQ tests or tests of academic aptitude usually view themselves positively, in both academic and social terms. Despite many such studies, educators, including teachers of gifted students, express grave concerns about gifted children's mental health and socialization.

But some parents do not share such concerns, and these parents tend to encourage their children to meet academic challenges. In cases where parents of the gifted want to advance their children's academic achievement, they are, however, often the object of considerable criticism by educators. The presumption is that such parents are willing to sacrifice their children's happiness to their own (academic or intellectual) vanity. Certainly, some parents take a dangerous vicarious gratitude from their children's successes. But more educators — and more parents — need to acknowledge that aspirations for intellectual development are legitimate. Parents who entertain such aspirations for their academically talented children are by no means more likely to harm their children than parents who entertain similar ambitions for the athletic performance of their athletically talented children.

The exception to the general rule about the emotional well-being of gifted children seems to be gifted underachievers. These children quite often — and quite understandably — harbor less positive images of themselves than other gifted children (Shore et al., 1991). Although their underachievement is sometimes attributed to personality traits or family dynamics, schools themselves contribute to the problem in a number of ways (Whitmore, 1980). In addition to failing to provide a stimulating, challenging curriculum to gifted students, the schools' conventional association of classroom competition with relative personal merit may actually *cause* some gifted students to perform poorly.

Whitmore (1980) noted that some quite young gifted underachievers were very uncomfortable with the competitiveness of their classroom. French and Cardon (1968) found bright high school dropouts to be critical of what they perceived as unfair judgments teachers made, based on classroom performance. Apparently, some gifted children regard as offensive the competitive climate so typical of schooling. The social climate of the classroom may well distract such students from the intellectual issues at hand, which can, in the midst of this climate, seem irrelevant. These students are perhaps right to regard the cutthroat struggle for good grades as counterproductive and possibly immoral.

Some students continue to articulate this view even as they successfully pursue their schooling in undergraduate and graduate programs (Friedenberg, 1965; Katchadourian & Boli, 1985). Katchadourian and Boli, in particular, identified a group of Stanford undergraduates who valued intellect, but not on the institutional terms promoted by Stanford. They were less concerned with grades than other students, and much less concerned with their career prospects. For these students, valuing intellect did involve certain risks (Katchadourian and Boli called this group "the dissenters"), but the risks were evident prerequisites of these students' intellectual and emotional fulfillment.

The Threat of Normative Emotional Balance

The way society enforces normative emotional balance is by placing a higher value on social amenities than intellectual endeavors. In this view devotion to intellectual pursuits over material comfort is unhealthy.

The story of William Sidis, one of the most famous "failures" in the literature on gifted education, is sometimes used as a cautionary tale (e.g., Montour, 1977) for parents or teachers who might be tempted to push their students to achieve beyond the norm for bright students. Recently, for instance, Margolin (1994) repeated the Sidis story to suggest the questionable validity of efforts to identify giftedness in children. The Sidis story, in our view, harbors another meaning.

Sidis met the requirements for entry to Harvard at the age of 9, though he did not enroll until he was 11. Some reports compare his brilliance to Albert Einstein's and Norbert Wiener's; whatever the case, Sidis was obviously precocious in the extreme. As an adult, however, he refused to take any job that made use of his extraordinary mathematical ability. He dressed sloppily, remained single, and earned little money. This "eccentric" behavior led to reports that Sidis was unhappy and neurotic. What sort of intellect, after all, would choose *poverty*?

Perhaps it is true that his refusal to use his abilities in the employ of a major university, government project, or corporation reflected weaknesses as well as strengths. Perhaps misguided parenting played a part; perhaps he also reacted badly to the snide and insulting articles about him that appeared in the press, beginning when he was a youngster. But his rebellion also may have come from a genuine commitment to pursuing his personal interests in the context of a principled refusal to employ his talents for ends he considered unworthy (Wallace, 1986).

Whatever the source of his refusal to strive for the wealth and fame that his intelligence and training might otherwise have earned him, recent discoveries establish the injustice of the charge that Sidis was a "failure."

As a young man, Sidis wrote a book that predicted the presence of black holes before their existence had been empirically detected. According to Wallace (1986), Sidis's book went unreviewed in the press and unacknowledged by the academic community, perhaps because of its difficulty. She reports that in 1979, the book was brought to the attention of Buckminster Fuller, who had been one of Sidis's classmates. Wallace quotes from Fuller's letter to an editor of *Scientific American*:

> Imagine my excitement and joy on being handed this xerox of Sidis's 1925 book, in which he clearly predicts the black hole. In fact, I find the book to be a fine cosmological piece. . . . I hope you will become as excited as I am at this discovery that Sidis did go on after college to do the most magnificent thinking and writing. (Fuller cited in Wallace, 1986, p. 157)

Sidis also wrote a weekly column for a Boston newspaper, wrote a book on subway tokens, and conducted original research on the influence of American Indian government on the development of the U.S. Constitution (Johansen, 1989). Although we cannot judge how happy he may have been, the historical record clearly demonstrates Sidis' continuing commitment to scholarship and intellectual integrity of a high order.

Concern for ensuring the "normalness" of bright students also inspires educators' persistent and zealous warnings about the dangers of exposing such students to extra-normal (i.e., appropriate) academic challenges. The practices of acceleration and retention constitute a telling example. On the one hand, schooling employs acceleration very seldom, despite the consistently positive research (which ought logically to dispel resistance). On the other hand, schooling routinely employs retention-in-grade, even though research shows that the practice results in little academic benefit with some risk for emotional harm. The contrast between how acceleration and retention are practiced reveals a characteristic pattern behind the commitment to normalness: Devotion to intellect is abnormal universally, whereas concern for emotional well-being is allocated differentially according to the perceived worth of the child.

Happiness Over Achievement

Because they generally associate happiness with normalcy, teachers and parents tend to believe that gifted children are at risk for unhappiness. This belief appears to relate to the strategy of mainstreaming, whereby mentally impaired students are "normalized." For such students actually to *become normal* (or to be perceived as indistinguishable from normal) would constitute a positive change, one likely, in fact, to improve otherwise grim prospects faced by many students with impairments.

But the attempt to normalize gifted students for the alleged sake of their happiness is misguided. We have frequently heard parents and some teachers vow that gifted students "have to get along with average people anyhow" as a justification for not altering the standard educational regimen in any way. Still, we cannot see how putting up with boredom and drudgery is necessary training for happiness.

The association between normalcy and happiness, however, does not hold, not for mentally impaired, average, or gifted children. In particular, the opposition of happiness and achievement, popular among educators and the lay community, overlooks the more sensible view that achievement and happiness are intimately related and in complex ways. Abraham Maslow, for one, argues that achievement is a necessary element of happiness; the people he considered self-actualizers seemed to him to have integrated the cognitive and affective elements of their personalities (Maslow, 1968). Schooling, however, implements an instrumental approach to both cognitive and affective development, a tendency that further distances intellectual from emotional understandings (Howley, 1987).

Unrealistic concern over the happiness of gifted students runs the risk of making them stupid, which doesn't necessarily mean having a low IQ. Stupid also means "stupefied, stultified, sedated." As Maslow (1970) points out, Goerling, a Nazi war criminal, had a high IQ, but was, in this sense, stupid nonetheless. Seligman (1992) claims that all of the major Nazi war criminals were quite intelligent (with high measured IQs), but apparently their *intellects* could not grasp the meaning of their horrific actions. Arendt (1977, p. 4), observing the trial of Adolf Eichmann, reported the apparent inability of the defendant to consider the suffering he caused:

> The deeds were monstrous, but the doer — at least the very effective one now on trial — was quite ordinary, commonplace, and neither demonic nor monstrous. There was no sign in him of firm ideological convictions or of specific evil motives, and the only notable characteristic one could detect in his past behavior . . . was something entirely negative; it was not stupidity but *thoughtlessness*. In the setting of Israeli court and prison procedures he functioned as well as he had functioned under the Nazi regime but, when confronted with situations for which such routine procedures did not exist, he was helpless, and his cliche-ridden language produced . . . a kind of macabre comedy. Cliches, stock phrases, adherence to conventional, standardized codes of expression and conduct have the socially recognized function of protecting us against reality, that is, against the claim on our thinking attention that all events and facts make by virtue of their existence. If we were responsive to this claim all

the time, we would soon be exhausted; Eichmann differed from the rest of us only in that he clearly knew of no such claim at all.

Both the kind of stupidity Maslow meant and the kind of thoughtlessness that Arendt had in mind are failures to integrate thought and feeling. We are not suggesting that education in the U.S. is preparing fascists, though the anti-intellectual bias of our public schools could lend itself to such a project under somewhat different political economic circumstances. Our schooling nonetheless *does* prepare us to tolerate injustice thoughtlessly as the natural order of things.

Education that cared for intellect would enable students to integrate knowledge so that they could frame questions in the context of enduring human dilemmas, and instruction to foster intellect would help students regard immediate experience from a critical distance. But the need for critical distance is not widely appreciated. The institutions of business and government are more vitally concerned with "how" than "why." And no matter what, the key objective is to augment the power and influence of these organizations.

So long as the professionals and managers who are most desirable to powerful business interests are those who are not hampered in their efficiency by the ability and inclination to ask questions relating to broad human issues, we can expect most schooling for gifted children — under the auspices of ensuring happiness — to devalue intellect to the same extent that schooling for other children does.

SCHOOLING, TALENT DEVELOPMENT, AND PROVISIONS FOR STUDENTS WITH TALENTS

Recent critical works (e.g., Margolin, 1994; Sapon-Shevin, 1994) question, as do we, the ethical and pedagogical assumptions on which many gifted programs rest. Although we agree with much of this criticism, we believe that it generally exhibits insufficient concern for the development of talent and care for the intellect. Possessing demonstrable talent is no more the fault of children than poverty is the fault of the poor, however. Neither justice nor good sense warrants steps to repress the learning of demonstrably able students — regardless of how they got that way.

Margolin (1994) sidesteps the question of alternatives because his analysis does not address the question of whether or not there "really are" gifted children. He is concerned primarily with how the concept *gifted children* is constructed and used. His admirable book, *Goodness Personified*, limits itself to an analysis of discourse about giftedness and the gifted. So far as it goes, the story he tells is compelling and, we believe, accurate. But it does not concern itself with the practice of schooling and the implications of such practice for culture, intellect, and the development of talent. Such practical problems — important to parents, teachers, and students — are outside the scope of Margolin's analysis.

Other critics, including Sapon-Shevin (1993), seem to believe that gifted children should remain in the regular program for all of their academic instruction. In principle, we agree. Hence, we have always strongly endorsed acceleration and advanced instruction. But we also recognize the damage done in actual practice when the circumstances of instruction restrain the development of talent — as they widely do in American schooling.

Tracking, for example, is bad for all students not because it groups students, but because its groupings, especially in large public high schools, are so rigidly maintained. Once a high school student lands in the "general track," escape is uncommon in most public schools (Gamoran, 1992; Oakes, 1985). Adam Gamoran reports, in particular, that public school tracking is ineffective in comparison with tracking practices in Catholic schools; it tends to reinforce rather than break down social and academic distinctions between African-American and white students (Gamoran, 1992; Lucas & Gamoran, 1993).

Ability grouping in elementary school, while possibly less rigid than high school tracking, confines "low groups" to inferior instruction (e.g., Wuthrick, 1990; Young, 1990; Young & McCullough, 1992). It thus prefigures and helps shape the results of tracking observed later, in high school.

Schooling is a system of delivering combined educational and custodial services widely and at low cost. While parents hold jobs, students are kept safe (in most neighborhoods and communities), fed, and instructed in basic skills. This is a valuable service, but it sacrifices true education as it provides custody. The system for delivering this odd combination of custodial and educational services so efficiently is an uncomfortable compromise maintained at the cost of an inflexibleness that accommodates well neither childhood nor learning. The system has much in common with the methods of mass production industries, which, indeed, served as models for the construction of the system of schooling. The system is socially entrenched, however: This is how we think schools must be run, despite the fact that what schooling accomplishes does not resemble a true education at all. Change is difficult not merely because the system is so rigid, but because this is the only system of schooling most of us can imagine.

One feature that schooling lacks — a feature that affects all students — is the flexibility to attend closely to the educational and intellectual circumstances of individuals who present themselves (a feature that might be called "responsiveness"). Many schools and many teachers make valiant attempts to notice individual students, but the requirements of cost efficiency and the rigid procedures of schooling ensure that such efforts are exceptions. Such-and-so is supposed to take place in the third grade; it is mandated to occur, and it usually does, more or less (Brown, 1993). This syndrome persists through the end of high school, so that in many high school classrooms students who can barely read encounter absurdly inappropriate textbooks.

Gifted children deal intellectually with this system about as well as other children do; that is, badly. No one of right mind would conceive of such a system, except that its existence makes such a conception quite unnecessary. Schooling, in fact, victimizes talent development among *all* the children it is supposed to serve. But because gifted children usually negotiate the basics with ease, and because most eventually secure comfortable jobs, people assume that schooling has succeeded, at least, in developing the talent of able students. It is easy, therefore, to conclude that such students require nothing different from what they already get during the course of their schooling: Talented children will succeed — and should succeed if they are not somehow morally lax — despite all obstacles.

This widespread view is the dark side of society's commitment to provide everyone with a standard, functional schooling. In reality, it means that whenever an uncommon talent presents itself in school, it *should* be ignored. The commitments of schooling (to custodial care and functional skills) contribute widely to the destruction of talent, and not only (or even principally) among the gifted. The system of schooling is positioned to discount the value of developing talent — incredible as that conclusion will seem to many people.

With substantially greater flexibility we could accomplish much more at comparatively little additional cost. For gifted students, the flexibility to implement acceleration and advanced courses is critical because age-grade placement serves them badly.

Recent studies document this assertion. In regular age-grade placements gifted children receive the same instruction in academics as the other children in the class (Westberg, Archambault, Dobyns, & Salvin, 1993); modifications in curriculum are minor (Archambault, Westberg, Brown, Hallmark, Emmons, & Zhang, 1993); and the simplest changes in instructional materials are seldom adopted. Despite the fact that classroom textbooks may be too easy for many students in the regular classroom (Chall & Conard, 1991), only one textbook per subject per grade is adopted in many public schools (Bernstein, 1985).

Differentiation in itself, however, is of little benefit to gifted students, because most such differentiation involves enrichment. Reis and colleagues (1993) found that 95% of the teachers they studied used enrichment to differentiate curriculum for gifted students, whereas only 18% also used acceleration. In reality, differentiation seldom occurs; and when it does, it seldom includes acceleration.

As school districts move to more heterogeneous classes and use cooperative learning more widely, they justify inflexibility with a misguided argument: Gifted children ought to remain in age-grade placements to benefit their chronological peers. Nancy Robinson (1990, p. 19) puts bluntly the plight of gifted children thus confined:

> *In the classroom, time is a fixed resource.* If children are organized in cooperative learning groups studying grade level material for the majority of their school day, they will have time to do little else. They will not have time to learn anything new to *them*.

Instead of holding able children captive, providing acceleration and advanced classes, and making them available throughout a school, would have the effect of mixing chronological ages and maximizing the benefits of cooperative learning — on a much wider basis than under a regime of thoughtless adherence to age-grade placement.

Providing acceleration and advanced classes for the gifted (and indeed for any students who could benefit from such provisions) is both just and pedagogically sensible. Moreover, gifted children, under such circumstances, would progress through school much more rapidly than they do now, and the funds that otherwise would be spent (largely for custody alone) could be diverted to better purpose.

We note that in providing acceleration and advanced classes, schools need to ensure the equal participation of both genders, locally represented ethnic groups, and underprivileged students. Once school personnel realize that many students — and not only the officially gifted — can benefit from acceleration and advanced courses, they can envision schooling that makes genuine progress toward ensuring equity. Talent development, as contrasted with schooling, requires careful and responsive nurture (Bloom & Sosniak, 1981). Indeed, the practice of broadly elaborating intellectual options for students has the potential to change the climate of a school.

CHAPTER 4

Effects of Poverty, Sexism, and Racism on Intellect

Edwina D. Pendarvis and Aimee Howley

In the previous two chapters, we looked at the particular mechanisms by which schooling belittles intellect and deflects talent toward instrumental ends. Those mechanisms implicate all of schooling, kindergarten through graduate study, and all participants in schooling—parents and students as well as educators. Moreover, the anti-intellectual culture of schooling assumes singularly peculiar distortions as it seeks ways to discourage the development of *intellect* among those children presenting the most evident *intelligence*. This chapter concerns other distortions of schooling that operate to sustain social and political inequities. It examines in some detail how schooling operates to limit the academic and life chances of underprivileged and working-class students, women, and students from racial and ethnic minorities.

SCHOOLING AND CLASS

According to Navarro (1991, p. 3), "How people live and die depends largely on their class." Although this claim runs counter to popular belief in individuals' ability to succeed no matter how adverse their circumstances, strong empirical evidence supports its validity. Discussion in this chapter focuses on the ways in which class affects the type of schooling students receive. Much of what determines the class that people in the U.S. belong to is their gender, ethnic, or racial membership. A larger percentage of women than men, and a much larger percentage of African Americans, Hispanics, and American Indians than members of northern European ethnic groups, are assigned membership in the working class. Among descendants of northern Europe, a larger percentage of rural than urban descendants find themselves confined to low wages or poverty.

For purposes of this chapter, class is categorized in fairly unconventional terms: the underprivileged, the working class, and the privileged. We use these rather idiosyncratic categories in an attempt to call attention to the effects of class location. The terms "lower class," "middle class," and "upper class" do not, in themselves, denotatively refer to any qualitative characteristics of class membership, and, connotatively, they stigmatize the poor as "below" the other classes. Since one of the purposes of this chapter is to correct the misconception that people who live in poverty are less worthy than others, the conventional categories of socioeconomic status are particularly inappropriate. In contrast, Marxist structural categories, which do distinguish among discrete classes based on their relationship to the production process (e.g., Wright, 1979; 1985), seem inadequate here, even though in other contexts they are most useful in depicting the dialectical relationship between classes—particularly between the two major classes, workers and capitalists, whose interests conflict.

Marxist class categories seem inadequate for discussion in this chapter, which refers to a group—commonly referred to as the "underclass"—that is prohibited from selling its labor—which is not to say that its members do not work. We refer to this group as "underprivileged" in order to focus on their circumstance as a group from which even the most ordinary privileges are withheld and in order to avoid the negative connotations of "under-class." Marxist categories have also been criticized as too limited for a complete understanding of the nature of white-collar workers' role in the political economy (Wright, 1979; 1985). Professionals and managers, particularly, do not fit neatly into structural categories. Like other workers, their livelihood usually depends on their labor, but many white-collar workers tend to align their interests with the capitalist class. They may, for example, own stock or rental property that supplements their incomes. Hence, we include them among the privileged. We make no claims that the classification system we use is better than conventional systems—except insofar as a different angle may offer new insights—just that it addresses more directly the main issues included in this chapter.

The Need to Allocate Poverty

Many families became wealthier during the 1980s, but more families lost money. So many families lost money that by the end of the 1980s, one-fourth of the children in the United States were living below the poverty level. This proportion, which has risen since then, was the highest it had been for over 20 years (Kellogg, 1988). As in the past, the increasing poverty was allocated primarily to vulnerable working-class families, especially families of minority racial or ethnic descent and families headed by women.

Poverty increased dramatically for a number of reasons, chief among them the globalization of corporate interests (Sweezy, 1992), increased foreign competition, accelerated computerization and automation in the workplace, and conservative economic policies at the federal and state levels of government (Heilbroner, 1993). Changes in business practices and in government policies, including the export of jobs to other countries and investment in financial trading rather than in production, resulted in significant reductions in demand for skilled and semiskilled labor in this country. While a small percentage of the population made a great deal more money than in the previous decade, the majority had to endure a *lower* standard of living. The status of some people changed so drastically that society adopted the newly coined term mentioned above, the "underclass," to describe them. The term "underclass" was used to describe the growing number of people who live in substandard housing—or no housing, who depend on charity or welfare for their livelihood, who have little or no health care, and who have virtually no prospects for improving their circumstances (Leman, 1986).

This recent deepening and expansion of poverty clarifies the function of the working class in U.S. society. Greater poverty results primarily from the reduced corporate need for so large a working class. Reduced need for workers implies that the limited material means allocated to workers to keep them sufficiently educated, healthy, and motivated to work now fall to a smaller proportion of the population. The function of the working class, for business purposes, is merely to provide labor. Because profit is business's reason for existence, people who are not needed for labor are, in effect, considered worthless and abandoned by the business community. To the extent that government serves business, it too abandons those who are useless for business's purposes. Moreover, the perspectives of government and business dominate public discussion. These circumstances conspire to ensure the virtual abandonment of a large segment of society, including millions of school children.

As Kozol (1991) points out in his critique of U.S. schools, *Savage Inequalities*, working-class and underprivileged children receive significantly fewer educational benefits than the children of wealthy parents. He also notes that parents who can secure educational advantages for their children do so even when these benefits are garnered at great expense to other children. Depriving other children of a "good education" gives the children of the privileged a competitive advantage, and it ensures a cheap labor pool for the future. Kozol (1991, p. 228) quotes the ironic observation of a school superintendent in San Antonio, Texas:

> If all of these poor kids in Cassiano get to go to real good schools—I mean,
> so they're educated well and so they're smart enough to go to colleges and

universities — you have got to ask who there will be to trim the lawns and scrub the kitchen floors in Alamo Heights.

This superintendent's pessimism appears warranted in view of the history of litigation regarding equitable pay, working conditions, and educational opportunities in the U.S.: So little has been given so grudgingly to poor workers and their children. Many of the children now in school will not be needed even for menial labor, much less for skilled or professional work (Krymkowski & Krauze, 1992). If current economic trends continue, the labor force will continue to decrease in size, and the number of children deprived of decent schooling will increase. The discrepancy between the educational opportunities for the rich and poor will continue to diverge.

To the extent that popular opinion regards wealth as the just reward for superior merit, it supports the increasingly unequal distribution of resources among the populace. Business corporations together with government institutions heavily influenced by them promote this opinion, and schools reflect as well as promote an ideology that justifies inequality as proceeding from such natural phenomena as inborn individual differences in ability and motivation. Seligman (1992, p. 3), for example, decries affirmative action and other efforts to create equity in society by attributing success and failure to inborn ability:

> IQ is positively correlated with just about all major measures of success and well-being: occupational status, socioeconomic status, income, marital stability, even good health and life expectancy. The correlations tell us the U.S. is very much a meritocracy, and the kind of "merit" that matters most is intelligence.

Schooling plays a contradictory role in society. Under liberal ideologies, its role is to equalize opportunity in the development of a competent citizenry. Nevertheless, much evidence shows that, whatever educators' intentions, school policies and practices actually make use of *putatively equal* opportunities to enforce *inequality*.

Schooling sustains social inequities by discriminating unfairly against vulnerable groups in a number of ways, deploying several forms of power to achieve its goals (Lukes, 1974). One form of the school's power is overt: The threat of punishment is inherent in school policies and rules, which represent the power of the state. Another mechanism of power in the schools is instruction itself, which, especially through the hidden curriculum, persuades students to accept particular beliefs and normative behaviors. The content and form of schooling perpetuates ruling-class ideologies among students (e.g., the importance of the restoration of America's global economic dominion). Institutionalized schooling also exerts power by controlling the agendas of decision-making forums (e.g., school-board meetings, IEP meetings, and school improvement council meetings). These mechanisms of localized power help to maintain the power relations that prevail throughout society.

Underpinnings of the Meritocratic View

The most insidious form of power is the ability to control ideas, especially ideas that determine how people regard themselves and each other. Schools base pedagogical practice on research and theories that support a meritocratic explanation of academic and career success. The major underpinnings of the meritocratic rationale are a paradoxical mix of deterministic and libertarian philosophies and theories, ranging from sixteenth-century Puritan asceticism to twentieth-century sociobiology, all of which attribute academic, social, and economic fate to inherent qualities of the individual.

According to the meritocratic view of achievement, individuals have the ability to change their economic circumstances through the exertion of will. Free will, with its related, particularly American, concept, "will power," is an important component of the popular view that capitalism establishes a meritocracy. Subscribing to the concept of free will allows privileged members of society to regard members of the working class and members of the underprivileged class as responsible for their own poverty.

The will to succeed financially plays an essential role in the U.S. political economy and has since the beginning of the industrial age. In *The Protestant Ethic and the Spirit of Capitalism*, Weber (1904/1958) explains the relationship between salvation and wealth as conceived by John Calvin and his followers. According to what Weber calls the "worldly asceticism" of the Puritans, prosperity was a sign of grace, and good husbandry was a means to salvation. Although Calvin, one of the earliest founders of Protestantism, was a determinist who believed that the Elect were predestined for salvation and that no one could *earn* salvation, other influential Protestant leaders confounded Calvin's concept of a calling as a sign of grace with the concept of a calling as an avenue to salvation.

Unlike medieval asceticism, which valued contemplation, hard physical labor was regarded by the Puritans as the most desirable means of avoiding temptation and glorifying God. The end of work was salvation, not wealth, but wealth was not considered undesirable in itself — as it had been under medieval asceticism — but only in so far as it tempted the wealthy to leisure and sensuality (Lasch, 1991). The religious spirit of the Protestant ethic has almost disappeared, but the summary ethical judgments that derive from it persist in a context very different from seventeenth-century New England. Today, joblessness, different from failing to receive a "call," is still somehow the mark of ill favor (the lack of grace). Often without understanding the source of this belief, the public regards the poor as immoral and pitiable.

One result of this ethic is the tendency to discount the social conditions that inhibit success: poor nutrition, inadequate health care, miseducation, and institutionalized abuse (e.g., racism, sexism, and classism). This ethic bolsters the feeling of entitlement shared by privileged members of society. According to the Center on Budget and Policy Priorities, 70% of the heads of impoverished rural families are employed (Maharidge, 1992), yet the myth that the poor are too lazy to hold jobs predominates. To illustrate this myth, Robert Coles (1977, pp. 491–492) reports interviews with children of wealthy parents:

> My daddy says the Eskimos . . . sit around all day, waiting for their welfare checks, or for the money they're getting from the oil companies. They're always trying to get more out of the state of Alaska . . . welfare bums and loafers, that's what my father says they're turning into. My mother says that the trouble with this country is that people are becoming soft; they want a lot of things, but they're not going to work as hard as they should to get them. They want jobs. But do they really try hard on the jobs? They want things for nothing. But do they know that you can't get something for nothing? There has to be someone who pays for everything. It's getting so that the people who work hardest and make the most money end up paying for everything, and the people who want to loaf all day end up expecting to get anything they want just by snapping their fingers. If it keeps on being like that, you won't see many people with any money left, and then the country will fall apart because there will be millions and millions of loafers, and the ones who don't loaf won't have any money left, because of taxes.

Perhaps even more influential than the Protestant ethic is the use of social Darwinism, Herbert Spencer's misinterpretation of Darwin's theory of evolution, to legitimate the social stratification that fostered the growth of industrial and postindustrial capitalism. Darwin's *Origin of Species* (1859) proposed that individual species arise from a natural principle: The organisms that are most adaptive are most likely to live long enough to reproduce. According to popularizers of Darwin's theory, psychological and social characteristics of individuals and groups of people conform to the same natural laws—of adaptation, variation, and inheritance—to which physical characteristics conform.

Herbert Spencer's conception of this principle as the "survival of the fittest" justified the ill results of the competitiveness inherent in the capitalist system as not only natural, but beneficial to the species and the economy. Spencer's "social Darwinism" maintains that capitalism is the best economic system because it fosters the operation of natural law in the marketplace. Unimpeded operation of this natural law supposedly results in the success of the biologically elite and, consequently, in the establishment of a meritocracy (the aristocracy of the most able). In the allegedly classless and democratic capitalism of the U.S., everyone is destined to succeed except those who are biologically inferior. Because intelligence is regarded as the most important biological trait for human adaptation, reduced levels of intelligence are supposed to reflect biological inferiority.

According to the logic of social Darwinism, less intelligent people are unlikely to succeed in a democratic meritocracy. They are less likely to procreate than in a class-based society in which *biologically* inferior people of the aristocratic class are "artificially" protected under a monarchy or oligarchy. By contrast, in a capitalist democracy, intelligent people, of whatever economic origins, become wealthy and thereby gain a reproductive advantage. Following this logic, capitalism should result in the development of a superior race of humans. Although comparatively few educators wholeheartedly endorse this logic—and virtually all would agree that it oversimplifies matters—social Darwinism forms a relatively unexamined ideological legacy that continues to influence public policy (Gould, 1981).

Gifted education has historically been associated with social Darwinism through the hereditarianism of Francis Galton, Cyril Burt, and Lewis Terman. In *Hereditary Genius*, Galton (1869/1972) reported that inborn ability, combined with two other innate qualities—zeal and the willingness to do hard work—was certain to manifest itself in high achievement. Although Darwin himself did not share Galton's conviction that achievement was solely a function of innate qualities, Galton believed that natural selection was the major factor in determining individuals' achievement. When his study of eminent literary figures, statesmen, musicians, and others showed that most had relatives with similar talents, he interpreted the findings as support for his hypothesis that talent was inherited. He did not acknowledge that these findings also support the equally plausible hypothesis that particular family environments create conditions favoring the development of particular talents.

Like Galton, Burt considered heredity to be the primary source of variation in levels of intelligence. Unlike Galton, however, Burt distinguished between potential ability, that is, intelligence, and realized ability, or achievement (Hearnshaw, 1979). He believed that the environment could expand ability but only up to an innately determined limit. This view is hardly arguable in theory—most scientists would agree that humans can do no more than their physical limitations allow. Burt and his colleagues, however, posit a comparatively narrow margin between potential and achievement.

Burt's studies, which correlated the IQ scores among family members who were related in varying degrees, and his studies of the IQ correlations among siblings, including identical and fraternal twins and non-twin siblings, served to buttress hereditarian theory and research from the 1940s until the 1970s. Although most of Burt's work has been discredited by the discovery that he fabricated findings, data, subjects, and even coresearchers, the hereditarian viewpoint continues to influence psychologists and educators (Gould, 1981).

Galton and Burt's work was admired by Lewis Terman, principal investigator and primary author of *Genetic Studies of Genius* (1925). Although many researchers and educators have questioned Terman's methods of identifying gifted children, his study is arguably the most influential in the field of gifted education. Few of the critiques of his study have questioned Terman's basic assumption that exceptional ability is inborn.

Beginning in the 1960s, another admirer of Galton and Burt, Arthur Jensen, put forth the hereditarian argument in a series of studies in which he concluded that higher socioeconomic status groups are innately superior to lower socioeconomic status groups. His conclusions offended many because he claimed to have found scientific evidence of the intellectual inferiority of African Americans. His findings supported the contention that the greater relative poverty of African Americans was due to their inferiority rather than to a long history of oppression. Although eminent sociological researchers (e.g., Jencks et al., 1972) challenged Jensen's findings, the predominant view — both professional and popular — remains hereditarian (e.g., Seligman, 1992).

Another hereditarian argument, advanced by Edward O. Wilson, an entomologist, considers evolutionary adaptation retrospectively: If the fittest survive, then *whatever* survives must be fittest (Wilson, 1975). Wilson's invalid logic leads him to the Panglossian view that all long-standing social *behaviors* are natural and important for survival. According to his view, behaviors — such as submissiveness in women and aggression in men, represent *genetic traits* that have survival benefits. The longevity of these so-called "traits" validates their evolutionary advantage. Wilson's version of social Darwinism, of course, argues against *all* social change. Any change in long-established social behaviors involves tampering with what Wilson believes are genetically programmed, inborn traits. Such tampering could, in Wilson's view, have disastrous social consequences.

Sociobiological and certain other innatist theories reflect and justify popular opinion. Incorporated into the curriculum in higher education, they influence future educators. Administrators, teachers, and counselors often use these theories, consciously or unconsciously, to discount their own effect on students' performance. For example, many teachers attribute learning disabilities and behavior disorders to inherited brain dysfunctions even when evidence of neurological impairment is lacking. By assuming that physical disabilities *cause* students' low achievement, teachers accept the inevitability of such poor performance. Belief in students' inevitable failure permits teachers to overlook the role that schooling (including poor teaching) plays in conditioning students' low achievement.

Similar beliefs contribute to the anti-intellectualism of programs for the gifted: Curriculum and instruction are regarded as less essential than innate ability for the development of talent. If educators think "talent will out," as Galton proposed, then they may regard activities to promote socialization as more important than those to cultivate students' intellectual abilities. This emphasis is likely to have particularly insidious effects on the achievement of gifted students from economically disadvantaged homes. Such families often lack the resources to compensate for schools' derelictions; they depend on the public schools to give their children an *academic* education.

According to Lewontin, Rose, and Kamin (1984), biological differences do not account for differences in academic achievement, nor does research support the belief that complex manifestations of human cognition and personality (e.g., intelligence, creativity, and motivation) are inherited. The arguments of biological determinism — that these manifestations represent inborn traits and that such traits account for differences in academic and life achievement — primarily serve ideological purposes. They legitimate social institutions responsible for unequal distribution of resources, and they conveniently relieve educators of responsibility for developing talent. The arguments of biological determinism, however, are not the only arguments claiming that the most successful are also the best and brightest.

In its way, the purportedly egalitarian position of liberals also advances this claim. Whereas political conservatives tend to attribute the achievement of individuals to inborn characteristics, political liberals tend to attribute it to environmentally induced characteristics. According to this view, the deficiencies of working-class and underprivileged individuals result from inadequacies in their cultures. The poor are said to be "culturally deprived," a condition more of their own making than inferior genetics ever could be. According to this view, parents with low incomes do not provide enough intellectual or linguistic stimulation nor do they value education sufficiently. Their children's failure is seen as a direct consequence of inadequate child-rearing practices. Hence, the liberal view — as much as and possibly more than the conservative one—may misrepresent the sources and consequences of poverty.

Barbara Ehrenreich (1987, p. 188) explains the popular tendency to attribute undesirable and self-defeating characteristics to the poor as a form of projection: The public attributes to the poor the very traits that it fears in itself.

> In the case of the poor, liberal ideology about the "culture of poverty" colludes with right wing ideology to make the poor the ideal symbolic victims of consumerism. Those traits that liberals saw as central to the "cycle of poverty," an incapacity for deferred gratification, a lack of self-discipline, and a lack of future-orientation—are from another point of view those of the ideal consumer.

In truth, however, the meager material pleasures of the poor are dwarfed by the excesses of the privileged classes (Schor, 1991). The poor may make sacrifices for their pleasures that the wealthy can avoid, but the mere good fortune of the wealthy simply hides the fact that the two groups share fundamental values (i.e., those centered on consumption). The good fortune of the wealthy certainly does not imply that they are wiser, more sensible, or more capable of delayed gratification. On closer inspection, in fact, this attribution of self-indulgence to the poor misconstrues reality. Some critics of food stamp programs are fond of repeating anecdotes about the misuse of food stamps to buy alcohol or other luxuries; however, Stallard, Ehrenreich, and Sklar (1983, p. 43) note,

> The average food stamp allotment per meal, per person is 47 cents—less than the price of a cup of coffee at a diner. No wonder, then, that a study by the U.S. Department of Agriculture found that food stamp recipients were far more economical and careful shoppers than non-food stamp shoppers.

The underprivileged, according to some culture-of-poverty theorists (e.g., Oscar Lewis and Daniel Moynihan), are too fatalistic to take action in their own behalf. Gaventa's (1982) discussion of power and powerlessness in an Appalachian coal mining area, however, explains the apparent quiescence and "fatalism" of the poor. In his view, the inaction of the poor reflects a rational response to the oppressive domination exercised over every feature of their lives by wealthy corporations. Such domination is particularly insidious because it is carried out not by alien businessmen in distant cities but by members of the *local* community: functionaries such as judges, school superintendents, teachers, and health-care providers. Although Gaventa's discussion focuses on rural Appalachian miners, his observations apply to other oppressed groups as well.

When inaction or ineffective action is recognized as a product of circumstance, not an acquired or inherited "personality" trait, one can make the quite tenable claim that changing the balance of power will immediately change the behavior of the poor. The "culture of poverty" no longer provides a convenient mask for the structural features of our society that condition the "failure" of the poor. Nevertheless, educators continue to invoke this explanation for the low achievement of certain students in part because it — like the hereditarian argument — relieves them of responsibility.

Moreover, the media and other representatives of dominant classes continue to blame the poor for their "failure," citing as moral exemplars the relatively few individuals who grow up in poverty but manage to succeed nonetheless (Ryan, 1971). These success stories serve both to inspire and to reproach those who remain impoverished.

All of these strategies help to convince members of the working and underprivileged classes that they are poor because they are unlucky, unintelligent, weak willed, or lazy, and, for the most part, these strategies work. Sennett and Cobb (1972) quoted the disparaging remarks that manual laborers made about themselves: "I really didn't have it upstairs to do satisfying work, if you know what I mean. I just wasn't smart enough to avoid hauling garbage" (p. 118). Sennett and Cobb concluded, however, that the workers whom they interviewed were not totally convinced of their blameworthiness. These workers understood that they had never really had the chance to develop themselves in the ways that privileged people have. Many of them had strongly conflicting feelings, blaming themselves for their relative poverty and, at the same time, sensing that they had been cheated out of a better life because the odds were against them.

Working-class and underprivileged students who *are* aware of the odds against them, however, may be in even greater jeopardy than other students. Paul Willis's *Learning to Labor* shows how working-class youths' attempts to resist the dominant culture doom them to the most menial role within it, that is, to low-paying, manual labor. These students' "partial penetration of the really determining conditions of existence of the working class . . . [is] definitely superior to those official versions of their reality which are proffered through the school and various state agencies," according to Willis (1977, p. 3). This savvy, however, occasions resistance, which much more surely conditions failure than would naive acquiescence.

Working-class parents are also suspicious of educators, as the following interview with a mother and father about an open-school night makes evident (Willis, 1977, pp. 73–74):

> *Father:*　The headmaster irritated me . . . if I could have been in a
> room with 'im [the headmaster] you know on his own, without any-
> body hearing us, I could have said . . .
>
> *PW:*　Could have said what?
>
> *Father:*　You're full of bull.
>
> *Mother:*　They say, "Children's night," go down, they ain't interested
> really in what you'm saying am they? They don't want to know.
>
> *PW :*　What's the whole thing in aid of then?
>
> *Mother:*　I don't know.
>
> *Father:*　I think it's trying to show you what good they'm doing for
> your kid. . . . They don't tell what they'm doin' wrong for him, they
> tell you exactly what they're doing right for 'em, what good they're
> doing.

Inhibiting Intellect Among the Working and Underprivileged Classes

The most fundamental power of public schooling is its power to force children to attend, regardless of whether the effects of the school program are beneficial or harmful. Parents who fail to send their children to school can be fined or sentenced to jail. Students who drop out of school can be penalized, in some states, for example, by having their driver's licenses revoked. The only students who can legally avoid public school attendance are those who attend private schools and those who receive state-approved "home schooling" from their parents. Neither of these options is available to most working-class and underprivileged families. Even many privileged families struggle to exercise these options.

Although many state constitutions explicitly require thorough and efficient systems of schooling for all students, states fail *much* more often to provide for children of the poor than for children of the affluent. This failure is perhaps most obvious in the squalid buildings and grounds, dilapidated equipment, and inadequate supplies provided in schools for working-class and underprivileged children. But it is also evident in other features of schooling relating to curriculum and instruction, remediation and discipline, and access to opportunities for higher education.

Inadequate facilities. Vast discrepancies exist between schools for children who are poor and schools for privileged children. Kozol (1985) reports that in Massachusetts, for example, the poorest school districts spent $1,500 per year per child, and the richest spent more than $6,000. This range — a 1:4 ratio — is typical, but in some states it is much wider and in some (e.g., impoverished West Virginia) it is much narrower. Litigation to reduce these discrepancies has sometimes proven successful in court, but the court decrees are, in fact, *unlikely* to be carried out (Kozol, 1991). Supportive court decisions have not often been translated into action to promote equity.

Kozol writes primarily about urban schools, but rural schools show similar discrepancies. In West Virginia, for example, parents in a poor, rural county filed suit because conditions in the schools were so much worse in their county than in more affluent counties (Pauley v. Kelley, 1979). The conditions in some schools in this mountainous, sparsely populated county were so bad that they were unsafe. Sewage disposal systems became saturated and seeped to the surface of playgrounds. Some schools had no on-campus source of potable water. In the high schools, only 40 textbooks were assigned to each classroom. Since most classrooms served over 100 students a day, students typically had difficulty taking books home. Consequently, relatively little homework was assigned. Laboratory equipment was outdated or missing. Most science classes were taught in regular classrooms, and teachers had to bring materials from home for the few science experiments that could be conducted under such conditions. In some counties in the state, conditions were not much better, but in most, buildings were safer and more sanitary. Furthermore, some counties had excellent facilities.

The West Virginia Department of Education responded to the judgment in favor of the plaintiffs by developing a "master plan," intended to raise standards all across the state and provide a more equitable school system. Five years later, however, educational researchers in the state reported that the plan "is not being implemented at this time" (Meckley, Hartnett, & Yeager, 1987, p. 186). More than a decade later, the plan still has not been implemented. Funding, if still terribly inadequate, is now more equal, however (Hughes, 1993).[1]

These events took place in a state that is forty-ninth in income, but twenty-second in spending on education. In spite of the state's general poverty, it spends more than an average proportion of its taxes on education, as do many school systems in impoverished areas, rural and urban. Even this *exceptional* commitment to education has not been expressed in actions to provide an equal and adequate education to all students in the state. It is even less likely that more affluent states, which spend a smaller proportion of their tax monies on education, will implement such action.

Although gifted programs, which predominantly serve children of the privileged, sometimes have better facilities than other programs in the schools, facilities for gifted programs vary greatly, as well. Gifted classes in poorer districts often have to meet wherever they can find space — on the stage in the auditorium or in the gymnasium, for example. But those in wealthier districts may have the use of their own, special facilities: laboratories with sophisticated equipment and computer classrooms with state-of-the-art hardware and software. The gifted children of privileged parents enjoy such benefits, while others, less fortunate but equally capable, are denied access based on their residency in impoverished communities.

Inappropriate curriculum and instruction. One means of allocating poverty is to make sure that some children fail to learn the concepts and skills needed to succeed (or at least to continue in school for long enough to earn credentials for particular jobs). Poor children and children from racial or ethnic minorities are most vulnerable. Research shows that these children are more likely than others to be retained or placed in remedial classes (Oakes, 1985). Retention in grade is probably the most effective means of delaying academic progress, but placing children in low groups or in remedial classes also ensures that they receive instruction at a slower pace (Oakes, 1985). In these slower paced classes, children may cover only part of the text or use a lower level text, so that at the end of the year, they are further behind than they were at the beginning.

This situation is particularly disturbing because instructional decisions about retention and grouping are not made solely on the basis of children's instructional needs. For example, the lowest achiever in the class is not necessarily the child who is retained. Educators' stereotypes about poor children affect such instructional decisions. Moreover, privileged parents find it easier to intervene when the possibility of retention or placement in a remedial class is broached. Parents who are members of the business or professional community are often neighbors of the teacher or principal, but even when they do not know the teacher personally, they share similar styles of dress, speech, and behavior. They regard themselves as the teachers' equals. Underprivileged and working-class parents who wish to intervene face a more formidable task than these parents.

Lareau (1989, p. 50) describes working-class parents' interactions with teachers: "parents appeared nervous and genuinely anxious in front of their children's teachers. Many shifted from one foot to another, had trouble maintaining eye contact, spoke very rapidly, and, in a few cases, stumbled over words." She contrasts this with the interactions of "upper-middle class" parents, who "easily maintained eye contact, did not blush or stutter, and did not appear visibly nervous" and who "joked with the teachers in their conversations, which were longer than at Colton [working-class school] and were more likely to include social conversation (e.g. the weather, community events, vacations)" (p. 76).

In working-class schools, the "really existing" curriculum tends to be mechanical, often involving rote memorization, practice of routine, and very little decision-making opportunity for students (Anyon, 1980; Brown, 1993). Teachers rarely explain why the work is assigned or the concepts behind procedures. Teachers often use worksheets. For example, in studying grammar, instruction considers rules, rather than discussing rhetorical reasons for selecting different styles of punctuation or diction. An essential message communicated by the curriculum for working-class children seems to be that work is boring, but must be done anyhow. According to Anyon (1980), assignments are highly structured and require primarily convergent answers; teachers' directions are phrased as orders rather than explanations or requests.

Students in predominantly working-class schools seldom have the opportunities offered to children in schools where students are predominantly affluent; working-class students are given fewer chances to design experiments or projects, to analyze ideas, or to express themselves in creative work (Brown, 1993). In high school, the curriculum for working-class students emphasizes manual and technical skills rather than scholarship. This type of curriculum is justified as more practical for "low achievers," but it effectively limits the college and career potential of bright underprivileged and working-class students (Gamoran, 1992; Oakes, 1985).

Remediation and discipline. The misconduct of underprivileged and working-class students arises in large part because of the type of instruction and curriculum they endure (e.g., Pink, 1982). Educators, however, tend to ignore the effects of poor educational practice and to regard only the students – and their families – as responsible for their indiscipline. Consequently, punishment is the school's usual response to the misconduct of such students. Although punishment, such as detention, paddling, suspension, or expulsion, has not been found to be effective, it is consistently preferred over interventions that *are* effective (Kauffman, 1993).

Characteristics of successful programs have been documented; such programs usually apply principles of reinforcement in highly structured ways to improve students' academic achievement, social skills, and progress toward graduation. More sophisticated programs acknowledge the relationship between students' indiscipline and schools' coercive agenda; but thus far the success of such programs has been ephemeral. Nearly *all* effective programs, however, are short-lived because of lack of fiscal support (Safer, 1982).

Privileged students are less vulnerable to pressures to fail; hence, they are less rebellious than their working-class or underprivileged peers. The privileged are also more likely than working-class or underprivileged students to attend schools that foster internalized responsibility and self-control. In fact, the classroom regimens in schools that serve impoverished communities stress obedience to external sources of authority, and even to *arbitrary* authority (e.g., Anyon, 1980; Brown, 1993; Wilcox, 1982; Willis, 1977). The two sorts of schools apparently pursue the cultivation of different sorts of character: one to accept leadership and rule, the other to submit to subordination and manipulation.

These distinctions help explain why infractions yield punishments that fall more heavily on working-class and underprivileged students than on their privileged peers. Preparation for leadership and responsible self-direction entails risk taking, so that among the privileged a certain degree and frequency of rebellious action can even be encouraged. Among those destined to be ruled rather than to rule, however, frequent counterproductive rebelliousness can be expected, but certainly not tolerated. Students from privileged backgrounds are not only *less likely* to receive punishment when they do indulge in rebellious behavior, but they are also *more likely* to receive and to respond to therapeutic intervention (e.g., counseling), a technology of the middle class (Bellah et al., 1985). In addition, they are more likely to be given over to the custody of their parents, and to have lawyers who can reduce the burdens that serious infractions might entail (see Colvin & Pauly, 1983, for a theoretical explanation of these circumstances).

Economically disadvantaged children often suffer poor health and uncomfortable or dangerous living conditions. Nevertheless, punishments are meted out to these children by schools and legal systems with *more* severity and *greater* certainty than to other children (Pink, 1982). Despite comparatively adverse circumstances, most working-class students are well-behaved. Nevertheless, the few who misbehave serve as examples that reinforce meritocratic myths; thus, according to Jencks and colleagues (1972, p. 139), we find that "the deviant minority seems to shape popular stereotypes of working-class values and behavior."

Inadequate access to college. Working-class and underprivileged students, no matter how capable, are much less likely than their more privileged counterparts to attend college. Data from the longitudinal survey, *High School and Beyond*, show that by 1986 approximately 38% of upper socioeconomic status (SES) students from the high school graduating class of 1980 had earned a bachelor's degree and approximately 16% of the middle SES students from this nationally representative sample had earned such a degree. By contrast, only 7% of the lower SES students had earned the B.A. degree (National Center for Education Statistics, 1991, table 289).

There are financial assistance programs for economically disadvantaged students, of course, but such programs offer limited support. Most assistance packages combine scholarship and loan monies, requiring students to work at least part-time in order to pay living expenses and to begin paying back loans as soon as they graduate. Students who must work while they are in college find it harder to get adequate time to read and prepare for class discussions, tests, and assignments than do students whose college attendance is fully subsidized by their parents. As a consequence, the students who are least well prepared by their high schools to attend college, are further impeded by the conditions under which their college attendance is made possible.

Evidence of the difficulty working-class and underprivileged students have in completing college work comes from the NCES survey *Recent College Graduates*. African-American, Hispanic, and American Indian groups take considerably longer, on average, to complete bachelor's degrees. For example, 41% of American Indians, as compared to 18.5% of whites take more than 6 years to complete B.A. degrees (NCES, 1993). Institutionalized racism and classism, of course, contribute to the circumstances that make college attendance and graduation more difficult for some groups than for others even when some financial assistance is available.

SCHOOLING FOR THE SUBSERVIENCE
OF WOMEN AND MINORITIES

College attendance and graduation are not just a function of class; they also vary dramatically on the basis of race and ethnic origin. Whereas approximately 29% of Asian Americans and 21% of white students from the high school graduating class of 1980 had received B.A.s by 1986, only 10% of African Americans, 7% of Hispanics, and 9% of American Indians had received comparable degrees (NCES, 1991, table 289). Among African-American students who attend college, more than half fail to complete their degree programs (Steele, 1992). White college students are more likely to complete degrees, in part because they have the financial backing of affluent families: The majority of white college students come from families whose income is $50,000 or more (Reed, 1988).

In Willis's view, a person's cultural location, at least in part, decides his or her likelihood to succeed in school and in the marketplace. He finds that the concept of "cultural location" provides a more compelling explanation of social mobility than the concept of individual intelligence (Willis, 1977). Cultural location is a function of class, but it is also determined by gender, race, and ethnicity. Cultural location implicates mechanisms of institutionalized practice that systematically and unfairly discriminate against members of the working and underprivileged classes.

In Western capitalist societies, discrimination against women and against racial and ethnic minorities helps to ensure that a large proportion of the population is available as cheap labor. Moreover, as the need for workers in general decreases, the increasing numbers of unemployed female and minority workers drive down the wages of those who are employed. Discrimination against certain groups in this way sustains differences in class.

Institutionalized discrimination against women and minority groups clearly favors the wealthy, even though individuals from privileged backgrounds may feel little personal prejudice or animosity toward the victims of unfair discrimination. Institutionalized discrimination allows members of privileged groups to espouse liberal sentiments without giving up their privileges. Because it is diffused throughout government and private institutions, the mechanisms and effects of institutionalized racism, for example, tend to be more insidious than the more blatant hostilities expressed by individuals. Despite serious attempts to change discriminatory practices in the U.S. (e.g., the civil rights movement, the women's movement), our society still favors male members of the white, privileged class. This favoritism is less evident than it once was in policy, though it persists in practice even after policies have changed.

Personalized discrimination, though fostered by institutionalized discrimination, varies in form and intensity among individuals and among groups. Both forms of discrimination, however, produce hardships for those discriminated against: Out of proportion to their numbers, more women than men are poor, more blacks than whites, more Hispanics than Anglos, more American Indians, and more of the rural populace. Exceptions occur, and extraordinary individual successes are documented in the popular and professional media — often as exhortatory examples.[2] In general, though, the chances of a minority child's growing up to become a well-paid professional or highly successful business person are much less than those of an equally capable child from the white majority.

Sexism and Women's Intellectual Development

Historically, women have been allocated more poverty than men. Nevertheless, as *Poverty and the American Dream: Women and Children First* (Stallard, Ehrenreich, & Sklar, 1983) shows, the poverty of women increased substantially during the 1980s. More than half of the families headed by women live at or below the poverty level, a poverty rate four times higher than the poverty rate for families headed by men (House Select Committee on Children, Youth, and Families, 1987).

Women *of all social classes* predominate in relatively low paying jobs. Working-class women earn low wages as fast food waitresses, clerks, and aides in day-care nurseries or, if they have access to more resources, as teachers, social workers, secretaries, and nurses. Privileged women may be judges and CEOs, yet they almost always earn less than their male counterparts (e.g., Matthews, 1985). Furthermore, the working wives of professionals and business executives often are employed in less prestigious and less well-paid jobs than those of their husbands.

Subotnik, Karp, and Morgan (1989) found that the male graduates of Hunter College's school for gifted students earned about twice as much per year as the equally gifted and equally well-educated female graduates. The mean income of the women was $47,391 and their median income was $40,000, compared with a mean of $105,000 and a median of $75,000 for the men. Part of this difference can be explained by the women's occupations. For example, as compared with 1.4% of the men, 13.4% of the women taught school at the elementary or high school levels. Nonetheless, the authors found that even when men and women were matched by profession, the women earned less than the men.

Hereditarian claims about women's intelligence. Although the media still portray women as less intelligent (i.e., more "dippy") than men, scholars seldom make this claim. Some research on highly gifted children, conducted under the auspices of the Johns Hopkins study of mathematical precocity, however, does make such an assertion. The finding used to advance this claim relates specifically to the mathematics achievement of mathematically talented girls. These high achievers never quite match the high scores on the math portion of the SAT obtained by their male counterparts. Benbow (1986) attributes the girls' lower scores to genetic, specifically hormonal, gender-specific characteristics. Of course, she could just as easily have offered an environmental explanation: Considerable research shows that girls receive less instruction than boys in advanced math.

Benbow's hereditarian reasoning is based on Geschwind's (Geschwind & Behan, 1982; Geschwind & Galaburda, 1984) hypotheses about brain dominance. According to Geschwind, right-hemisphere dominance results from excesses of testosterone or sensitivity to it. This right-brain dominance is associated with left-handedness and, sometimes, with learning disabilities and immune deficiencies. It also is associated with extremely superior mathematical ability. This reasoning suggests that individuals who show signs of having testosterone-induced right-hemisphere dominance (i.e., because they are left-handed or have allergies) are likely to perform extremely well in mathematics.

A recent study attempting to replicate Benbow's findings (Wiley & Goldstein, 1991) found no support for the link between allergies, left-handedness, and mathematical ability, casting doubt on Benbow's argument. Wiley and Goldstein found no higher incidence of left-handedness among highly mathematically precocious boys than among other adolescents. Moreover, they questioned Benbow's research methods. Benbow found a higher frequency of left-handedness, they say, because she compared the frequency in the experimental group of adolescent boys with the frequency among males in the total U.S. population. Her findings are the artifact of this decision.

According to Wiley and Goldstein, had Benbow used adolescents as her comparison group, she would have found no significant difference because there is a greater frequency of left-handedness in the 10- to 20-year-old age groups than in adults. Wiley and Goldsmith account for the higher incidence of allergies as relating to class differences rather than intellectual differences. They believe that a higher incidence of *identified* allergies exists among the gifted because middle- and upper-income families can afford to seek medical help for allergic conditions. Benbow's sample came primarily from this privileged group.

"Culture-of-poverty" claims about women's intelligence. Until this century, women in Europe and the United States were effectively excluded from higher education. Their lack of formal schooling — private or public — affected intellectual development. Mary Wollstonecraft (1792/1986, p. 100), an early feminist, astutely observed,

> Men complain, and with reason, of the follies and caprices of our sex. . . . Behold . . . the natural effects of ignorance! The mind will ever be unstable that has only prejudices to rest on, and the current will run with destructive fury when there are no barriers to break its force. Women are told from their infancy, and taught by the example of their mothers, that a little knowledge of human weakness, justly termed cunning, softness of temper, outward obedience, and a scrupulous attention to a puerile kind of propriety, will obtain for them the protection of man. . . .

When girls enter schools today, they score slightly higher on standardized academic tests than boys. As with economically disadvantaged children, girls have a better chance of qualifying for gifted programs in the early grades than in the later ones (Silverman, 1986). By high school, however, girls score lower than their male peers on standardized tests (Sadker, Sadker, & Steindan, 1989). The greatest difference in scores is in mathematics. In elementary school girls have higher math scores than boys; but by the time they take the SAT in junior high or high school, boys typically score about one-half standard deviation, or 50 points, higher (Dorans & Livingston, 1987). Moreover, based on their scores on the Preliminary Scholastic Aptitude Test, girls are awarded far fewer—slightly more than one-third—of the National Merit Scholarships (Sadker et al., 1989).

Declines in girls' achievement result from their socialization, via the "hidden curriculum." Without thinking about it, teachers convey messages that reinforce and reproduce behaviors associated with gender stereotypes. Teachers, for example, reinforce girls' quiescence by giving more attention to the boys in their classes. They initiate more contacts with boys (Acker, 1988) and engage them in more verbal interchanges—more criticism as well as more praise (Jones, 1989; Sadker et al., 1989). Teachers encourage male achievement by referring boys to high-level groups more often than they refer girls, even when the girls are equally bright (Hallinan & Sorensen, 1987; Irvine, 1986; Mickelson, 1989). In addition, some evidence suggests that teachers respond more positively to gifted boys than to gifted girls (Solano, 1976).

Receiving the messages that they do, girls—even gifted girls—express less confidence in their abilities than do boys (Fox, 1976). They are particularly skeptical of their abilities to excel in science and mathematics. Consequently, girls are less likely than boys to pursue advanced studies even when they have the ability to succeed (Fox, 1976). Although increasing numbers of women are studying mathematics and science at the college level (Mickelson, 1989), women are still grossly underrepresented among math and science majors (Jones, 1989). The majors they select most often lead to relatively low-status, low-paid work like nursing and teaching.

Some advocates for women's rights have marked off an area of expertise as belonging essentially to girls and women. They view women as tending to be more intuitive than analytical. Cixous (1975/1988) for example, uses the metaphors "intelligible" for masculine and "sensitive" for feminine. Although women and men do exhibit some characteristic differences in interests, there is no clear empirical evidence for differences in reasoning or intuition. Nevertheless, objectivity is often regarded as masculine, and analytical thinking is sometimes associated with male domination.

Efforts to assign intuition as a special expertise of women, while well-intentioned, may actually limit women's intellectual development. Girls and women who—because of their special "gift" for intuition—have been discouraged from learning to think analytically are at a disadvantage in the intellectual realm. Of course, men, who often fail to cultivate a sensitive outlook on life, are disabled by a similar oversight. Stereotyping mental abilities as masculine or feminine denies both women and men development of a broad range of intellectual powers (Belenky, Clinchy, Goldberger, & Tarule, 1986).

Racism and the Intellectual Development of Minorities

The most vicious forms of unfair discrimination are those based on differences in the physical appearance of different races or ethnic groups. To this day, many people adhere to the unfounded belief that such traits as skin color, physique, and facial features signify more profound differences in mental faculties. Unfair discrimination against various ethnic groups *is* a form of racism. Racism in the treatment of African Americans in the United States may often appear more virulent than racism in the treatment of other groups. General economic conditions and cultural heritage, as well as physical differences contingent on race and ethnicity, seem to be salient in determining the degree to which different groups are discriminated against at different points in time. This assertion carries considerable weight in the U.S., with its history of exterminating American Indians and enslaving Africans.

African-American students. The most chilling evidence of the effects of racism appears in comparisons of the mortality rates of different racial groups. According to 1988 statistics, life expectancy at birth was 75.5 years for whites, but only 69.5 years for African Americans. Moreover, the discrepancy appears to be widening (Navarro, 1991). This difference results from the greater poverty of the African-American minority, poverty that results from a long history of oppression (Navarro, 1991).

Of course, such oppression persists, even if the privileged classes — given voice through the mass media — prefer to blame African Americans for the unfavorable circumstances in which they live. For example, liberal politicians from the 1960s liked to attribute African Americans' poor school performance to the failure of African-American culture to value education.[3] This view, however, reflects an ahistorical misconception. Since before the Civil War, African Americans *have* struggled ardently to provide education for their children. The white majority, not African Americans themselves, have impeded these efforts through such overt mechanisms as "separate but equal" schools and continuing (perhaps worsening) de facto segregation (e.g., Rumberger & Willms, 1992).

An illustration of the conditions that hindered the efforts of African Americans to educate themselves is provided by the history of the Freedmen schools. Gutman (1987) describes how former slaves and white schoolteachers from the North fought to set up and operate schools despite opposition from white southerners. Except for Florida, which imposed a separate education tax on African Americans, no state in the South made budgetary provisions to assure facilities, materials, and teachers for the former slaves. Three years after the end of the Civil War, the federal government allocated a half million dollars to the Freedmen's Bureau to set up or rent schoolhouses, but white opposition continued to impede the establishment and operation of schools for African-American children. Evidence of African Americans' commitment, however, is ample. They "purchased schoolbooks, hired, fed, boarded, and protected teachers, constructed and maintained school buildings and engaged in other costly (and sometimes dangerous) activities to provide education for their children" (Gutman, 1987, p. 260).

Whereas today there may be less overt hostility toward African Americans, impediments to the education of African-American children are still considerable. Segregation is nearly as prevalent now as it was 40 years ago when the Supreme Court handed down the landmark *Brown v. Board of Education* ruling (Rumberger & Willms, 1992). There are fewer resources to support schooling in African-American communities, despite the fact that such communities often tax themselves at higher rates than those of the neighboring suburbs. Because property values are low, however, high taxation rates often fail to provide adequate funds for schools (Kozol, 1991). As a consequence, children attend schools that are dilapidated, often to the point of being dangerous.

Because of poor conditions in public schools many African-American parents struggle to send their children to private or parochial schools. These schools are safer, have better discipline, and are more academically focused than public schools. According to one study (Jones-Wilson, Arnez, & Asbury, 1992), African-American parents in Washington, DC, ranked inadequate discipline in the public schools and poor curriculum and standards as the two most important reasons for seeking alternatives to public education.

Although most privately schooled African-American children attend Catholic schools, many attend independent African-American schools (Ratteray, 1992). New York City has 55 such schools (Foster, 1991). The majority of African-American students, however, attend public schools despite the harm such schools may cause them: Their achievement relative to that of other students is often lower when they leave public schools than when they enter (cf. Brown, 1993; Wilcox, 1982; Wilcox & Moriarity, 1977).

African-American males usually have the lowest academic achievement of any group, but African-American females also perform poorly (Garibaldi, 1992). As a consequence, African-American students are disproportionately assigned to remedial and special education programs. They are, for example, three times as likely as white children to be identified as mentally retarded but only half as likely to be identified as gifted (Kozol, 1991).

The blame for low achievement among African-American students has traditionally been assigned to the family; however, schooling itself appears to inhibit the intellectual development of these students. Teachers often regard African-American students as less capable than other students and, consequently, hold low expectations for them; they assume that African-American students will not have the interest or the ability to attend college. Furthermore, when African-American students are educated in integrated classrooms, they are given relatively little attention (Williams & Muehl, 1978).

The content of the curriculum also contributes to the disenfranchisement of all minority groups, perhaps especially African Americans and women. As McCarthy (1990) notes, both African-American and feminist writers have commented on the devaluation of African Americans' and women's identity; James Baldwin, Ntozake Shange, and June Jordan, among others, cite schools as "principal sites for the production and naturalization of myths and ideologies that systematically disorganize and neutralize minority cultural identities" (p. 46).

As a consequence of such treatment, African-American students often regard the school environment as a hostile one. Despite the best intentions of many educators, African-American students nevertheless experience political and cultural conflict within their classrooms and schools. Such conflict—rather than inherent or cultural deficiencies—accounts for the low achievement of these students (Jackson, 1992; cf. Labov, 1972). Nevertheless, the conflict contributes to low self-esteem and persistent feelings of hopelessness.

Minority students identified as gifted, however, tend to be more hopeful and positive about their schooling than other students. As Ford and Harris (1992, p. 59) speculate, "Perhaps students, by virtue of being identified as gifted and placed accordingly in gifted classes, have more hope for their educational futures and career prospects than do those placed in regular classes." But African-American students have limited access to gifted programs, and the gifted programs that do serve them tend to have fewer resources than gifted programs in more affluent, white communities (Kozol, 1991). Whereas only 1.4% of African-American students received resources or services through gifted education programs in 1981, 3.7% of white students received such services (Grant & Snyder, 1986).

African-American students also have limited access to higher education, as we mentioned above. Historically, they have been underrepresented in college programs, and their college enrollment rate has been *declining* since 1978 (Reed, 1988). Those who do enroll in college cannot hope for the kind of family support available to white students. Compared to the $50,000 family income of more than half of the white college students, the family income of more than half of the African-American college students in 1985 was under $20,000 (Reed, 1988). Not surprisingly, African-American students are more likely than white students to leave college for financial reasons.

Hispanic students. The patterns of discrimination that inhibit the intellectual development of Hispanic students are similar to those affecting African Americans. But for many Hispanic students, the problems of racism and poverty are compounded by the fact that English is their second language. Hispanics may, in fact, have the highest drop-out rate of any minority group (Ruiz, 1989). On average, 32.4% of Hispanics as compared with 13.2% of African Americans and 12% of whites were classified as high school dropouts in 1990 (NCES, 1991, table 98).

These findings, however, can be misleading. Among Hispanics, different subgroups seem to meet different fates as they assimilate into American society. The differential success of Hispanic subgroups results in large part from class differences in their native countries. Many Cubans who immigrated to the United States, for example, came from wealthy families. Their move to this country was an attempt to retain wealth and privilege in the face of the egalitarian policies of the communists (Bean & Tienda, 1987). Mexican-American immigrants, by contrast, usually come from impoverished communities, bringing few resources with them to the U.S. (Bean & Tienda, 1987).

The differences in the relative achievement of the different Hispanic subgroups are, of course, obscured in statistics that consider Hispanics as a single ethnic group. Moreover, the achievement of Hispanic students reflects factors such as length of residence in the U.S. and socioeconomic status. For these reasons, the school achievement of Hispanic students is quite variable. On average, however, their achievement in many subjects, while lower than the average for white students, is typically higher than that of African-American students (Hardeo, 1989).

Like African Americans, Hispanic students are more likely to be retained than white students. Those who are from large families, particularly single-parent families, are more vulnerable. By the time they are in high school, they are more than twice as likely as non-Hispanic white students from comparable family types to have been retained at least 2 years (Muller & Espanshade, 1985). Their relatively higher retention rates may reflect the combination of discrimination, poverty, and linguistic and cultural differences.

Hispanics—like African Americans—share a legacy of public humiliation. Many African-American and Hispanic students hear from their parents stories about being required to use separate restrooms, drink from separate fountains, and eat at different restaurants. Though perhaps less public, discrimination continues against the current generation of minority children. As Rodriguez (1989, p. 38), recalls, "I had a sense that it was not so good to be a Mexican . . . in sixth grade, when my mother enrolled me in a different school, the school administrator commented, 'Oh, her last name is Rodriguez, just put her in the slow class.'"

Hispanics not only have lower achievement than whites, they are also underrepresented in gifted programs. Relatively few Hispanics are identified as gifted. In the Los Angeles Unified School District, for example, Hispanics represent 56% of the total student population, but they represent only 29% of the population identified as gifted (Perrine, 1989). Similarly, Hispanic students are underrepresented in higher education programs (Schroeder, 1991), including graduate programs, especially in mathematics and science (Thomas, 1992). In 1988–1989, for example, 86.2% of those earning doctoral degrees were white, whereas only 3.8% were African American and 2.7% were Hispanic (NCES, 1991, table 274).

American Indians. American Indians are the most impoverished of all of the minority groups; and the effects of their poverty are reflected in their high drug-abuse, murder, and suicide rates (e.g., Szasz, 1992). These conditions are the legacy of whites' attempts to destroy the Indian nations through genocide from the moment of contact through the nineteenth century; but they also reflect the vicious discrimination that followed (see Zinn, 1980). Whites' mistreatment of American Indians was so horrendous that by the turn of the twentieth century, the Indian population had been reduced at least 90% by murder, disease, and starvation. The Indian population has risen almost tenfold since 1900, and the federal government today recognizes over 400 tribes.

Given the historical circumstances, the effects in the present are no surprise. Indians' achievement test scores, for example, approximate those of African Americans and Hispanics. Of the Indians graduating in the high school class of 1980, only 9.2% had completed college degrees by 1986 (NCES, 1991, table 289); and Indians have the highest level of unemployment of any ethnic group in the U.S. population.

Indians' academic performance suffers not only because of political and economic discrimination but also because of cultural hegemony. Whites typically devalue (or patronize) Indian culture—circumstances that adversely affect Indian children's achievement and ability test scores (Guilmet, 1983). Differences between native culture and school culture, ignorance of native culture, language differences between students and teachers, differences between students' and teachers' values, cultural differences in learning styles, poor motivation of students, students' home and community problems, and inappropriate use of tests with Indian students all contribute to the underachievement of this group (Gilliland, 1986; Swisher & Deyhle, 1987).

In response to such conditions, Indians have traditionally struggled to wrest control of their education from white institutions. Institutions like the Bureau of Indian Affairs now favor the employment of Indians as teachers and school administrators. The infamous boarding schools have mostly closed or changed dramatically, and many Indian schools are tribally controlled. Most Indian children, however, attend *public* schools (either on reservations or elsewhere). But despite the legacy of oppression and genocide, many whites nevertheless continue to view Indians' successful efforts to establish their control over Indian education as a form of rebellion.

Asian-American students. In contrast to the academic achievement of African Americans, Hispanics, American Indians, and women, that of Asian-American students is higher than average. Specifically, Asian-American high school students score significantly higher on tests of mathematics than other students (Hardeo, 1989), and they tend to select majors in math and science in college. The high academic achievement of Asian-American students has received much attention in the popular media as well as in scholarly journals. Curiously, the high achievement of these students is usually attributed to environment—specifically, to cultural values communicated through the family—rather than to heredity.

Chauvinistic attitudes may be responsible for this representation. For instance, the success of Asian Americans neatly confirms the American myth that poor immigrants who work hard can succeed in this country regardless of the odds against them. Asian Americans can, in this way, serve as exemplars to other minority groups.

Some studies have examined the relationship between families' valuing of education and Asian-American children's high achievement. To discover specific family variables that are associated with high achievement, one study (Caplan, Choy, & Whitmore, 1992), surveyed 200 Indochinese refugee families. The 536 school-age children in the families had been in the U.S., on average, 3½ years. Despite their limited familiarity with English, the tragedy and disruption many had suffered in political and military conflicts in their home countries, and the poverty in which they lived in the U.S., these children performed as well as children born in this country. They had GPAs slightly above 3.0 ("B") and average scores on the California Achievement Test.

Surprisingly, GPA was *positively* correlated to the number of children in the family—the opposite of what is usually found. The investigators attributed the positive correlation among the Asian Americans to two circumstances: (1) Asian-American children spend more time on homework than native-born children do and (2) siblings help each other with school work in the evenings. These researchers concluded that the nature of the family is the key to these children's high achievement.

Although Caplan and colleagues' causal attributions are not justified by their methods—correlational studies such as this one cannot establish cause—their explanation is plausible. It would be difficult to argue that additional hours of homework and devotion to learning do not contribute to good grades. But in suggesting that poverty and limited familiarity with English do not preclude achievement among children who receive support and encouragement in a stable home, this research tends to discount the real impediments to the achievement of children from other minority groups.

Unlike Asian Americans, children from African-American, Hispanic, and American-Indian families grow up under conditions of institutionalized discrimination: Their families have endured *generations* of poverty and exclusion from school.

Studies of second- and third-generation Asian-American children may find that high educational achievement does not have the returns for them that their families predicted. If this is the case, we can expect that these generations will show lower achievement. Studies that have, indeed, found lower achievement among subsequent generations of Asian-American children attribute decreases in achievement to changes in family values—the children have been Americanized.

Investigators usually stop their analyses at this point, unwilling to speculate about the sources of these changes. We suspect, however, that such changes may reflect acquiescence to a covert class system as much as or more than they reflect pressures on children to conform to the norms of the mainstream. We worry, too, that the decreasing achievement of Asian-American students may become even more pronounced as states like California institutionalize practices—for example, quota systems in higher education—that discriminate against high-achieving Asian Americans.

PROSPECTS FOR CHANGE

All forms of unfair discrimination serve to undermine the efforts of the poor and minorities to improve their circumstances. Sexism divides underprivileged and working-class men from women. Racism divides workers of different racial and ethnic backgrounds from one another. Sexism and racism prevent the underprivileged and working classes from uniting to exercise economic and political power. Considering these ideological

impediments, serious action against unfair discrimination, especially institutionalized discrimination, will require extraordinary effort on the part of
the underprivileged and the working classes: first to grasp the similarities of
their circumstances and then to act on behalf of their common interests.

Action of such extraordinary purpose ultimately resulted in the passage
of civil rights legislation in 1964, but its actions—the ongoing campaign for
the equal rights not only of African Americans but of all minorities,
women, and disabled people—were countered forcibly. Not only did the
angry sentiment of mainstream whites operate to thwart change, but the
agents of institutionalized racism (especially local political machines and
the police) aggressively sought to squelch the civil rights movement. Civil
rights legislation was passed, but not without substantial loss of life. And,
of course, legislation has merely made some racist practices illegal. Enforc-
ing the law and disestablishing institutional racism are other matters altogether.

The events and consequences of the civil rights movement are, however, illustrative of the sorts of commitments and sacrifices required to
effect substantive change. Any similar effort that seeks real change in terms
of the distribution of power will meet as much or greater resistance. If the
disenfranchised are to significantly improve their life circumstances, they
must be ready to join forces for a long, and possibly bloody, battle.

This devastating prospect leads many sympathizers to search for more
gradual, less tumultuous avenues for change. Reformers, in past and present times, have imagined that changes in schooling would foster such gradual improvements in society. Yet many of the school reforms proposed to
target problems of poverty and discrimination have as much potential for
sustaining as for relieving oppression. Two such proposed reforms—school
choice and site-based management of schools—exemplify the contradictions inherent in the project of using schools to promote political economic
change.

Reform Proposals

In the hopes of motivating school improvement by sponsoring healthy
competition among schools, some reformers have recommended "school
choice." Advocates believe this strategy would produce two salutary effects:
It would force schools to improve in response to market pressures, and it
would involve parents in the schooling process by giving them the option to
select the schools that their children attend (Chubb & Moe, 1990).

Many school choice plans involve the use of vouchers—subsidies to parents that pay all or part of the tuition at public or private schools. Despite
their purported benefits, school choice plans pose particular dangers to poor

and minority children. For instance, some voucher plans involving cross-district choice among public schools require the school district the student leaves to pay the cost of the child's tuition in the school of his or her choice. Poor schools whose students opt to leave find themselves in the position of paying per pupil costs—often much higher than their own—to wealthy school districts. Parker (1992) gives the example of one school district, which spends $4,600 per student, having to pay another district $10,200 for each student choosing to attend its schools. Such arrangements drain the resources of districts that already are the most poorly funded; yet students who benefit most from school choice are likely to be the most privileged within their districts.

Voucher plans that include private as well as public school options are even less likely to provide substantial benefits to poor and minority students. Such plans usually give students a fixed stipend—often a fraction of the cost of private school tuition—to spend at the school of their choice. Because poor families cannot pay for the unfunded portion of private school tuition, however, they cannot exercise this "choice." Wealthy families find, by contrast, that they are supported in their efforts to educate their children outside of the public schools. This arrangement is doubly damaging to underprivileged and working-class children: When sizable numbers of wealthy parents select private school options, they become much less willing to pay high taxes whose primary purpose is to support the education of other people's children.

The fact that some African-American parents, as well as parents of other minority groups, support school choice indicates their recognition of the failure of the public schools to educate their children properly. Under some circumstances vouchers may, in fact, give options to low-income families that privileged families have long exercised. Nevertheless, because public schools are contradictory sites of struggle in the political economy—informed not only by the market but also by democratic ideals—they hold more promise for equity than do private schools.

A second reform proposal aimed primarily at public schools is site-based management. Like school choice, this reform promises structural changes in the institution of schooling. Site-based management is put forth as a democratic reform intended to make schools responsive to communities' needs and aspirations. But it, too, poses particular dangers for poor and minority children.

Unintended consequences may result when local schools are given autonomy to design and regulate their own programs. Of most concern for underprivileged and working-class children is the possibility that site-based management will substantially deregulate the schools. Whereas we, like most educators, would welcome the elimination of much of the intrusive

regulation that currently exists, we worry about the elimination of regulation intended to ensure adequate and equitable education. This concern
is particularly acute when we imagine what might happen if site-based
management were implemented widely without provision for the *equal
funding* of schools.

School choice and site-based management plans may be less forward-
looking than they appear. They may actually represent efforts to revoke
some of the equity provisions achieved through the civil rights movement
and other popular movements. We find it curious that much of the "bureaucracy" that conservatives claim hampers the schools (e.g., Chubb & Moe,
1990) exists in order to provide due process protections for handicapped
students, women, minorities, and the poor (Lowe, 1992).

Changing the Students

Can students who are underprivileged or who belong to a minority
group be taught to help themselves? Willis (1977) and Giroux (1983) believe that resistance to inequity as it is usually expressed by underprivileged
and working-class youth is ineffective and self-destructive. Willis points out
the effects of capitalist ideology in the racism, sexism, vandalism, and
alcohol abuse of the "lads" who reject the school's authority. Their ill-
informed resistance is met by punishment that effectively prevents them
from finishing school—by being held back in grades, by being channeled
into vocational tracks, and by imprisonment—often under circumstances in
which privileged children would simply be reprimanded or given probation
(cf. Jackson, 1992).

The "cultural revolution" of the 1960s, nonetheless, suggests that students *can* accomplish significant change. The majority of the student activists of the 1960s—most of them privileged and many of them gifted—would
probably agree, however, that what was accomplished is far short of the
just legal system and more equitable distribution of resources for which
they worked.

A more contemporary youth subculture, commonly labeled "punk," is
composed primarily of working-class youth whose families subscribe less to
mainstream values. Though members of this group may not have particularly high IQs, they nevertheless seem to be making an *intellectual* statement. Their critique of society is articulated through their clothes and hair-
styles, just as the hippies' was. But the punk movement is cynical. The
clothes acknowledge how bad things are, refusing to pretend that things
will get better—an attitude that is an insult to the enterprising spirit of
Western capitalism. However, as Willis notes, this kind of rebellion is only
a beginning—a partial penetration. The violent racism of some "skinheads"

provides evidence of the misdirection of such rebellion. Willis and Giroux, among others, would argue that the racism of these "punkers" derives from their inability to recognize the privileged class as the true source of their oppression.

Giroux (1983) believes that resistance can be effective if it is channeled into more acceptable forms of rebellion. He suggests that teaching critical theory and critical thinking in a context that values students' lived experience will empower students to play a more active role in creating an equitable society. Furthermore, his suggestions seem to recognize the contradictions endemic in reforms that merely seek to improve the academic success of underprivileged and working-class students: Greater academic success often results merely in the cooptation of bright underprivileged and working-class students.[4]

Like most educational reform proposals, Giroux's approach overestimates the potential of schools to change society by making changes in students. Moreover, his approach fails to take into account the severe constraints under which teachers normally work within the public schools. In our view, structural changes in the political economy must precede and then inspire changes in schools.

Limited Effects of Educational Change

Although business tends to blame the schools for high unemployment — suggesting that workers are not competent — the schools are not the main problem (Berliner, 1993). If every student now in school graduated with excellent reading and math skills *and* with computer skills, there would not be nearly enough jobs for them.

There are so many poor people today, not because of problems with schools, but because of problems with our political economy. Unemployment is the result of the elimination or export of jobs, not of inadequately trained employees. It is due, also, to the failure of the wealthy to invest in the production of new goods. Instead, they have employed their wealth and expertise to buy and sell existing companies, often using risky methods and outright scams (Jacobs, 1992). Slowly, smaller companies are being bought out and subsumed under the aegis of large, multinational corporations. As this trend continues, power is concentrated into fewer and fewer hands, and the wealthy have less and less of a stake in their own nation's well-being (Barnet, 1974; Sweezy, 1992).

Increased poverty is understandable if the goal of capitalism is, as frequently seems to be the case, to make as large a profit as possible. Under this regimen, cheap labor is a distinct advantage. And if business's goal is to maximize profit, then to the extent that business influences government, people who make a living through their own labor should expect no more government protection than the minimum needed to supply the cheapest possible labor to business. This analysis suggests that improvements in education will merely be instrumental — minor technical refinements of the efficiencies of training. Significant education reform, however, will not be achieved without significant structural change in the political economy, and such change can take place only through widespread popular action.

Yet we observe that such changes are not forthcoming. Instead, we see sharper divisions between the privileged and the poor, the educated and the uneducated, the vocal and the silenced. Moreover, the future does not promise easy improvement. With a rapidly growing world population and the attendant competition for scarce resources, the scope of poverty will continue to widen and its circumstances worsen.

Even the most dire vision does not excuse educators from the important work of nurturing talent — of all students, from all backgrounds — in ways that give them the greatest chance of realizing their potential. The chance to realize one's potential is a birthright to which all people are, as a consequence of their humanity, entitled. This entitlement implicates an academic education.

And an academic education for poor and minority students entails affirmative action. In defending the selection procedures of an Illinois gifted program, Fetterman (1988, p. 74) says that the Illinois superintendent of schools wanted "an affirmative action program rather than an academic program." We do not regard these as incompatible. In fact, affirmative action *requires* an academic program; otherwise, academic knowledge will retain its identity as capital, available disproportionately to the privileged. And good academic programs require affirmative action; otherwise, the curriculum must include obfuscation and rationalizations that compromise the integrity of scholarship. Respect for the intellect and the development of talent depend, in our view, on equity.

CHAPTER 5

The Intellectual Potential of Schooling

Craig B. Howley and Aimee Howley

Previous chapters have considered the historical and cultural roots of anti-intellectualism and how it works in schooling, the role of gifted education in anti-intellectual schooling, and the particular ways schooling hobbles intellect among the disenfranchised. Having established the scope of our critique and presented evidence and argument to warrant it, we consider in this chapter and the next the features of schooling that might nurture intellect much better. The discussion is necessarily speculative, even tentative.

In the present chapter, we develop the idea of culture as it applies to our position. Culture, in this view, has a great deal to do with care for the intellect over the long term, from generation to generation. The discussion considers the importance of intellect in the so-called "postmodern" ethos, as conventional ways of viewing the human condition have come under increasingly sharp attack. In general we find cause for hope in the demise of some conventions and cause for alarm in others. Of particular concern to us, and to care for the intellect, is a prospective role for the liberal arts, an appreciation of the character of human potential, and the place of ethical reasoning as a key manifestation of the intellect.

KNOWLEDGE AND MEANING IN CONTEMPORARY AMERICAN CULTURE

Culture, in one sense, is the realm of "universal" meaning made manifest in works of the intellect (Bell, 1976). Formal education professes care for this culture. But, as we have seen, the rhetoric seldom carries very far into practice, either in K–12 or postsecondary schooling. Instead, our scheme of schooling has submerged culture of the intellect in an instrumental regime where the production of loyal jobholders is the aim. Common sense would locate the home of intellect in academe, particularly in universities, yet academe is by no means so hospitable to intellect as people assume (Barzun, 1959, 1989).

In another sense, however, the performances of *local knowledge and belief* constitute culture and represent a meaning that does not consciously strive for universality (Lyotard, 1979/1984). Though the social sciences claim to have discovered this sense of culture, they in fact invented it. The mystery and allure of the civilizations that shared the planet with Europeans inspired this belated intellectual invention.

Initially, the motive for contact was economic. Europeans sought a global dominion — on the basis of their claim to spiritual superiority — through military conquest and monopoly trade; indigenous practices and beliefs that got in the way of conquest and trade were distorted or suppressed. Anthropologists subsequently concluded that indigenous cultures nearly everywhere had become endangered. They drew a major lesson from the debacle: Much that is meaningful escapes our notice, our understanding, and our respect. People make meaning wherever they are, and in much of what they do, and not only when they produce works of self-conscious intellectual significance.

Contradictions of American Culture for Schooling

Some critics (e.g., Bell, 1973) find that the relativism of an anthropological view of culture undermines the authority of intellectual culture (known to some as "high" or "elite" culture). In the absence of this authority, according to Bell, people cannot cope with the ethical and existential circumstances that comprise the human condition. Birth, death, loss; justice, liberty, security; work, labor, and pleasure — these are conditions that cannot be satisfactorily endured by a civilization without the accumulated works of intellect (works insured by literacy) to inform responsible action.

Other critics believe that the performances and beliefs of Western societies (an anthropological sense of modern doings) rest on intellectual practices that *inevitably* lead to the destruction of other cultures (e.g., Best & Kellner, 1991; Habermas, 1973; Lyotard, 1989). Ultimately, such "other" cultures would include the local practices in the traditional communities of Western nations as well, so that nothing but the arrogant practices of intellectuals, generalized and disseminated throughout the world, would remain. Western intellectual ("universalist" or "high") culture is said inevitably to be "totalizing" by some of these critics because it seeks to subordinate all performances and beliefs to its own (e.g., Lyotard, 1979/1984). Information technologies and academic disciplines (e.g., psychology, sociology, criminology, medicine, and the law) are among the methods used to subordinate or dismember other cultures—whether they are located in the third world or in localities in America (e.g., Foucault, 1973, 1979; Postman, 1992).

These two criticisms are equally serious, but we find their antagonism spurious. On the one hand, intellectuals are often as foolish and full of mistaken ideas as other humans. But it is not only intellectuals who represent the intellect. Barzun complains, for example, that intellectuals are among the principal *enemies* of the intellect (Barzun, 1959). After all, in our postindustrial society, the research and development departments of major corporations, the military, and government agencies and contractors—as well as the universities that these other entities dominate—are the places in which most intellectuals are likely to hold *jobs*. These institutions employ the mind to advance their particular concerns and secure their existence. The arrangement is not hospitable to care of the intellect.

On the other hand, how might indigenous performances and beliefs effectively oppose the "totalizing" tendencies of our postmodern culture, except with the aid of the intellect? Legacies of considered thought, wisdom, and meaning must also be brought to bear in such opposition. Without the contributions of a culture that engages in literate reconsideration of the enduring dilemmas of the human condition, humanity *will* become increasingly vicious (cf. Bell, 1990). A culture—and perhaps most especially an intellectual culture—that avoids this task of literate reconsideration will self-destruct (Postman, 1992).

The legitimacy of each sense of culture, literate "elite" and anthropological "local," seems to us clearly to depend on the other. Any account of the human condition, broadly written, cannot succeed without paying considerable homage to its local roots (Lasch, 1991). At the same time, the meaning of local performances and beliefs is more richly understood when it takes account of the human condition more broadly interpreted. This intertwining is neither a mystery nor a conundrum. Humans are creatures that make meaning by developing their capacities in association with one another. They require a context that nurtures them and which they, in turn, can nurture.

We acknowledge that the generalized performances and beliefs of the West (e.g., accumulation of private capital, conspicuous consumption, bureaucratic domination) have entailed extreme forms of exploitation that have spread misery widely (cf. Foucault, 1979; Habermas, 1975; Lyotard, 1979/1984; Wallerstein, 1984). Perhaps other cultures, not inventing these performances and beliefs, simply lacked the power necessary to do so much damage. However, the idea that technologies can develop and apply in only one way (i.e., catastrophically) strikes us as false. Tool-making and tool-using developed with cultural logics other than technical rationality[1] would produce quite different circumstances for human action (cf. Fay, 1987; Habermas, 1973; Marcuse, 1955).

Perhaps, however, the very troubles that beset intellect stem from just those performances and beliefs that have so damaged *other* cultures. In this case we are reaping the whirlwind previously sowed. Bell (1976) himself cautions against the tendency to misinterpret dilemmas of the human condition as problems soluble with technology and money. According to Bell, this tendency, which he calls "the economizing mode," inevitably debases culture of the intellect (not to mention its nurture through a true education). The economizing mode also debases indigenous cultures, as it markets commercially deformed practices and beliefs as widely as possible ("mass culture"). Intellectual jobholders are *clearly* among the culprits. And their schooling does not teach them otherwise, for the most part.

The two views of culture (anthropological and intellectual) seem to clash more dramatically in the United States than in any nation. Because American immigration policies have been historically more generous than those of many nations, American society exhibits a variety of cultural forms unseen in most nation-states. For this reason, U.S. educators have recently debated conflicting notions of "multicultural education." Neither curriculum nor instructional methods can be agreed on, but many of the apparent adversaries do seem to agree that, for the sake of public order, citizens with diverse backgrounds must learn to live amicably together. The superficiality of this agreement continues the largely instrumental and sentimental goals of schooling (safeguarding a polity in which all can pretend to happiness, but in which few actually realize fulfillment).

No matter how misguided the acrimony over multiculturalism, the substantive issue pertains to the agenda that the machinery of schooling is meant to *serve*: global economic dominion. Citizens are the natural instrumentalities of this agenda; indeed, they are the only possible instrumentalities of such an agenda. They should, under this agenda, be so narrowly trained that they will neither reflect nor comment on matters of public interest; they should disdain both intellectual and anthropological culture. Technocrats would take care of public administration, and citizenship would be synonymous with jobholding.

A true education, an education in which the enlargement of the mind is the chief aim, would proceed *much* differently. We believe it would enact the interests of self-determination and justice. At the very least, however, such an education of necessity involves the sorts of cultivation and caretaking (i.e., culture in both senses) that defy schemes of global dominion.

We hold, therefore, that development of intellect does not require external justification; it is its own justification (Dewey, 1916; Greene,

1982). Enlargement of the mind enables humans to make their own wise judgments, whereas one that narrows the mind (e.g., to the specialized skills of a particular job in the mode of technical rationality) hobbles wise judgment. Nurture of the critical faculty of the mind — the intellect — is grounded in what Habermas calls the "emancipatory interest." Habermas (1971) identifies three fundamental interests — technical, practical, and emancipatory — as uniquely human. Whereas technical interests concern the material reproduction of life and practical interests concern the social reproduction of life, emancipatory interests concern the fuller realization of human potential. Realizing the emancipatory interest depends, according to Habermas, on "critical reflection."

The Shrinking Realm of Meaning: Loss of the Particular

Mass public education developed in the nineteenth century amid a self-conscious lack of intellectual culture and a fear of diverse immigrant cultures. Schooling developed as a "one-best-system" to supply the lack and bridge the differences. Systems of schooling then, as now, were essential tools for nation-building, a process that submerges distinctions of place, culture, and person in order to fashion a single, purposive national identity (Curti, 1943; Katz, 1968; Meyer, Tyack, Nagel, & Gordon, 1979; Tyack, 1974).

In this scheme, patriotism, rather than works of intellect, looms as "universal meaning." Nation-building, of course, continues in the present. The high patriotic purpose to which schooling now seeks to commit citizens, teachers, and children is establishing (or safeguarding) America's global economic dominion (Shea, 1989). Neither view of culture is very relevant to this purpose: All human interests are to be subservient to the technical interest as implemented within the American political context (cf. Habermas, 1971).

Rhetoric about "accountability," for instance, implies that taxpayers are entitled to schooling that accomplishes its purposes. With the power of state departments of education on the rise (e.g., Tyree, 1993), however, the voices of individual taxpayers figure hardly at all in the conversation about educational purpose. Instead, it is the *state itself* that seeks to hold individual districts, schools, teachers, and students accountable to its own purposes. These purposes are detailed in state goals, systems of curricula, and minutely specified "learner outcomes." Accomplishment of learner outcomes is the official point. The whole complex apparatus bears on holding *students* accountable for what the state intends for them. Teachers and administrators become functionaries of the state for accomplishing this purpose.

Schooling, then, is no more the vehicle for cultivating universal meaning than it has been the vehicle for valuing local meanings. Both senses of culture become submerged in the process of nation-building, and the further task (in industrial and postindustrial eras) of developing human capital (Arendt, 1958; Best & Kellner, 1991; Lasch, 1991).

The Shrinking Realm of Value: Loss of Authority

Educational worth — or the commitments we make on behalf of raising our children — is today most often validated with the technologies of science. Beginning with the *Novum Organum* ("new tool") of Francis Bacon (1620/1944), science has been construed as the ultimate authority for *how* we know the world (epistemological warrant) and *what* we know of it (ontological warrant). The authority of science legitimates the knowledge of most worth (Spencer, 1860/1963; Bush, 1991); the methods of pedagogy (e.g., Gage, 1979); the means of educational administration (e.g., Odiorne, 1965); and, most certainly, the route to educational progress (e.g., Dusewicz & Beyer, 1988).

Throughout the modern period, many observers took the evident utility of technology, especially its skills and knowledge, to constitute the ground on which societal progress rests (e.g., Becker, 1964; Inkeles & Smith, 1974; McClelland, Atkinson, Clark, & Lowell, 1953).[2] But the accretion of scientific thought does not necessarily entail social progress, ensure justice, or secure liberty (Heilbroner, 1960; Lasch, 1991).

At mid-century, Robert Heilbroner (1960, pp. 197-198) noted that Americans deceive themselves about social progress because they misinterpret history:

> The very assumption that the growth of technical skill, political equality, or economic well-being will automatically lead to "progress" — rather than to increased destructiveness, heightened social disorder, or vulgar opulence — already takes for granted an environment in which rationality, self-control, and dignity are paramount social attributes. But this is hardly the impression one gets from an examination of the panorama of human existence.

The conditions for social progress simply do not exist, according to Heilbroner. We have not nurtured reason or self-control, nor do our "social systems" function with respect for the human condition. If society managed the dilemmas of the human condition (e.g., natality, mortality, plurality, individuality) more ethically, social progress might then become possible. Instead, critics have advanced convincing arguments that technical rationality has in fact altered the human condition for the worse (e.g., Lyotard, 1979/1984; Postman, 1992; West, 1989).

Rather than inferring social from technological progress, therefore, one might instead take the position that thinkers in our society have misused science to reconstruct the human condition as a set of problems amenable to technological solution. The misinterpretation consists in viewing all dilemmas as problems and validating only that knowledge which promises to "solve" the "problems." The imperative to solve problems has been so great that applications parodying the methods of science are now required in places where their use is problematic.[3] The cultural tendency to apply the methods of science indiscriminately throughout society is known as "scientism." The development of social science, behavioral science, political science, and administrative science — though producing meaningful and important works — also tended to regulate other constructions of social circumstance, historical analysis, politics, and human action and agency (Arendt, 1958; Habermas, 1975; Lyotard, 1979/1984).

Scientism is one of the features of our anti-intellectual culture (Barzun, 1959), and it dominates the thinking behind the public school project in America (Callahan, 1962; Cuban, 1992). Ironically, the claim that educational research is without practical value often rests on the perception that such research lacks adequate scientific rigor. We fail to learn the facts, in this view, because of bad methods. The "solution" to this "problem" is better science, not a different way of thinking about schooling or a different appreciation for the constitution of a true education.

Larry Cuban, however, reminds us that educational circumstances pose dilemmas, not problems. He advises educators to nurture such relationships and conversations as would allow them to consider these dilemmas more fully (Cuban, 1992). Pretending that persistent dilemmas are problems amenable to solutions fabricated by sufficiently rigorous researchers misinterprets the human condition as an imperfection of nature that technology and its cadre of experts will correct. This circumstance undermines the critical purpose of intellect, which is the birthright of every human.

This account of authority helps explain why American culture finds such little value in the humanities. The humanities comprehend the human condition as founded on enduring dilemmas that are in need of continual reexamination, reinterpretation, and redemption. The meaning they try to construct is tentative; it does not fix problems, nor does it manipulate social relationships (as new technologies do). The humanities are products of intellect that belie many of the performances and beliefs of our society: accumulation of private capital, conspicuous consumption, and bureaucratic domination. On such terms the humanities are useless. The notion of enduring dilemmas that characterize the human condition is disruptive to a technological conception of knowledge, social progress, and the educational purpose of global dominion (e.g., "being first in the world in math and science").

The authority of science no longer seems an adequate warrant of either educational purpose or educational method. Indeed, the warrant of science as the surest path to certain knowledge is in *most* doubt among eminent scientists (e.g., Hawking, 1988). Observing the intractable misery of the world, many people conclude that the promises of technology are hollow. Though what we observe as progress is a convincing display of power, it takes us further than ever from the good life.

THE IMPERATIVE FOR THOUGHT
IN POSTINDUSTRIAL SOCIETY

Around 1900, scholars, artists, and other intellectuals began to appreciate the sort of dramatic alterations to which the new century would bear witness. Ferdinand Tönnies (1887/1957) emphasized the terms *gemeinschaft* ("community") and *gesellschaft* ("society" or "corporation").[4] His work provided the theoretical basis of sociology for the next 75 years (Lasch, 1991). Whereas Marx concerned himself with theories that would help workers transform the conditions of their existence, Tönnies tried to describe the momentous changes that seemed to be taking place worldwide. Tönnies, in fact, observed the later history of many of the same phenomena as Marx.

Industrialization and urbanization were among the most important material changes taking place. But these changes — viewed almost as unavoidable natural processes — also entailed social changes: the rise of bureaucratic corporations and state agencies; changes in the nature of work (e.g., "rational" organization of tasks through their division into smaller and smaller scopes of work); the breakup of extended families (associated with rural life and livelihood); and, in general, more impersonal relationships among all people (Durkheim, 1933/1964; Tönnies, 1887/1957; Weber, 1947). How long urbanization will (or can) continue is anybody's guess, but some demographers (e.g., Ledent, 1982) expect that in third world nations such as Honduras and India, about 75% of the population will live in cities by the year 2050 (approximately the degree of urbanization in the United States in 1990).

As the current century comes to a close, social theorists have begun to suggest that capitalism has entered a new stage, or even that capitalism has already been superseded by an historically new system of economic organization. Changes in families, the growing influence of computing and telecommunications applications, major changes in the political economy within and among nations, and dramatic dissolutions of post-World War II alliances — all these seem to many to foretell a much larger change. Interpreting these signs has involved intense debate that may itself constitute some evidence that major changes in the character of our institutions, ideologies, and cultures are underway (e.g., Harvey, 1989).

The tentativeness of the object of scrutiny is indicated by use of the prefix "post" to describe it: postmodernism, postindustrialism, postpositivism (for increasingly more narrow domains). Nonetheless, the various analyses encompass the same issues, for the most part. Material issues concern:

- The spread of conspicuous consumption as the necessary counterpart to industrial productivity
- The increasingly larger share of employment in jobs that produce services rather than in jobs that produce goods
- The myriad effects of computerization and robotics on production, consumption, and culture and
- Cultural, social, and ideological changes within late capitalism, particularly including perception of diverse backgrounds and perspectives.

The issues dealt with in this debate, however, do not fundamentally concern material reality. Rather, they fundamentally concern *claims* about material reality: What is real? How do we know? What does it mean? The ongoing debates deal with such dilemmas as:

- The nature of the world and its relationship to individuals (the nature of reality)
- The role of language and discourse in forming who we are (semiotics and subjectivity)
- What phenomena constitute the tools of thought (images, words, the methods of scholarship) and
- How or whether we can change the world for the better (implications for action, especially political and cultural practice).

People whom schooling has narrowly prepared to implement specialized technical roles cannot hope to examine such claims as those listed. Were such considerations widely necessary (we believe they *are*), then this sort of schooling (i.e., *mis*education) has already helped to deny people a voice in their own futures.

But the point is *not* that we now need a different sort of schooling to "prepare individuals for the twenty-first century." Schooling that would prepare people to consider the material and philosophical issues that the world presents would have been a good idea from the start; it has always been a good idea. It was the sort of education colonial leaders like Thomas Jefferson recommended but which their descendants found to be inapplicable in an industrial society, where what was good for General Motors was good for America (Lasch, 1991).

Standardization and Diversity

The difference between anthropological and intellectual culture gives rise, in the present era, to the peculiar distinctions of modernist culture, those between elite ("high") and mass ("low") culture. The widely diffused performances and beliefs of modernist mass culture do not actually consist of indigenous, or local, practices. Rather, they consist of performances and beliefs fabricated and disseminated usually for profit by corporate entities not only ignorant but purposively and openly destructive of local practices.

A national mass medium is unfit to represent local practices because it is in competition with them. It seeks to replace them altogether. Its national venue, moreover, means that purely local performances and practices are irrelevant to its sought-after audience. Securing the greatest possible profit requires a cutthroat self-indulgence and absolute disregard of manners; narcissistic, exploitative, and pornographic performances yield the most secure results (since they sell best). The standardization of this mass culture overwhelms local performances and beliefs. Debased national meanings displace the rich, varied meanings of local performance and belief. More intellectual fare—as delivered nationally by public broadcasting, for instance—not only attracts a small following, but suffers the same debasements that characterize the mass media generally.

The critical danger, for both the integrity of the intellect and the integrity of democratic action, lies in the tendency of contemporary society to produce conformism. Society has assumed the activity that was once the province of the family (i.e., economic production) and society exacts unparalleled conformity from all quarters. Such conformity, Hannah Arendt (1958, p. 40) tells us, destroys the self-directed agency of individuals and corrupts our public life:

> It is decisive that society, on all its levels, excludes the possibility of action. . . . Instead, society expects from each of its members a certain kind of behavior, imposing innumerable and various rules, all of which tend to "normalize" its members, to make them behave, to exclude spontaneous action or outstanding achievement.

Behavioral science interprets the laws of chance in such a way as to render acting, variable humans as behaving, conforming animals. The transformation is socially useful because society seeks to organize humans, extensively and intensely, as instruments of economic growth. Schooling normalizes children to this end, and the profession aptly calls this function "socialization," for schooling inducts children from the archaic family and into society where their function is to hold jobs and swear fealty to the nation-state. The particularities of individuals' origins, of indigenous performances and beliefs, and even the development of intellect for its own sake threaten the socialization function of schooling, unless carefully channeled, curtailed, and frequently subverted altogether.

Schooling in its present form is part of the fabricated mass culture that includes television and movies (both family-oriented escapism and pornographic display), preposterous tabloids, and theme parks that simulate a hyperbolic reality (from science to theology) for the masses. Such technologies constitute methods that national and transnational elites can use to exert power throughout a basically liberal, democratic society (cf. Foucault, 1973, 1979). Mass culture effectively imposes the conformity and discipline that the capitalist system of production and consumption requires. Its ubiquity (e.g., schooling in which attendance is compelled) and universal appeal (e.g., excessive television watching) make the extreme violence and overt repression that characterized early capitalism largely unnecessary in otherwise stable circumstances in the contemporary, developed world.

Postmodern theorists counterpose diversity to the standardization and extreme conformism that characterize modern society (Best & Kellner, 1991). With few exceptions, these theorists take the view that the concerns of individuals, especially those who (as above) have been *denied* a voice in considering their own destinies, must be "privileged" in the future.

An analogy of biological and cultural diversity is perhaps in order. One may view a culture as an organic system (cf. von Bertalanffy, 1968). Diversity serves organic systems well, but modernism imposes controls for diversity, in the name of efficiency. The voices suppressed are akin to species or varieties sacrificed in the name of bigger yields. In each case, the sacrifice reduces diversity, with serious implications for the future, since diversity of biological substance and cultural practice constitutes the only source of flexibility among species and cultures alike. A one-best-system for dealing with the future cannot be constructed without knowing what the future will bring, and that knowledge lies outside the human condition.

In education, construction of a "one-best" system of schooling has sought to control variability in the name of economy (Callahan, 1962; Tyack, 1974). In this system, indigenous cultural practices are suppressed because they—like indigenous agricultural varieties or species—are inefficient accumulators of capital. The regime of accumulation requires a single set of education goals, a single set of curriculum frames, a single set of validated "best practice," and, ultimately, a singular context in which to accomplish all this work.

This commitment to economy, however, is frustrated in modern (and particularly postindustrial) America by the difficulty of securing a singular context. Longing for this security partly explains the conservative fascination with Japanese education, which seems to implement the one-best-system so much more profitably than the nation that invented it. The usual observation is that Japanese educators do not have to struggle with racial diversity, as must U.S. educators. But Americans have a long history of struggling *against* all sorts of diversities: language, religion, ethnicity.

This may be true, but, at the same time the Japanese have another secret. Theirs is perhaps the ideal postindustrial culture because the *traditional* culture is a magpie, successfully accommodating, adapting, and integrating elements of other cultures from at least the seventh century forward. Because this diversity is integral to their culture, the Japanese may be much better positioned to deal meaningfully with postmodern realities than Americans, who have so long sought to suppress diversity in their culture.

The Alternative of Local Knowledge

The cultivation of local knowledge is an alternative to the suppression of diversity. This alternative looks like a shabby curiosity if judged by the terms of the modernist project — construction of one-best-systems governed by standard operating procedures in which "lesser" alternatives are eliminated.

Local knowledge even seems preposterous because our experiences in modernist culture teach us that local knowledge cannot really exist. And this judgment conforms with the experience of increasing numbers of people raised within the confines of mass culture. Knowledge, such an experience tells people, comes from certain textbooks, marketed by familiar firms, to be delivered in certain ways to students whose circumstances are best ignored.

The scientism of the modernist project denies the significance of local perspectives as irrational, provincial, and inefficient. At the same time, meanings and commitments must enter the world, for in these things lie the motivations that spur people to action. Habermas claims that the modern world, dominated by technical rationality, draws such meanings out of the "life-world," otherwise abandoned by technical rationality (Young, 1990). The life-world, then, is a key center of meaning; indeed, the life-world germinates local knowledge.

Local knowledge is, in fact, a realm of meaning that we might reclaim; it represents voices and perspectives that have been suppressed for the sake of profitable accumulation. Teachers can help restore the silenced voices, but they can do so only if they see clearly the connections between local performances and beliefs (anthropological sense of culture) and the universals of the human condition (intellectual sense of culture).

Wendell Berry's view of local knowledge. The poet and essayist Wendell Berry articulates such a notion of local knowledge.[5] In his view, commitment to a "beloved place" is a necessary condition of resistance, but the commitment also entails an understanding of the wider world, for one cannot otherwise understand the threat of destruction in and to such places. Place, in this sense, encompasses not only a geographic environs, but care for its circumstances, relationships, and meaningfulness. All this is implied by the status of "beloved," a status that implies *cultivation* (Berry, 1970/1989, 1990).

A deformed and irresponsible intellectualism dominates our (modernist) world and the condition of humans in it, in this view, and Berry (1990, p. 116) applies the criticism to the humanities as well as to the sciences:

> The scientific ideals of objectivity and specialization have now crept into the humanities and made themselves at home. This has happened, I think, because the humanities have come to be infected with a suspicion of their uselessness or worthlessness in the face of the provability or workability or profitability of the applied sciences. The conviction is now widespread, for instance, that "a work of art" has no purpose but to be itself. . . . A poem, in short, is a relic as soon as it is composed; it can be taught, but it cannot teach.

Berry, with Barzun, believes that intellectuals are among the chief enemies of intellect in our culture. But in his view, all the major institutions of (modernist) mass society—the churches, the schools, the corporations, the law, the governments—participate eagerly in the act of plundering local places (cf. Habermas, 1975, on the fate of the life-world). When Berry describes our society as "mind-dominated," he is not advocating thoughtlessness. Instead, he is speaking both of domination by abstract cleverness (value-free intelligence), employed for whatever purpose pays well, in combination with the disdain, so commonplace in modernist society, for physical labor.

The most curious feature of local knowledge is that it necessarily entails a defense against local ignorance. Actual local knowledge—as contrasted with the *idea* of local knowledge—is in utter decline in many places, according to Berry. In his view, the national political economy cultivates disregard of particular places, it degrades the affections *and* thinking of those who live there, and it wastes these things in order to secure the profligacy of those who live elsewhere. Hence, cultivation of the intellect can and must — in this view — proceed on a local basis. The "universal" and the particular meet in caring for a beloved place.

Objections to local knowledge. Three objections may be raised to the idea of local knowledge as a source and object of culture. The first is that local knowledge may be no more than parochialism. Just as elite culture can be hegemonic when imposed as the dogma of ruling-class ideology, parochialism is the dogma of local knowledge — the narrow views of the powerful in an unenlightened parish. Parochialism, however, can be understood as a means to dominate local people in ways that subvert local knowledge. In fact, parochialism in the postmodern world tends to become the principal manifestation of domination by the *national* culture among local citizens, with radio and television as its pulpits. This circumstance is one reason, in fact, that attending to the intellect is now necessary for the strengthening of local knowledge. True local knowledge, in the sense of caring for a beloved place, cannot manifest itself as thoughtless practice.

The second objection, from a conservative vantage, is that the project of cultivating local knowledge is simply another misguided ("modernist") quest for authenticity. Daniel Bell (1976) objects that modernist culture, in its quest for authenticity, values the idiosyncracies of individual experience *over the commonalities of the human condition.* Berry's response to this objection is that modernist culture, operating through the norms of the academy, has also severed the connection between life as it is lived (e.g., Habermas's "life-world") and the content of important works of the intellect. These works persist, but people cannot connect them to authentic experience, and neither can they recognize in them the commonalities of the human condition (cf. Moretti, 1993). True local knowledge is by no means an unmediated, "natural" authenticity: It is instead a cultivated authenticity.

Simultaneous care for local knowledge and for the intellect are by no means at odds with one another; to care for one, but not the other, inevitably destroys both, as the course of modernist culture well illustrates. Modernist culture, in our view and that of others, has neglected the intellect, much as it has neglected local knowledge.

The third objection to local knowledge, a pedagogical objection, concerns practicality. Incorporating local knowledge in the regimen of schooling would require teachers not only to cultivate the intellect in authentic ways, but to do so while accurately distinguishing authentic local knowledge. It is not apparent how, under existing circumstances, such teachers could be prepared in this way by teacher training institutions, nor if so prepared, how they could survive professionally in the real world. The power of their insight would make them dangerous to themselves, as well as to others who see matters quite differently from them.

These practical objections are telling, and they are the most serious. They suggest that the entire argument in favor of cultivating local knowledge is idealistic. But surely the argument is ethical, and it is not less practical simply because it would encounter great difficulties. In fact, the ability to distinguish between legitimate and illegitimate knowledge is by far the most important contribution teachers can make in the lives of their students. If we fail to make such distinctions ourselves and if we fail to nurture our students in making such distinctions, we implement only miseducation. Though miseducation is common, we cannot entertain the position that miseducation is our only choice.

Like the view of community as tragedy (cf. Berry, 1990), this view of schooling is also tragic. Fatal flaws are everywhere: Domination is the legacy of the one-best system, teachers are ill-prepared, modernist culture is narcissistic, literature and art are marginalized, scientism makes serious commitments look irrational, and everything must have its price. The ultimate tragedy may be that the efficiency of the one-best-system (educational, economic, political, and cultural) threatens the existence of the planet, though the timing of the ultimate tragic event is in question.

Observe, however, that the "problems" of environmental degradation, like other worldly circumstances, are profound manifestations of a failure to deal thoughtfully with dilemmas of the human condition. Cultivated minds, like cultivated communities, are endangered species. Other cultures, which our society has done its best to silence or exterminate (e.g., American Indian cultures), have cherished quite different views of the earth, views that might have helped us serve the future better.

It is possible to hear these voices again. Principled reason suggests that schooling could abandon the quest for the one-best system and, in its place, construct an institution that represents diversity, tolerates "inefficiency" and divergence, and does less damage to children. It might also actually help cultivate communities in which the care of local knowledge entails care of the intellect, and vice versa. It would be difficult to imagine any other sort of *ethical* community in the postmodern circumstance.

THE ROLE OF THE LIBERAL ARTS

From ancient times, liberal studies have provided a disciplined way by which the intellect develops itself. According to Cardinal Newman (1852/ 1959), the pursuit of knowledge through liberal studies cultivates reason and, thereby, both demonstrates and enables human potential. In contrast, knowledge that is merely useful limits potential. This limiting effect necessarily results from the instrumental aims of such knowledge, which determine its narrow scope and content. By its nature, such knowledge constrains humans to the immediacy of their everyday experience rather than permitting them to reflect on, examine, or critique it.

Reasoned examination of everyday experience is quite different. First, it enables self-determination: People can direct the course of their experiences and make sense of the things they experience. Reasoned examination of experience also enables the sorts of intellectual dispositions that sponsor ethical reasoning and dialogue (though they do not necessarily entail virtuous *action*). Finally, the habit of such scrutiny puts experience in ever more expansive contexts, allowing people to see the crucial links between past and present, local and remote, determined and indeterminate.

Interestingly, traditions — resilient patterns of collective experience — constitute an inherently expansive context in which to reach such understandings and insights. All traditions link past and future with the present, but intellectual traditions cultivate the cross-generational link especially well. And the substance of these linkages, recorded in intellectual artifacts, make the cultural project unusually explicit and accessible (at least to literate minds). They are ready at hand to help people examine and, if warranted, transcend the immediacy of their circumstances. Healthy intellectual traditions predispose their heritors to contemplate the persistent commonalities as well as the diverse circumstances of the human condition (cf. Hampshire, 1983).

Traditions and Roots

In important ways, liberal education provides access to the intellectual traditions — and the knowledge derived from those traditions — that develop the mind. According to Hirst (1973, p. 98), "To acquire knowledge is to become aware of experience as structured, organized, and made meaningful in some quite specific way, and the varieties of human knowledge constitute the highly developed forms in which man [sic] has found this possible."

This structured knowledge, embodying the emerging wisdom of a culture, is not, as some (e.g., Bloom, 1987; Hirsch, 1987) insist, immutable and eternal. Instead, it is the substance of an ongoing conversation (Moretti, 1993). Oakeshott (1962, pp. 198–199) writes about the character and educational purpose of this conversation:

> As civilized human beings, we are inheritors, neither of an inquiry about ourselves and the world, nor of an accumulating body of information, but of a conversation, begun in the primeval forests and extended and made more

articulate in the course of centuries. It is a conversation which goes on both in public and within each of ourselves. Of course there is argument and inquiry and information, but wherever these are profitable they are to be recognized as passages in this conversation, and perhaps they are not the most captivating of the passages. . . . Conversation is not an enterprise designed to yield an extrinsic profit, a contest where a winner gets a prize, nor is it an activity of exegesis; it is an unrehearsed intellectual adventure. . . . Education, properly speaking, is an initiation into the skill and partnership of this conversation in which we learn to recognize the voices, to distinguish the proper occasions of utterance, and in which we acquire the intellectual and moral habits appropriate to conversation. And it is this conversation which, in the end, gives place and character to every human activity and utterance.

Such a conversation, it should be clear, is recorded in the intellectual traditions of many cultures (including European, Asian, and African). And the conversation is only partly transmitted through the fields of disciplined study that comprise the liberal arts.

Neither the source of the conversation, nor, in particular, the basis for its continuity is restricted to intellectual disciplines. Less formal traditions are at least as important to the elaboration of shared meanings. The local knowledge that infuses such traditions continually interacts with the more formal, disciplined knowledge that constitutes the intellectual legacy of the literate culture. Certain forms of local knowledge, therefore, will realize their inherent potential to both enrich and become significant parts of the formal cultural legacy. Indeed, the ultimate source of intellectual traditions *is* local knowledge, certain performances and beliefs that have entered wider circulation across time and space (e.g., in the form of liberal studies).

Jazz, for example, offers rich possibilities for expression, but its classics have only recently become part of the accepted musical canon. Only in recent years have scholars recognized the contributions that jazz has made to the musical heritage of the culture; and, as a consequence, they have included jazz among the musical studies considered important for the well-educated person.

Of course, by their nature, the insights derived from a less formal tradition are more difficult to describe and to share with people outside the tradition. Moreover, the forms of local knowledge that will influence the formal tradition at any historical moment are contingent on power relationships in society (e.g., Foucault, 1979; Lyotard, 1979/1984). The modernist era, in its disregard of local circumstance and practice, has made the mistake of attacking the most vital sources of meaning in the world (e.g., Arendt, 1958; Habermas, 1975; Postman, 1992).

Whatever their content, intellectual traditions provide bridges between thought and expression that occurred in the past and thought and expression that will occur in the future. Such bridges seem more necessary in some fields of study than in others. History, for example, interprets the past and, as a consequence, is totally dependent on it for its content. The historical lineage seems so clearly embedded in prior events that the historian's relationship to the past seems self-evident. The nature of this relationship is, however, not nearly so obvious as it might at first seem. Because the past can never be reexperienced, the historian cannot merely recount it. Instead, the historian must interpret the past, and such interpretation depends on a tradition of historical constructions and methods. As a consequence, any particular historical interpretation is, itself, dependent on the traditions of historical writing, just as it is dependent on the historical record that it endeavors to explain.

As with history, the legacy of other of the humanities—literature and philosophy, for example—is ancient. In the humanities, "new knowledge" often consists of scholars' reinterpretations of classic texts or of refutations or revisions of earlier interpretations of such texts (Shils, 1980). Sometimes, scholarship in the humanities consists of identifying or constructing new texts. These texts elaborate or expand the more or less continuous thread of thought that conjoins ideas to produce coherent traditions.

But all fields of study, no matter how forward-looking, depend on the past for much of their content and method. Even the natural sciences, which aim to wrest progressively more accurate factual knowledge from the evident world, formulate and test problems that derive from a legacy (Shils, 1980). Scientists, however, regard the legacy of their disciplines in somewhat different ways from the ways in which scholars in philosophy, literature, and history view their intellectual heritage.

Whereas for humanists, any part of the legacy may be as important as any other, for scientists, the most *recent* contributions to the tradition are usually the most salient. Scientists seek to reaffirm, refute, or elaborate discoveries of the recent past. They have little regard for discoveries of the more distant past, even when they recognize that such discoveries were in fact responsible for making the more recent ones possible (Shils, 1980).

For scientists and humanists alike, however, the intellectual legacy contextualizes and circumscribes thought. It does so because it produces the cultural frame of reference—or "ethos"—that makes particular types of thought possible at particular points in time.

The development of technology is the driving force in the modernist ethos. Scientific discovery and technological innovation are taken to propel society forward, while social engineering, the scientific approach to understanding and manipulating social relations, is supposed to smooth out the discontinuities and ameliorate the dysfunctions that inevitably result from rapid — but necessary and wholesome — progress (Aronowitz, 1988). In this view, social concerns, whether in the guise of local knowledge or as knowledge of the humanities, constitute a somewhat retarded realm of development in need of remediation or amelioration.

By contrast to the modernist ethos, the contemporary postmodern ethos questions the idea of technological progress. Rather than presuming that society develops in step with the progress of objectively revealed truth, postmodern theorists believe that society unfolds many subjective, parallel realities. This view of the world, of course, tends to reaffirm the interpretive traditions of the humanities and the worth of local knowledge and, simultaneously, to make suspect the universal truth claims of positivist science.

According to postmodern theory, knowledge is located in a personal and social context. Theorists of the postmodern tend to promote a more democratic view of knowledge and a more skeptical view of all truth claims, including those of science. Furthermore, the postmodern ethos construes the legacy of literate culture in a radically different way: It gives many new voices access to that legacy, and, at the same time, it sanctions inventive interpretation and pointed critique of the cultural canon.

Good Works and Bad

This postmodern conception makes curriculum development a bit troublesome for educators who want to select the knowledge of most worth but who can no longer rely simply on the conventions of the past. Such conventions now seem surprisingly naive to those who understand the postmodern perspective (and, one must admit, to those, like Moretti [1993] who truly understand the classical perspective).

Neither Herbert Spencer's argument that science is the knowledge of most worth nor E.D. Hirsch's (1987) prescription for cultural literacy provides a compelling rationale for considering a certain text or type of study more worthy than another. Both Spencer's and Hirsch's claims are based on the suspect belief that certain products of human intellect have universal, if not eternal, significance. In the postmodern era, science is no longer defended as the clear path to the truth, and the privileges enjoyed by certain groups (e.g., white males, European intellectuals, Italian fresco painters of the fourteenth century) no longer warrant universal appreciation of their cultural artifacts. Such artifacts, in this view, can therefore no longer serve *unquestioned* as exemplars.

Yet the question of worth, particularly with regard to the educational benefits of certain studies, can never be moot. In order to elaborate criteria for including particular content and excluding other content from the curriculum, we need to examine two views that contrast with the one we advocate in this book.

The first is the extreme "classicist" or "culturist" view, which holds that certain texts are quintessential products of world civilization. According to this view, students must understand these classic texts, often referred to as "great books." Such understanding aims to grasp the most universally applicable insights, especially of Western civilization. Allan Bloom (1987, p. 344) elaborates this position in *The Closing of the American Mind*:

> A liberal education means reading *certain generally recognized classic texts*, just reading them, letting them dictate what the questions are and the method of approaching them — not forcing them into categories we make up, not treating them as historical products, but trying to read them as their authors wished them to be read [emphasis added].

A necessary corollary of this position explains how one distinguishes between "great" and lesser texts: The "great books" are those that have withstood the test of time. They are the products of a literate tradition that is both transmitted and validated by an elite class of scholars residing in the academies of the distant and more recent past.

This approach to liberal studies is discordant with the contemporary postmodern ethos. The entanglement of exploitative elites with the works of intellect presents a dilemma that observers like Bloom overlook much too easily. Many observers regard this oversight as unwarranted.

With the postmodern theorists, we recognize that *throughout* the course of history certain voices have been silenced and certain literate traditions have been disqualified. History has its winners and losers, and only fools would presume that the winners always (or even often) prevailed because they were virtuous or because their positions best implemented justice (Lasch, 1991). This legacy (a legacy of distortion) is one of the dilemmas of the human condition that requires interpretation, not neglect (Habermas, 1985).

Our responsibility now and in the future is to widen the conversation that constitutes intellect, to make it more thoughtful and aware of itself, and to reclaim it from distortions — in the past and in the present. This is a project that is never finished. At no point will one be entitled to say, "It is done."

For such reasons as these, we question the ability of any person or group to identify a collection of works, all of which are *objectively* or *universally* or *eternally* good. Moreover, we suspect that the goodness of any text, by which we mean its ability to assist people in understanding their experiences in particular and the human condition in general, depends principally on its transformative value for readers. Consequently, texts can be considered "good" only in reference to how well they help us make sense of the world, the degree to which a text reveals or clarifies meaning. Obviously, some texts have such value for more people than others, but the virtue of any canon is time-bound and "the canon" is inherently mutable. To take any other view is to deny the human condition (as one bounded by birth and death) altogether.

So we do believe that certain influences are preferable to others and that certain learning experiences are more likely than others to exert such influence. Hutchins (1968, p. 103) claims:

> A certain critical distance is necessary for the comprehension of one's own society, just as a certain externality is required for the comprehension of one's own language. The methods of getting this distance are innumerable and immaterial. The aim and the result are what count.

We agree. So, apparently, did John Dewey. His view (Dewey, 1916, p. 76), moreover, illustrates the transformative value that we impute to liberal studies:

> Education is a constant reorganizing or reconstructing of experience. It has all the time an immediate end, and so far as activity is educative, it reaches that end—the direct transformation of the quality of experience. Infancy, youth, adult life—all stand on the same educative level in the sense that what is really *learned* at any and every state of experience constitutes the value of that experience, and in the sense that it is the chief business of life at every point to make living thus contribute to an enrichment of its own perceptible meaning.

Hutchins and Dewey indicate that, while "innumerable" experiences are educative, it is not true that all experiences, indiscriminately, are educative. Simply, we learn better from some experiences than from others.

Some educators, however, take the contrary position that any experience is as likely as any other to cultivate "transformative" reflection. Critical pedagogues, for example, claim that the immediate experiences of everyday life (even the manifestations of popular culture) are the most likely to contribute to critical, reflective thinking (e.g., Giroux, 1983, 1988). Further, they regard education in the intellectual traditions as likely to suppress rather than to cultivate intellect.

We view this position with skepticism because we know that intellectual development results not from direct, but from mediated, encounters with experience. The choice of experience and the way instruction mediates the experience are important: an insight that is not foreign to many critical educators. The most promiscuous view, however, that *all* experiences are equally valuable, also implies that *none* is particularly valuable. But if all experiences, no matter how harmful, were equally educative and all representations of knowledge were of equal worth, no matter how meaningless, then thought would be unnecessary, history would have ended, and the construction of meaning would be pointless and perhaps impossible.

Moreover, we have found in our lives that the sources of such mediation are seldom readily accessible from within life experience itself. Teachers inevitably mislead us, curricula misrepresent the truth, institutions distort the conversation. The sources of mediation that reside in the intellectual traditions, the languages and forms of expression of an ongoing literate dialogue, provide a more reliable source of mediation. These sources connect students to traditions whose rich histories — read freely — *challenge*, rather than accommodate, a too-literal reading of life experience (cf. Moretti, 1993). For example, serious literature in any tradition — European, feminist, third or fourth world — offers insight and intellectual stimulation that is not possible from reading mass-market romance novels. Such novels, like commercial television programs, are self-contained and amusing diversions. But they *are* diversions; they can easily divert people from the painful, imperfect, and long-standing quest to interpret the human condition (including personal and collective experience).

The Meaning and Value of Liberal Studies

Of course, unreasonable demands to read inaccessible works serve no one well, and there is surely an important place for entertainment, recreation, and relaxation in the world. Certainly, good teachers *can* use romance novels to help students learn to read and perhaps to begin a conversation about the human condition. Schooling for most people, however, ordinarily treats such necessities as the outer limit of intellectual development for most students. This "default position" is the legacy of life adjustment pedagogy (Barzun, 1959).

We articulate our claims about the value of intellect and the role of liberal studies in developing the intellect in order to oppose the all-too-common view that intellect should dedicate itself to serving the instrumental purposes of society. Though this most common view accords highest status to scientific and technical knowledge, it does not dismiss the humanities altogether. In the instrumental view, the humanities are an adornment, a diversion that provides the elite with a utility that parallels the utility of romance novels among "the masses." The appropriation of the humanities by the elite also confers distinctions of *status* that are inherently less accessible to the masses. The appropriation is abetted by schooling, and people who do not belong to the elite come to regard the humanities – and the intellect itself – as elitist.

As for the *meaning* of the humanities, in this view, it becomes a purely private matter (Bell, 1976). Individuals confront an array of expressive forms and styles (which are merely fashionable). The meaning or value of a particular form or style lies not in the thing itself (or its content or in the issues with which it deals), but in the "individual consumer." This interpretation is regarded as common sense. As intellectual culture is "privatized" in this way, art, literature, and *even knowledge* (as interpretive meaning) become areas of the human experience that are *not properly subject* to public discussion. Not only does public discussion offend common sense (cf. Bell, 1976, pp. 129–130), but it constitutes an impermissible invasion of privacy.[6]

The view of humanities as fashionable diversion does, however, provide for a form of progress in the humanities. Progress, in this view, consists of ever-changing fashion. This debasement accomplishes two things. First, it obscures the legitimate project of the humanities (i.e., interpreting the human condition), which becomes less important than trendiness. Second, and perhaps more importantly, such debasement renders the humanities harmless by construing them as high-class diversions of economic and social elites. It would be bad form, in such circles, to suggest that the humanities *were* essential to constructing the good life.

As diversions, the humanities – literature and the arts, in particular, but also philosophy – serve the dictates of pleasure. Their value comes to be measured in relationship to their ability to amuse each individual, and, as a result, judgments about their worth become a purely personal concern. Elaborate works of literature vie with situation comedies to provide audiences with pleasure, and, since both compete in the marketplace, the terms of the competition are, in fact, set. Serious arts and letters receive scant attention; the amusement they offer has too many prerequisites. As a result, contemporary artists and writers are tempted to banality, public discussion of important issues is curtailed, and a long conversation becomes ever more distorted by the marketplace.

These results do not, however, constitute a direct exhibit of popular choice. Instead, they are the product of an ideology – transmitted through schooling and acted out in the marketplace – that subordinates meaning to acquisition. This ideology also contributes to the complicated stratification of tastes that determine the cultural capital of different social classes (cf. Bourdieu & Passeron, 1977). This ideology recasts the artifacts and traditions of "elite" and "mass" culture as social markers that signify status distinctions, and, in consequence, it diminishes the inherent value of such artifacts and traditions, whether they represent local knowledge or works of intellect.

Classical music, for example, serves as a signifier of the ruling class, and, in reaction, distaste for such music marks working-class resistance to the perceived snobbishness of the privileged elite. The decision to avoid classical music altogether is largely a response to the messages embedded in the social constructions that surround music, not an informed judgment with regard to the music itself, with which most people are not at all conversant.

Our analysis in no way suggests that the arts should stop trying to provide pleasure or that educated people ought to shun the pleasures of popular music. It does, however, argue that the arts have the potential to provide rich interpretations and inventive transformations of experience and that the role of education ought to be to help everyone realize such possibilities.

Similarly, the analysis *by no means* calls for the demise of practicality. Rather, it suggests the dangers of using immediate utility as the best criterion of practice and, hence, as the guide to human potential and the realization of the good life. It also suggests that study of the arts and sciences gives individuals multiple ways to interpret, critique, transform, and, when needed, transcend the particulars of their experience. Moreover, such study connects individuals to an ongoing conversation about ultimate and situated meanings, allowing them to participate in shaping as well as understanding the ethos of their time on earth.

LEARNING FOR ITS OWN SAKE: EDUCATION AS FAITH IN HUMAN POTENTIAL

The virtue of developing the mind for its own sake makes no *explicit* appeal to utility (Cremin, 1961), whereas the educational project of business (i.e., "investing in our children" in order to develop human capital) invokes utility to *justify* its aims. Maxine Greene (1982, p. 99) summarizes Dewey's view of this matter:

> Dewey . . . objected to finding ends "outside of the educative process to which education is subordinate." An imposed aim, he thought, is rigid; "it is not a stimulus to intelligence in the given situation . . . it is a limit set to activity." Thus he rejected the whole notion of education as preparation for a remote future; the primary aim of education was to enable persons to continue their education.

The notion of doing anything "for its own sake" also sounds elitist, self-indulgent, and even unethical, so, many people would conclude that schooling to develop the intellect is either useless or immoral, if not both. Nothing could be further from the truth, however. Humans, after all, are what they are by virtue of their minds. When the purposes of schooling are construed primarily in instrumental terms, development of human potential is radically deformed. The familiar hyperbole about preparing students for the twenty-first century is, on these terms, ill-founded because it limits the potential of human beings to engage in self-development.

Small-mindedness diminishes humanity because to be human entails enlargement of the intellect, which is the aim of a true education. Much of what passes for education in America, however, is small-minded, and this small-mindedness is implemented systematically as schooling (cf. DeYoung & Howley, 1992). The conservative critique ascribes the failures of schooling to inefficiency, the liberal critique to inequity and inadequacy of funding, and the radical critique to exploitation.

Our view is closest to the radical critique, but shares Dewey's faith in learning for its own sake. Such faith has been most severely tested by the debacles of the twentieth century, which have provided ample reason for thoughtful people to question the wisdom of allowing either human potential or progress to take its own course. Despair and cynicism are so common that we can barely recognize them in what passes as educational common sense (i.e., production of patriotic jobholders as the mission of schooling). We now build such misconceptions into the basis even of our efforts to change things.

The draft preface to one state's new curriculum framework, for instance, begins with this surprising statement:

> While this nation, and this nation alone, has committed itself, at least in principle, to the concept of educating the masses, other nations have educated only the economically and socially elite.

Nations such as Zimbabwe and Vietnam have, in this century, achieved remarkable and widespread improvement in literacy under circumstances that Americans neither understand nor acknowledge (Bhola, 1987). Similar observation can be made about many other nations, including America's once-and-future arch rival, Russia. Denial, of course, is a convenient way of keeping despair at bay, but the sort of denial required can sound both ignorant and arrogant.

Catastrophe and the Utility of Despair

Lasch (1991) points out that engaging the subject of catastrophe and despair constitutes *pessimism*, a form of bad manners. American schooling was supposed to have been an *optimistic* venture, widely underwriting democracy and guaranteeing affluence and social mobility for successive generations. Questioning this educational purpose constitutes bad manners because it appears to challenge the very roots of the American experience, that exuberant adventure in the wilderness that sought to show the world the "true and only" path to the good life: progressive, practical knowledge necessarily bringing social amelioration in tow.

It has not worked out the way Americans wanted; the rich are getting richer, the poor, poorer, and social mobility is declining in America (e.g., Krymkowski & Krauze, 1992; Lichter & Eggebeen, 1993; Thurow, 1987). The Great Depression, the second global war and its legion of regional successors (especially, for Americans, in Vietnam), an evil and wasteful high-tech arms race, and the emergence of an horrific culture of self-destruction (cf. Lasch, 1979; Mumford, 1934/1961) make continued optimism difficult. According to Lasch (1979, p. 222),

> Democratization . . . has accomplished little to justify . . . faith [in the wonder-working powers of education]. It has neither improved popular understanding of modern society, raised the quality of popular culture, nor reduced the gap between wealth and poverty, which remains as wide as ever. On the other hand, it has contributed to the decline of critical thought and the erosion of intellectual standards, forcing us to consider the possibility that mass education, as conservatives have argued all along, is intrinsically incompatible with the maintenance of educational quality.

Schooling turns out to have been (or to have become) a technology for delivering children from their parents to society as jobholders (DeYoung, 1989). Not only have we lost *meaning* in this enterprise, but (perhaps as a long-term result of the loss of meaningful education) equality continues to elude us.

Catastrophe. Americans have so far been spared the most horrible effects of the century's catastrophes. The catastrophes involve the carnage of scores of millions killed in each of two world wars (on other continents); tens of millions killed in meaningless imperialist adventures (e.g., in Vietnam); and tens of millions killed to carry out political hegemony (e.g., in the Soviet gulag). Related catastrophes involve wholesale economic attack on indigenous communities and cultures on all continents, often precipitating famines and other calamities of previously unknown scale (most notably in Asia and Africa).

At the very least, the progressive knowledge of science and its resulting technologies haplessly enabled the crescendo of conquest and exploitation that culminated in such catastrophes. But most postmodern theorists believe more than this. In their albeit diverse views, the knowledge and tools of the West were not merely misused by thoughtless men—quite the contrary. Thoughtless men developed the knowledge and tools *for this purpose*. In this reading of history, many of the great cultural heroes, no matter how thoughtful, inevitably became the tools of more powerful people and organizations. Perhaps Albert Einstein's work illustrates this reading better than the work of many. Einstein was a life-long pacifist and socialist, yet his work has been passed on to all subsequent generations as humanity's very worst catastrophe. This bequest is *not* the actual event that may terminate humanity, but the distortions of faith in human potential resulting from the inescapable and continuing threat of global nuclear war.

In previous centuries, apocalyptic circumstances provoked revivals of faith; in the twentieth century, the enormity of the threat has provoked despair, reflected in the existentialist analysis so popular among intellectuals in the 1950s. Traditional metaphysics, ethics, and politics cannot, in the existentialist view, cover over the despair that the human condition now entails. The existentialists, while not succumbing to this despair, nonetheless wrote from its shadows; they articulated a view of the absurdity of human life that would have outraged the moralists of the nineteenth century, much as it did outrage ordinary Americans in the 1950s.

Because the American way of life (i.e., its mode of production and consumption) requires progress, alternatives are considered unpatriotic. The economy rests on the accumulation of capital, and that accumulation requires ever-expanding production and consumption (Heilbroner, 1985). The desire for unending economic growth is the essential meaning of the word "progress," now and into the next century.

Corporate and political leaders whose interests are vested in this system of accumulation *must* oppose the idea that natural or ethical limits to growth exist (e.g., the incapacity of the earth to support such an economy or the increasing division of the world's population into the starving and the fat). In this view, only naysayers, doomsdayers, and all who are unpatriotic would question faith in progress (Lasch, 1991). Their objections, in this view, are "idealistic."

Technology is the mechanism of the accumulative process. The social critic Lewis Mumford (1934/1961, p. 321), writing about technology in 1934, astutely observed that technology allowed for a peculiar representation of reality in the image of the machine:

> The mass of mankind learned . . . that certain parts of the environment can neither be intimidated nor cajoled. To control them, one must learn the laws of their behavior, instead of petulantly imposing one's own wishes. Thus the lore and tradition of technics . . . tended to create the picture of an objective reality.

In Mumford's view, people develop technology to manipulate the environment in accord with natural laws, but technology inevitably confronts them as an alien representation of the world. Machines appear as representatives of an inescapable economic, cultural, and natural order; they objectify misconceptions about the power of humans to subjugate nature.

One of the worst effects on the human condition, however, is how this circumstance cultivates thoughtlessness. Machines automate the effort, attention, and patience that production previously required. As a result, people lose the facility for such devotions, which are a *necessary* part of the human condition. Machines have contracted time for most people, but the machine chimera of instant, effortless attainment deludes us. Wise control and genuine creation still require time—time for false beginnings, judgment, and redirection; time for reflection; and much time for making meaning, which is the essence of devotion.

The delusion of effortless control constitutes much of the popular appeal of the computer; we are unduly impressed by the speed with which it carries out functions previously carried out much more slowly by human brains. When Mumford wrote the preceding passage, machines had merely begun to reform nature and to deform thought; now, with computers and with the development of artificial intelligence, it is possible not only to automate the deformation of thought, but for the deformation of thought to deform material reality (e.g., the perils of genetic engineering). Writing 25 years after Mumford, Arendt (1958, pp. 125–126) predicted this circumstance:

> We . . . forced open the distinguishing boundaries which protected the world of human artifice from nature . . . delivering and abandoning to [natural processes] the . . . stability of the human world.

Arendt thus took an unusual stance on the question of control. In her view, the issue was not whether humans controlled machines, but whether machines could remain part of the human artifice. She believed that by destroying the line between human artifice (culture) and nature (the prehuman cosmos given to human perception), humans had violated the basic condition of their existence. Technology, in short, was diminishing humanity (cf. Lyotard, 1979/1984).

The utility of despair. The twentieth century presents a surfeit of despair. Communities have vanished, plundered out of existence; catastrophes barely imaginable in 1900 have swept the globe, and the distinction between humans and monsters is ever more difficult to make. Reality itself is in jeopardy according to a host of postmodern thinkers, who observe that people experience simulations (television, computer applications, Disney-like theme parks) as far more compelling than the banality of ordinary time and space (Best & Kellner, 1991).

The extreme individualism of the American circumstance, however, permits private despair and public optimism to coexist. Lasch (1979) was among the first to note the function of therapy in creating the conditions for this coexistence, though Bellah and colleagues (1985) show more clearly how the therapeutic outlook constricts public discourse about commitment, justice, and the meaning of the good life. Lasch (1979, pp. 99–100) explains the link between therapeutic distraction (narcissism) and bureaucratic dis-interest (conformism) that helps maintain the political conditions required to sustain the regime of perpetual accumulation:

> The individual endlessly examines himself for signs of aging and ill health, for tell-tale symptoms of psychic stress, for blemishes and flaws that might dimin-ish his attractiveness. . . . Modern medicine has conquered the plagues and epidemics that once made life so precarious, only to create new forms of insecurity. In the same way, bureaucracy has made life predictable and even boring while reviving in a new form, the war of all against all. Our overorgan-ized society, in which large-scale organizations predominate but have lost the capacity to command allegiance, in some respects more nearly approximates a condition of universal animosity than did the primitive capitalism on which Hobbes modeled his state of nature.

America's comparatively good fortune during the twentieth century allows despair to serve a useful function. Despair is expressed as narcissism, which not only distracts people from public issues (attention that might subvert vested interests) but also helps increase demand for new goods and services.[7] When schooling, as it does, takes up the project of producing patriotic jobholders, citizens become slaves. They engage an endless cycle of producing and consuming, and many lead desperately unexamined lives. Progress, in the form of new products and services, offers a different kind of salvation through eliminating flaws, pain, boredom, and effort (Lasch, 1991).

Wendell Berry (1970/1989, pp. 65–67) begins his book *The Hidden Wound* with a list of precepts about the desperately useful misconceptions that characterize American thoughtlessness. Berry notes that Americans think of society as a pyramid, with honor and happiness accruing to those at the top. Getting to the top of the pyramid requires a peculiar series of sacrifices. Two of his precepts constitute major points of agreement with the views developed in this chapter:

> Knowledge was conceived as a way to get money. This seems to have involved an unconscious wish to streamline the mind, strip it of all knowledge which would not predictably *function*.
>
> We knew and took for granted: marriage without love; sex without joy; drink without conviviality; birth, celebration, and death without adequate ceremony; faith without doubt or trial; belief without deeds; manners without generosity; "good English" without exact speech, without honesty, without literacy.

Trapped in a despair most of us cannot recognize, and which can hardly be spoken, our delusions about the purposes of schooling persist. In preparation for the new millennium, many reports have proposed "retooling" the workforce. The instrumentality of this proposition is flatly obscene — with people, education, and society all conceived as tools for capital accumulation. Accumulation of human capital (Becker, 1964) has become the public good, while all virtues constitute strictly private acts of dubious worth and usefulness. This view of retooling, however, is very much in the nature of the American vision of education.

Schooling as Retooling

Retooling also implies that "the old factory model" of schooling — though once considered adequate by business — no longer suffices. The instrumental goal of efficiently producing human capital, though, is still considered worthy by business people.

Privatization is one scheme, first advanced during the 1980s, to improve the efficiency of schooling. The main point of privatization is to deconstruct the inefficient bureaucratic monolith of the public school system (McGinn & Pereira, 1992) and replace it with a host of competing, and therefore better and cheaper, private school alternatives. Whether from preference or economic necessity, private schooling has achieved what some observers (e.g., Coleman & Hoffer, 1987) claim to be better results under circumstances that the managers of public schooling long ago decided to reform (e.g., small school size, inadequate teacher salaries, sectarianism).

But for all the differences, private schools are organized much like public schools, with textbooks and whole-group work predominating in instruction. Moreover, it is unclear to what extent the comparative "success" of private schools, especially Catholic schools, derives from either (a) a somewhat different set of aims (centered on culture of the community of Christ) or (b) a clientele that is, for a variety of reasons, more academically "promising" than the clientele of the typical public school (Bryk & Driscoll, 1988; Bryk, Holland, Lee, & Carriedo, 1984).

Providing wider access to existing private schools, however, is not so dramatic a scheme of privatization as others that have been proposed. Among these schemes is Lewis Perelman's vision of "hyperlearning." Key assumptions of Perelman's (1992) high-tech view of more efficient schooling for patriotic jobholders include the following:

> "Capital" and "intellectual capital" become ever more the same thing. The creation of knowledge through learning and the embodiment of knowledge in software now hold the keys to wealth. (p. 2)

> The real threat posed to our economy by public education—colleges as well as schools—is not inadequacy but *excess*: too much schooling at too high a cost. (p. 3)

> There is no meaningful distinction between "education" and "training"; the most effective learning follows the process of apprenticeship. But that process is increasingly inherent in modern HL [i.e., hyperlearning] media; apprenticeship programs are superfluous. (p. 5)

> The right goals can be summarized in four simple words: more, better, faster, and cheaper. . . . HL technology already exists and is achieving these productivity goals in the segments of the national learning enterprise that are compelled by *competitive forces* to seek more and better learning in less time at lower cost: notably, in corporate and military organizations. (p. 6)

"Hyperlearning" is the absolute debasement of intellectual tradition in the cloak of reform. The vision dismisses liberal learning—reflection, thought, and intellect—as unproductive vanity. It preposterously misconstrues the knowledge of most worth as the expertise required to engineer software, a commodity whose significance is defined by its capacity to produce wealth. Worse, it insists that the interests of all humans coincide with those of corporate might. It denies any educative role for privacy, solitude, or community; students' minds comprise a human capital whose worth is validated exclusively by the accumulation of goods and money.

Perelman's vision—like others of similar purpose—is so terrible because it misrepresents the human condition and deforms human potential. In John Dewey's view, the loyal jobholding citizen was a slave of sorts, whom even the "marketplace of ideas" could not redeem, for, in fact, one can no more buy and sell ideas than one can learn by plagiarizing.

And, in spite of their insistence about what is best for public education, the representatives of business are much less clear about the need for society actually to provide jobs to those trained to hold them. They wash their hands of this commitment and place it in "the invisible hand," Adam Smith's[8] term for the expectation that all will be for the best when free trade prevails.

Despite its appalling material, ethical, and spiritual misconstructions,

Perelman's vision is only a scheme for a better mousetrap. Society *already* conducts schooling for the same purpose as Perelman espouses. In Perelman's dark vision, however, private enterprise is the reason schooling exists, the means of its operation, and the measure of its success.

Faith in Human Potential

We regard the diverse "progressive" views of education (and the contingent ideas of what schooling should be) as rooted in faith in human potential.[9] Like any faith, it is fundamentally nonrational. This observation is not to say that such faith is "unreasonable," "irrational," or "crazy." The faith, however, is not a faith in progressively more accurate scientific knowledge or progressively more beneficial technological innovation. Nor is it a faith that the unfolding of human potential is necessarily benign. The faith rests on commitment to the idea that the good life is *possible*, that it is the destiny of humans to articulate that life, and that the mission of education is to promote such articulation.

The conversation about the good life is the essential human project of long standing, even if participation is increasingly difficult because the way society parcels out work excludes many people from the conversation. Indeed, the worst nightmare, one that haunted Hannah Arendt, is that the jobholding and conformism of mass society would exclude the conversation itself from the human condition. If it is true that humanity shelters both good and evil, then the continued existence of the good is assured, and for us, that is the observation that warrants faith in human potential.[10] We believe, in fact, that the conversation about the good life continues despite all obstacles, no matter how horrendous.

Nurture of the good, as always, is up to us humans, and our actions and thoughts may help it thrive or wither. In education, nurture of the good consists of attention to the conversation about the good life: its quality, its extent, its depth, and its inclusiveness. Education can hardly aspire to a more important purpose, under any circumstances, but especially under the circumstances of contemporary despair.

Critics are doubtless correct about the dereliction of stewardship of the works of intellect, yet the works themselves do remain accessible to those who can somehow find their way to them — and many do find that way. The conversation that represents the faith of human potential to articulate the good life is carried on in many languages, by people of widely differing views, in many forms. The conversation is also carried out across many generations. This point is key: Without the intellectual habits of mind and heart that involve wide reading and reflection on the things read, participation in the historical dimension of this long conversation is virtually impossible.

Plato believed that the educated mind automatically seeks the good, but few contemporary philosophers would agree. We turn next, therefore, to a more detailed consideration of ethical reasoning and its role in the nurture of intellect.

ETHICAL REASONING AND THE LIFE OF THE MIND

The relationship between thought and ethical action is widely acknowledged (Albert, 1985; but cf. Arendt, 1977). Even extreme emotivists — philosophers who ground ethical decisions in socially determined affective responses — agree that reasoning plays a role in clarifying ethical statements and promoting dialogue about ethical issues (e.g., Stevenson, 1966). The common ground shared by these philosophers and those who believe that ethics is a fully rational process is the fundamental belief that ethical discourse necessarily involves the giving of reasons.

Where Do Reasons Come From?

The British empiricists John Stuart Mill and Herbert Spencer (key philosophers for the modernist ethos) claimed that ethical action could be warranted by reference to empirical truth. If one examined human action objectively, one could, in this view, scientifically identify the "good." Mill and Spencer concluded that pleasure must be "good" because most humans appeared to seek it.

Almost 100 years earlier (in the mid-1700s), however, Hume had discredited the association between knowledge and ethical action, and most contemporary philosophers favor Hume's rather than the empiricists' view of the matter. Contemporary thinkers, nonetheless, continue to debate the contribution of human judgment to action.

Existentialist thinkers, for example, claim that ethical action derives from commitment, which is a product of will, not of reason. Jaspers (1932/1970) states this case in its most extreme form: Ignorance necessitates will, and will promotes action. He claims, "I must will because I do not know. The Being which is inaccessible to knowledge can be revealed only to my volition. Not-knowing is the root of having to will" (Jaspers, 1932/1970, p. 167).

According to this view, the source of the will (and, consequently, of ethical action) is revealed truth, not empirical truth. Revealed truth is available to humans by means of what Jaspers called "reason," as contrasted with rational thought, which he called "understanding" (Passmore, 1966). Nevertheless, even Jaspers noted the importance of philosophical discussion, though he suggested that such discussion was ultimately rooted in faith. For him, the life of the mind entailed primarily a "nonrational" receptivity to revealed truth about the totality of existence.

Jaspers and the British empiricists represent two extremes. Most philosophers of the modern and postmodern periods take up intermediate positions. They view the ground for ethical judgments to reside neither totally in the objective, empirical domain nor fully in the realm of reason. More often than not, they accept the fact that there is no such thing as an ultimate warrant (e.g., Hampshire, 1983). Judgments of worth depend for their justification on some form of prior belief, however such belief is derived. Moreover, contemporary philosophers usually note the cultural basis of such foundational belief.

Even though they claim that views of worth are socially derived, these thinkers do not, by and large, claim that convention determines action. Nor do very many of them suggest that material reality shapes human experience so completely as to undermine any possibility for "agency" (self-directed action). Instead, most recognize the role of will (choice or intention) in the process of ethical decision-making and the role of rationality in the discussion of reasons (Albert, 1985).

Even emotivists see benefit to the rational discussion of emotive meaning. Urmson (1968, p. 147) explains the role that rationality must play if emotivist theories of ethics are to make any sense at all:

> The stress laid on emotion, imperfectly distinguished from and indeed confused with attitudes, led to the mistaken view that evaluation [that is, judgment of value or worth] was an entirely non-rational element in human behaviour, to which the concepts of truth and falsity, of validity and invalidity, could not be applied. . . . It is in attitudes so interpreted that we can find disagreement, not in emotion; disagreement is possible because attitudes are adopted and maintained, need to be rationally grounded, and can be attacked and defended.

Contemporary ethical theory, then, presupposes some form of reasoning before and after ethical action. Prior to such action, reasoning guides judgments of means and ends; following action, reasoning justifies the action to others (cf. Hampshire, 1983, for a slightly different dichotomy of "reason-giving").

One may, of course, engage in one form of reasoning but not the other. For our purposes, however, both occasions for the giving of reasons are pertinent. When people give reasons in anticipation of action, they call on personal understandings—ethical precepts, experiences with means and ends—and reflexive thought to inform or guide their decision making. By contrast, when they account for their actions to others, they necessarily rely on understandings and modes of discourse that are more widely shared. In both cases, the understandings that support ethical dialogue—either with self or among others—reflect something that is different from "knowledge." Instead, they reflect what numerous philosophers and sociologists refer to as "meaning."

Personal Meaning and Ethical Decision-Making

As individuals encounter the world, they interpret it to themselves. Such interpretations result from comparisons between new and previous experiences and reflections about what such experiences mean (Arendt, 1977). At any point in time, the sum of one's interpretations of the world represents a store of personal meanings.

"Meaning," in this usage, encompasses more than knowledge, though it clearly includes knowledge: "Meaning" takes account of understandings beyond those that can be known with certainty. Intuitions, beliefs, and commitments—as well as facts and truths—constitute personal meaning. Personal interpretations of the relationships between means and ends, as well as beliefs about the relative value of different ends, constitute significant guides to action. When someone intends to act ethically, that is, makes an ethical decision, personal meanings come to bear on the particulars. Personal meanings, first, help us to judge which of various possible consequences best approximates "the good" and, second, to determine the actions that are most likely to foster that consequence.

Intellect informs both parts of such an ethical determination. To make a wise judgment about "the good," an individual benefits from the ability to situate any decision within a larger frame of reference. Understandings derived from the study of history, philosophy, and religion seem particularly relevant. Moreover, if part of intellectual honesty is the requirement to warrant ethical principles, humans are *obliged* to elaborate such a rational derivation (Albert, 1985; Habermas, 1985; Hampshire, 1983). In order to construct a warrant of this type, however, they must have the ability to reason deductively from premises as well as the willingness to expose those premises to critical scrutiny (Hollis, 1982).

Both reason and knowledge help us construct a relevant association between means and ends. In the realm of human action, this association cannot constitute a law of behavior, since no one is able to predict with complete accuracy the reactions of others (Arendt, 1958). Nevertheless, a person must use past experiences with other people as well as introspections to make tentative predictions about the effects of intended actions.

Shared Meaning and Ethical Dialogue

Whereas some ethical decisions and actions take place in the private sphere, many ought to occur in a public arena. Such an arena, in theory, would provide every person access to an on-going debate about what constitutes the "good society." In practice, however, the institutionalization of private and public life may have deformed, or even destroyed, the forum and the language that enable such debate (Bellah et al., 1985; Brown, 1993; Habermas, 1985; MacIntyre, 1984; Poulantzas, 1980).

According to numerous critics of capitalism, large corporations, in league with a government bureaucracy that supports them, determine the "goods" of contemporary democracies and how such goods are distributed.[11] Under capitalism, such goods are equated with both material gain and personal happiness, two conditions that are themselves seen as inextricable (Heilbroner, 1985); in practice, such goods are distributed unequally among the various classes of society.

To maintain such an arrangement, in which material goods increasingly eclipse other possible goods (such as camaraderie or leisure) and in which some people have greater access to such goods than others, capitalism requires a system of justificatory beliefs. This system of beliefs, or ideology, rests on the premise that individuals *do* make rational decisions with respect both to their involvement in the marketplace and their participation in political life. This assumption, in fact, constitutes the key belief on which neoclassical economics rests (Heilbroner & Thurow, 1985).

In practice, however, such decisions are made neither at the individual level nor in a reasoned manner. Options for participating in the marketplace are, in large measure, determined by some interaction between one's social class background and luck, and participation in political decision making is almost totally illusory for most persons. According to Poulantzas (1980), the capitalist state endows citizens with the illusion of meaningful influence, while at the same time depriving them of effective control over production and distribution of the variety of public goods (e.g., access to leisure, to schools, to highways).

In Poulantzas' view, the capitalist state deludes its citizens into believing that the process of staking and getting support for economic and ideological claims takes place through involvement in the democratic mechanisms of government. By perpetuating this myth of consensus politics, the state maintains its power without obvious coercion. More importantly, the myth obscures the actual oligarchical diffusion and exercise of power, and it focuses attention on the illusory manifestations of allegedly democratic rule. As a consequence, the myth promotes the widespread, but mistaken, belief that the political arena gives every individual the opportunity to participate in decision making as well as giving every faction the chance to take over political stewardship. It is no wonder that for many people political cynicism and political idealism go hand-in-hand.

The reality of political participation is, as mentioned above, quite different. Not only are the important issues resolved elsewhere than in a public forum (Heilbroner, 1985), but also the language for their debate has become impoverished and dysfunctional. Among many observers who could be cited to similar purpose, Bellah and colleagues (1985, p. 204), make this point:

> The extent to which many Americans can understand the workings of our economic and social organization is limited by the capacity of their chief moral language to make sense of human interaction. The limit set by individualism is clear: events that escape the control of individual choice and will cannot coherently be encompassed in a moral calculation. But that means that much, if not most, of the workings of the interdependent American political economy, through which individuals achieve or are assigned their places and relative power in this society, cannot be understood in terms that make coherent moral sense.

These authors claim that if Americans are to begin to transform the conditions of their personal and collective experience, then they must arrive at important shared understandings about the relationship between self-identity and the common good. Such understandings derive from connections to unifying traditions – both religious and secular – that predate the ethos and institutions of modernity. Further, Bellah and colleagues suggest that a more legitimate and satisfying political dialogue will result if Americans intentionally invoke these traditions.

In our view, however, this interpretation is dangerously simplistic because it ignores the contradictory role that tradition plays in complex society (see Friedrich, 1972). Whereas tradition has the potential to support transformative thought and action, in practice, it frequently provides the rationale and the mechanism for repressing both. Such repression occurs most often when the authority that legitimates a tradition comes from beliefs that have no reasonable support (Friedrich, 1972).

We conclude, therefore, that the traditions with the greatest potential to be transformative may be those that call on reason to substantiate their authority. In this postmodern era, such a view is, ironically, identified as "conservative" and possibly even "hegemonic." From the postmodern vantage an emancipatory program seems to include the return to prerational thinking, linguistic distinctness, and local action. Where events seem, however, to conform to some of the features of this program — notably in the Middle East and in Eastern Europe — communities of like-minded individuals take the license not only to oppress, but to kill, their heterodox neighbors.

Such events cannot, of course, be taken to indicate that the postmodern ethos will inevitably sponsor a politics of regional and ethnic chauvinism. But they do suggest cautions for those engaged in nurturing the minds of the young. In our view, certain postmodern themes must be mediated by an understanding of their Enlightenment roots if they are to be used to help children make sense of the world.

CODA: INTELLECT AND TALENT DEVELOPMENT IN THE POSTMODERN CONDITION

In the emerging postmodern world, the imperative for thought is clear. Cultural contradictions have become sharper, especially as the drive for capital accumulation and for unbridled consumption have become aspirations of people worldwide. At the same time, the ferment of different cultures mixing in the United States and throughout the entire world, and of a technological environment in which knowledge (debased as information) figures with such prominent economic importance (cf. Lyotard, 1979/1984), points to a coming time — already upon us — of rapid and disturbing change.

Our analysis has sought to establish the importance of nurturing intellect widely, so that people can grasp, use, critique, and invent ideas. But our analysis does *not* suggest that such an expansive project can be adapted to a narrowly instrumental purpose. Indeed, we have articulated this position precisely in order to show how schooling might enact a true education, one that respects the capacity of the human intellect to develop itself.

The relationship of intellect to ideas, and of ideas to institutions of culture and society is inherent. But our schooling — as we typically (though by no means always) practice it — purposively *neglects* care of the intellect, and therefore of the ideas, meanings, and circumstances of the human condition. Ignorance on this score is not simply unaesthetic: It inevitably leads in time (and much time has already passed) to dysfunctional institutions and damaged relationships among people. The appalling violence of the twentieth century attests to this observation, and to the inchoate despair that follows us into our jobs and homes alike.

Insofar as gifted education is practiced in support of the mission of producing patriotic jobholders by selecting for elite and specialized job training children whose lives are already privileged, we definitely question its worth. In its small way, gifted education (as it is most often practiced) contributes to the despair and dysfunction that has characterized the modernist era (Margolin, 1994).

The project of "scientifically" identifying the cleverest (most "intelligent") children in schools and developing their talents (in accord with "their special needs") for productive service in the political economy has dubious ethical, political, and aesthetic value. Such a project exhibits many of the misconceptions of modernism, and many of its contradictions (Margolin, 1994). That the cleverest children should so frequently turn out to be those who lead the most privileged lives, and whose training (as a result of their identification) will ensure the continuation of that privilege has always seemed suspicious to us.

We believe that credible empirical evidence shows that, if our society (our world) privileged more children, we would discover more of them to be clever. In particular, the development of talent is not a "zero-sum" undertaking, though so far capitalism has unfairly allocated the benefits (and liabilities) of the sort of talent development it prizes.

The way past this dilemma is to practice legitimate care for the intellect and to pay much less heed to immediate instrumental results. We *could* nurture the conditions under which we *would* recognize and prize talent more widely if we were less concerned to make as large and quick a financial profit as possible from so doing. Schooling will always possess an intellectual potential, no matter how incompletely the institutions of society permit it to be realized. But people who are concerned with liberal learning, with the life of the mind, with ethical reasoning, and with the enduring dilemmas of the human condition must take a role in realizing the intellectual potential of schooling. The final chapter takes up the issues of schooling on this basis.

CHAPTER 6

Rethinking the Potential of Schooling

Aimee Howley and Craig B. Howley

Our arguments about the character of U.S. schools implicated the pervasive anti-intellectualism of our society as well as specific mechanisms by which that anti-intellectualism most often manifests itself as school practice. This chapter, more speculative than the preceding chapters, offers other possibilities for schooling that are based on care for, rather than neglect or denigration of, the life of the mind.

The authority for these alternative practices resides in the possibilities for improvement that our society harbors. These possibilities, although almost dormant in recent history, belong to political and intellectual traditions that nonetheless constitute the human legacy. So, while our society fulfills its potential and satisfies its taste for vanity, indulgence, and thoughtlessness, it has within its own past the roots of a much finer destiny. And this destiny shelters a conception of schooling broadly supportive of the alternative practices elaborated in this chapter.

We believe that these practices could dramatically alter the substance of schooling and its effects on the lives of students. For example, we imagine graduates who would leave school with as much intellectual curiosity as they had when they entered. Many, possibly most, of them would be independent people who could engage critique. Moreover, the vast majority would see themselves as active participants in the processes that make sense – both personal and collective – of the world. They would be prepared to keep themselves informed and to join the debate that fashions the public good and determines the best means to pursue it.

Yet, the world that they enter may be ill-prepared for thoughtful citizens with these inclinations. Economically that world may have fewer places for well-educated workers and, perhaps, fewer jobs of any sort to offer (see e.g., Schor, 1991), and the effects of such economic conditions on power relations are hard to gauge. We suspect, however, that as resources increasingly become concentrated in the hands of a few, power also will become less justly distributed.

Our hope, however, resides in the potential for change occasioned by the *mismatch* between citizens who are schooled in the intellectual habits of inquiry and critique and a political economy that is dependent on mute and compliant workers. We can, of course, imagine the possibilities for violence that might become manifest when such citizens confront an intransigent work place and an unreceptive political forum; but we can also imagine a slower, less cataclysmic process of change. As we have said earlier, though, we suspect that schools remain the way they are primarily to forestall such change. So, in truth, we do not project that these sorts of changes—either in schools or in the political economy—will take place in the foreseeable future. Elaborating their possibility is necessary, nonetheless.

In Chapter 1 we argued that the mission of schooling for social reproduction and economic competitiveness debases the school enterprise. Here we propose schooling premised on stewardship of intellect—both its traditions and its potential for transformation. Chapter 2 explored the anti-intellectualism of teachers and the culture of the schools and colleges where they work. In the discussion below, we consider the characteristics of the sorts of teachers and the cultures of schools and colleges that would support schooling with a predominantly intellectual focus. Chapters 3 and 4 looked at the particularly impoverished ways that schools seek to serve, and in the process manage to exploit, gifted students, on the one hand, and disadvantaged students, on the other. We consider alternatives to these practices based on aims that have both intellectual integrity and emancipatory intent.

Throughout our framing of alternatives, we warrant our presumptions with faith in the potential of human beings to shape a good society. Education is the cornerstone of such an endeavor, and our thoughts here are as productive of our own education as of anything else. We hope, however, they will stimulate and possibly fuel debate about issues of immediate concern to educators and of enduring significance to the lives of schoolchildren.

AUTHORITY, INTELLECTUAL STEWARDSHIP, AND SCHOOLING

Whereas we, with others, question the apparent consensus that the mission of schooling in the United States should be to produce patriotic jobholders, nearly everyone agrees that education, including the education that takes place in schools, cultivates knowledge of one sort or another (cf. Bennett & LeCompte, 1990). Moreover, most people can probably agree that carrying out this work successfully depends on some legitimate authority. This section of the chapter draws the implications of these essential relationships in light of our previous discussions.

In our view a true education is one that develops the intellect of students, particularly with respect to considering the enduring dilemmas of the human condition. Schooling that accomplishes this work would implement a three-part mission. It would promote students' ethical reasoning, it would build communities as "harbingers" of democracy, and it would nurture students' ability to make meaning. For us, the last of these missions is key to intellectual development and, in many ways, informs and augments the other two missions. In fact, we find that the making of meaning entails ethical, political, and aesthetic perspectives on knowledge and authority. We will deal with these perspectives in the context of difficult choices contingent on the nature of culture in American capitalist society and our view of the possibilities for schooling to contribute to cultural meanings in this country generally.

The Dilemmas of Capitalist Culture

In previous centuries, the local performances and beliefs of ordinary persons often *were* separate from those of the nobility (the elite). Local cultures were small-scale: Mass culture did not yet exist. The rise of the bourgeoisie from at least the sixteenth century forward, accompanied by the elaboration of science as the esteemed method of controlling the world, began new cultural forms, of which the novel is one of the most remarkable. But museums, schooling, hospitals, and a variety of public and private works conducive to commerce and practical learning also arose.

Capitalism began to bring the two forms of culture into increasingly closer contact. Both forms of culture changed as a result: Local performances and rituals in many places in the world have been supplanted by amusements marketed nationally and inserted locally by electronic means (the myriad forms of telecommunications); intellectual culture has aped science and tied itself to the service of national and global economic hegemony. The relative value of intellectual versus anthropological culture makes little sense in the contemporary world, as each depends for its vigor on the other.

Authority. Mass schooling has been a rather late development in the history of capitalism. In America, schooling was originally an entirely local effort, funded haphazardly, with much infighting among local boards, considerable teacher turnover (as young women married and young men sought careers in medicine, law, or the clergy), and, always, short terms to accommodate the great agricultural endeavor of the nineteenth century. In America the very need for mass schooling did not become apparent until the early years of the twentieth century; and it was not until 1917 that a majority of the U.S. population lived in cities. The American version of mass schooling was a strictly urban phenomenon (Tyack, 1974).

But the authority for its establishment was the legal power of each state to operate and maintain "thorough and efficient" systems of schooling within its borders. State departments of education were established throughout the nineteenth century, but remained small until the urban agenda (i.e., the need for mass schooling) became clear. According to Callahan (1962), urban educational administrators, convinced of the need for scientific management of the emerging system of mass schooling, "captured" state education agencies just as they began to exert statewide powers.

This institutional development is unique in history; though mass education seems inevitable, ubiquitous, and unchangeable to contemporary observers, it is, in fact, the careful creation of the twentieth century. The odd and grossly inequitable patterns of funding (Kozol, 1991) that persist are twisted legacies of the system's roots in the nineteenth century. But the vast similarities that permeate American classrooms speak of a "one-best-system" mentality that is characteristic of twentieth-century modernism (e.g., Bell, 1973; Harvey, 1989; Tyack, 1974).

The authority on which this system rests is legal and economic. This authority legitimates the existing mission of schools: schooling conceived as a factory for factory-workers, accommodating the great manufacturing project of the twentieth century. In this system jobholders, like automobiles, are mass produced. Whereas the schooling of the nineteenth century did not play a fundamental role in agricultural production, twentieth-century schooling clearly became an essential part of the industrial enterprise. The urban, industrial system of schooling was *designed* to produce punctuality and conformity; schooling had to be boring because jobs were boring. Work was equated with jobs (rather than with a call to higher purpose, as in the Protestant biblical tradition), and good-feeling (playfulness) strictly with leisure.

The authority for extracting instrumental products from the traditions of schooling came from the production process itself. This authority both restrained and exploited the potentials of schooling. Clearly, this same authority could not sustain, either simultaneously or subsequently, the true education of the intellect on which we place our hope. From where, then, might such authority come?

It *cannot* come from the state as it now exists. The state (whether a particular state government or the national government) has been and is now following the counsel of business organizations — the elite that *controls* the production process. In the past, this counsel advised efficiency, standardization, and life-adjustment training. Now it advises higher order problem-solving skills, computer technology, and flexibility. The motive in both cases, however, is the changing nature of capitalist production, and the methods are those of business (Weiner, 1990). In 1912, the method of choice was "scientific management" (and its cousins); in 1992, the method was "total quality management" (and *its* cousins). The conventional wisdom espoused in support of the new, "more flexible" approaches to mass education is that citizens were, at one time, well-served by the "factory model," but the "needs of the twenty-first century" indicate the necessity of radical change. In Chapter 5, we examined one program of change (Perelman, 1992) based on such premises. That program based its authority on the value of software as a method of accumulating wealth.

Stewardship. Schemes that try to warrant educational practices on the basis of trite claims about "future needs" and posturing for global dominion are unethical, undemocratic, and ugly. They are lies, in fact, that few believe, even among those who promulgate them.

Schooling must nurture intellect above all else, and this nurture must draw on both local knowledge and on intellectual tradition. The first source, as we have shown, comprises care for "a beloved place," for the immediate context of one's life with others. The second source — the intellectual tradition represented by liberal learning — constitutes care for the human condition and the artifacts that express human meaning. The local source both informs and depends on the second, which includes much more than the intellectual sources of the present, or of any particular canon past or present.

The authority for this sort of schooling is, of course, the substantive authority of the intellect. And the warrant for this authority rests on the human capacity for development, a capacity that schooling as we practice it now (and as we are exhorted to practice it in the future) too often constricts and distorts for thoughtless or greedy purposes.

It is true that even the intellectual authority necessary for a true education appears weak, in view of the debasement of local performances and beliefs and the distortion of intellect by "the economizing mode" (Bell, 1976). Our considerations can, indeed, be dismissed as impractical in the sense that the odds against them are heavy.

But in our view lack of deference to mere utility is a virtue when true education is at stake, and the scope of challenge these considerations offer is actually an advantage in practice. For to culture a true education is to assume a form of stewardship, of learning and of the human potential to learn. Mass education of the twentieth century realizes, and twenty-first century projection aims to realize, no such form of stewardship. The main preoccupation of such education has been, and will be, if unchallenged, an economic efficiency carelessly destructive of worthy things, relationships, and places.

Stewardship in education comprehends the need for humans to take pleasure in their work and to care for the human artifact. Stewardship also comprehends care for generations past and generations to come. This sort of stewardship is a commitment due students from teachers, children from parents, and the world at large from the people in it.

In an essay titled "God and Country," Wendell Berry (1990, p. 102) writes of the frightening burden of stewardship, but also of its hope. He insists:

> We can ally ourselves with those things that are worthy: light, air, water, earth; plants and animals; human families and communities; the traditions of decent life, good work, and responsible thought; the religious traditions; the essential stories and songs. . . . One is part of a remnant, and a dwindling remnant too, though not without hope, and not without the necessary instructions, the most pertinent of which, perhaps, is this, also from Revelation: "Be watchful, and strengthen the things which remain, that are ready to die."

American schooling, however, abandons stewardship. Instead, it is motivated by the view that any worthy thing and any meaning may be sacrificed to economic growth. But as the economic growth that sustains capitalism becomes more and more difficult, the sacrifices required are certain to become more onerous. The incredible productivity and requisite unbridled growth of capitalism have not only threatened the global environment, they have distorted, silenced, or eliminated many cultural forms altogether. Norbert Wiener warned nearly a half-century ago (in *The Human Use of Human Beings*, 1950) that the advent of computers would mean that no meaningful work would remain to be done by humans. Wiener advised that we get busy and figure out what people are for.

Wiener's prediction is beginning to come true; the computerized service economy is shifting from high-paying full-time unionized manufacturing jobs to low-paying nonunionized part-time service jobs (e.g., fast food, routine data processing). But we have still not come to believe that people are for making meaning, and, in fact, our schooling is largely constructed in order to deny this prospect.

According to Berry, these sacrifices (of meaningful work and of worthy relationships with one another and with nature) are the punishment for accepting the evil premises of a society like ours. But all cultures, our diverse one included, continue always with sources of hidden strength that can be nurtured or neglected, and we find in this circumstance cause for hope in otherwise desperate straits.

Avocation vs. vocation. A decent life requires meaningful work, a work that elicits one's deepest commitments by virtue of its significance in a larger scheme of things than short-term economic utility; in other words, a calling. Juliet Schor (1991) deplores the quality of Americans' work lives and use of leisure time. In her analysis, this circumstance leads to intellectual, communal, and spiritual impoverishment. Too many people occupy jobs that demand long hours, and too many people go without jobs or occupy jobs that ask them to accept fewer hours than are required for full-time pay and benefits. The business community identifies this unequal distribution of wealth and leisure as the flexibility required to compete in a global economy. Schor identifies it as a problem of distributive justice with practical implications for society. It propagates envy throughout society; it focuses people's efforts on consumption and away from meaningful thought and action; it takes satisfying leisure away from privileged but overworked jobholders, underprivileged jobholders, and the unemployed (i.e., the postindustrial reserve army).

As we see it, intellectual stewardship is an essential part of every calling, agricultural, industrial, commercial, or academic. By conceiving schooling as preparation for patriotic jobholding, however, our society has ignored the intellectual stewardship required for justice and decency. Those who do feel a "call," therefore, typically practice what is most important to them outside their jobs. Their real commitments are implemented privately, where public benefit is minimized. With more leisure, and less emphasis on consumption, Schor (1991) believes that people would discover the possibility of making contributions of time and effort that would have public as well as private benefits.

The Possibilities of Schooling for Culture

With Counts (1930), we see schooling as an "American Road to Culture," with an ethical, political, and, most critically, an intellectual function. The intellectual function is based on the notion that human development is its own warrant. This is a peculiarly aesthetic notion of intellect, and its conception of schooling is philosophical rather than narrowly instrumental.

At the same time, the purposes of schooling that we have articulated have practical relevance. The ethical, political, and aesthetic choices people make determine what their world will be: whether justice will be honored; whether many will undertake legitimate work; whether society can accommodate any sense of community; and whether essential meanings will be sought, elaborated, and prized. This sort of practicality differs sharply from the instrumentality of teaching skills and attitudes required for compliant job performance and perfunctory citizenship. It has more in common with Jefferson's view, as reported by Lasch (1979, p. 230), which

> stressed what the eighteenth century would have called useful knowledge, especially ancient and modern history, which Jefferson hoped might teach the young to judge "the actions and designs of men, to know ambition under every disguise it may assume, and knowing it, to defeat its views."

Assuming that a true education resembles the one described thus far, is it possible that schooling might encompass such an education? Three issues bear particularly on the answer. What body of works, or canon, ought to inform schooling that exerts intellectual stewardship? What relationship ought to prevail between the processes of education and the objects (products) with which it deals? And to what extent can schooling contribute to the intentional development of culture?

The problem of the canon. Because public schooling has employed such a narrow conception of education, the issue of the canon — that body of works authoritatively judged most worthy of study — has received little attention (in K-12 schooling) except as it pertains to high school English. In this case, surveys of texts used indicate many commonalities, but they also reveal some diversity and some change with time.

Our view of authority and the intellectual stewardship it represents, however, points directly to teachers for the consideration of any canon. The next section of this chapter takes up the role of teacher-scholar, which we construe as fundamental to a schooling that practices intellectual stewardship. Teachers must be capable of judging works most worthy of study, on the basis of issues considered, accessibility to students taught, and potential for promoting intellectual growth among their students. Teachers must also be willing and able to defend their positions to one another and to encourage such conversation among others.

The purpose of such conversation is not to devise an immutable canon. Any canon is inherently mutable, and one that seems to be immutable is one in which the conversation that intellectual stewardship tries to promote has died. This is, in fact, the canon that high school English students usually encounter.

The real shortcoming of this canon is not its inherent irrelevance to the lives of such students but its *presumed* irrelevance — manufactured by processes of schooling, with teachers acting, usually against their will, as helpless complicitors. At the same time, development of the intellect consists of an increasing ability to tolerate "irrelevance," construed as the distance between a work (or an event) and one's own circumstance. In this sense, the thing or event that appears alien becomes a strange, but intriguing, invitation to meaning-making. The problem of the canon thus leads to the problem of educational process.

The problem of educational process. The display to students of a body of works allegedly worth their consideration is important, but cannot itself help them accomplish an education. Levin (1993) rightly points out that conceptions of school reform almost always disregard the fact that students are beings *at work on themselves*. To honor this view of students would undermine the authority on which schooling is now conducted (i.e., schooling as a form of production). Educators, under the domination of scientism, have mistaken the seat of educational process, which in fact lies in students and not in the machinery of schooling.

The key act of the intellect is the making of meaning. An educated person, in our view, is one who becomes disposed to make meaning. How does this happen? What is the role of schooling in this development? Such questions must be answered if one views students as principal enactors of their own educations, as they must be in a schooling that nurtures intellect. How do they—and we—come to heed the call of intellectual stewardship?

A true education provides the conditions for what we are inclined to call "revelation" (or, much more blandly, "insight"). The key concepts here are "reveal," "hide," "vision," and "light." Insight provides a motive for meaning-making; one's vision penetrates a constellation of ideas and events, which tempts one to make sense of them all. Insight, however, is an ordinary event that comes often to those *already somewhat disposed to meaning-making*.

The term "revelation" applies more nearly to people from whom the objects of sight are hidden, and who experience a sudden and freshly experienced understanding. Such understanding comes as an epiphany. Revelation describes a more dramatic, more sudden, and more complex unfolding of meaning than "insight." Students are transformed by the revelations that comprise major events in their educations. In light of such revelations, students may proceed to a series of related insights, to new kinds or degrees of meaning-making, and to new actions in their lives.

A true education, one that entails the call to intellectual stewardship, would develop the conditions for such epiphanies. Most students now learn less than we intend, but with a true education most students would inevitably learn *much more than we intend*.

Epiphanies are inherent in the educational process, in a way that any body of works serving as canon can never be. While providing sudden access to a worthy source of meaning, such epiphanies make it possible for the meaning that students subsequently construct to help them reconstruct that source. It must be so, if the source of meaning is to endure.

Revelation concerns distance (from received wisdom) and vision (of individual insight). It also points to a preexisting meaning from which one is estranged, but which one may nonetheless seek. A true education endeavors always to bridge this distance. The schooling we practice, and the one that vested interests plan for the future, maintains rather than bridges this distance for most students, even those from privileged backgrounds.

This step is necessary because the power of any ruling class is constituted of a certain received wisdom, a certain sacred canon, whether the classical canon of humanism, the knowledge of science, or the word of God. If the received wisdom is *too* widely understood, *too* widely familiar, and *too* widely reinterpreted, then the basis of ruling-class power can be threatened. Mass schooling, as we practice it, ensures that meanings inimical to ruling-class power will remain obscure to most people.

Culture as intentional construction. A true education would constitute a commitment to culture as an intentional act of thoughtful beings through the practice of intellectual stewardship. A few teachers, working against the grain, always manage to convey this sense of education to their students. But most students still experience their schooling as unrelieved servitude that conditions them for a life of servitude to follow (Willis, 1977).

When schooling aims to produce patriotic jobholders, it removes itself from the realm of culture (cultivation, nurture, care for the intellect) and allies itself with manufacturing. The central activity is fabrication to order, with students conceived in great disrespect as the "raw material" on which teachers and administrators must work (Levin, 1993). A distorted scientism has tried to specify standardized procedures for this fabrication. The greatest distortion is the presumption that behavioral objectives, learner outcomes, graduation requirements, and world class standards will somehow yield learning and attitudes more agreeable to business. Bureaucrats, politicians, and functionaries describe all manner of actions and knowledge in terms of behavior in a vain attempt to ensure that teachers, children, and parents are sufficiently accountable to the state. These specifications are outrageous and offensive because they undermine the intentions of a true education.

Webb (1992), for instance, demonstrates the ridiculous implication of applying an outcome matrix to such objectives as "develops a sense of honesty." In Webb's example, the objective is attached to a matrix that would have teachers record "date taught" and "date mastered." This approach is not, in our experience, uncommon, despite its absurdity.

Such examples support a most unfortunate conclusion: American schooling, as an institution, is no longer capable of understanding the basis of a true education (i.e., culture, nurture, intellectual stewardship). Almost nowhere can one find a respectful attitude taken toward students as people whose learning depends most essentially on their own construction of themselves (Levin, 1993). Americans have almost no familiarity with the sort of schooling we imagine, except for the few teachers here and there who glimpse it for themselves and their students. Indeed, the principal reason *we* can imagine such forms of schooling is that such teachers have helped us.

Admittedly, the prospects for such a schooling are not very good, given the power deployed against it, a power that is already loudly proclaiming a quite different vision (e.g., Perelman, 1992). One may nonetheless enter the conversation, joined by good teachers always, about what schooling for a decent world would do and how one might get from the schooling we have to the schooling the world needs. The following sections of this chapter consider some of the features we imagine to be necessary and some of the strategies that might help them take shape.

THE ROLE OF TEACHERS

Schooling ought to cultivate a true education, assisting students to make personal and collective sense out of their encounters with the culture in both its intellectual and popular forms. This aim, which fundamentally overturns the conventions of schooling, calls forth teachers whose characteristics and practices would sustain their own intellectual growth and that of their students. In their classrooms such teachers would model virtues of reflection and action, and in their schools they would assume stewardship over the schoolwide practices that support an intellectual mission.

Interestingly, recent calls for educational reform—both from within and outside the educational establishment—appear to offer similar recommendations to these. On closer inspection, however, these reform proposals differ from those put forward here, construing the aims of education in different terms from those we elaborate. They frame concern for teacher competence and teacher empowerment in terms of the effects of these features of schooling on narrowly instrumental ends: students' scores on standardized tests, teachers' salaries, the global competitiveness of U.S. workers.

Throughout this book, we have made quite clear our reasons for judging such aims impoverished and, consequently, misdirected. Aims that accord with an intellectual culture of schooling, by contrast, presume a less instrumental interpretation of teachers' work. They depend on teachers to shape schools that are richer in, yet, at the same time, more skeptical of traditional academics than most schools, either those that already exist or those hoped for by contemporary reformers. Moreover, this reconception of teachers' work encompasses a vision of teachers who construct for themselves and honor through their customary practice a personal commitment to the life of the mind. Although this image of teaching is unlikely to take shape under current circumstances, we see a possible starting point for such revision in the programs within colleges and universities whose mission is to educate teachers.

Characteristics of Teacher-Scholars

Teachers who engage the intellect of their students must nurture intellect for and within themselves. Such teachers are, in important ways, perpetual students: They attend to significant works in their fields, they pursue scholarly projects of their own conception, and they take pedagogical encounters as opportunities for reflective inquiry.

Such teachers are rare, at least in contemporary K–12 schools, but they are not altogether absent from that context. In general, however, the work of self-consciously intellectual teachers—those whom we call teacher-scholars—has neither been examined nor reported, although the occasional exemplar earns public acclaim. Jaime Escalante, for example, an East Los Angeles math teacher, achieved widespread recognition for teaching calculus to Hispanic students whose backgrounds suggested that they would be less than apt pupils. And we periodically hear reports of programs that bring writers, artists, and scientists into public school classrooms as intellectual role models. Moreover, there are some inspiring accounts of reflective educators, including those whose work defies the conventional logic of the "hidden curriculum."

The intellectual qualities of teacher-scholars. Construed as central to schools' intellectual mission, teaching becomes an enterprise of considerable intensity and scope. Even under the current regimen of schooling, the work of teachers is physically tiring and, often, emotionally draining. Indeed, the physical and emotional demands of public school teaching actually seem to interfere with the potential of teachers to address its intellectual challenges. Within their work day, teachers typically lack the time (or the administrative support) to read pertinent literature, to design or carry out research, or even to engage in meaningful dialogue with their colleagues.

These are, nonetheless, the sorts of things that teachers ought to be doing routinely. Whereas this conception of teachers' work requires obvious changes in the culture of schools, it also requires that people with different views of their role and different proclivities choose to become teachers. Neither the characteristics of teachers nor those of schools exist independently of one another; and, in general, the teachers who are suited to or become tolerant of the nature of the work are the ones who remain in the classroom.

If that work were reconceived, different sorts of people would likely find it rewarding. Notably, we believe that schools whose mission was primarily intellectual would attract teachers who saw their identity bound up with some type of scholarly pursuit. These teacher-scholars would devote themselves to reasoned inquiry, and they would support their devotion through continual attention to the questions posed, answered, and reframed by the disciplines of the liberal arts. In addition, we imagine that many teacher-scholars would connect their teaching to generative practices acquired through sustained involvement with an artistic medium.

The cultivation of intellect requires teachers to articulate complex ideas and ask stimulating questions—practices supported in large measure by teachers' abstract reasoning. Moreover, reasoned inquiry undergirds the scholarly work that teacher-scholars pursue on their own, whether that work proceeds from reflection on subject matter or pedagogy. Although the disposition to reason abstractly does not assure reflective practice, it does augment teachers' efforts to make thoughtful interpretations of the complexities of classroom life. Such interpretations, coupled with the willingness to experiment with techniques of teaching, form the basis for teaching practice rooted in what Rexford Brown (1993) calls "the higher literacies."

We realize, of course, that many highly intelligent people—excellent abstract reasoners—would not make good teachers. Nevertheless, we cannot endorse the myth put forth by some teacher educators that abstract reasoning (often construed in this myth-making as "intelligence") and teaching ability are unrelated.[1] Furthermore, we suspect that a positive association between these characteristics would be more likely in schools whose focus was on intellectual matters predominantly.

To attend well to intellect, teachers would also bring to bear on their practice a strong academic grounding in the humanities and sciences. This background would enable them to draw upon and recount significant cultural understandings and to introduce students to various ways of constructing, deconstructing, and reconstructing meaning. Certainly, if K–12 schools were to incorporate a liberal arts curriculum, teachers would themselves need to be well-versed in such an approach to the production, transmission, and transformation of knowledge.

In addition, experience with one or more of the arts would enhance teachers' sensitivity to aesthetic modes of expression including, perhaps, teaching itself. By virtue of their own creative activities, such teachers would tend to be flexible and tolerant of ambiguity. Such characteristics should predispose them to nurture the inquisitiveness and divergent expression of students. Moreover, teachers who were accustomed to critiques — of their own artistic productions and those of others — would be likely to view critique as a positive feature of intellectual discourse. Permitting critique to infuse classroom discussion, such teachers would support the development of students' powers of discernment. Students would thereby learn to take an active part in the interplay of creation and interpretation that constitutes the making of meaning generally.

The moral virtues of teacher-scholars. As with the intellectual virtues, teacher-scholars would both model and guide students in the practices of moral reasoning and ethical action. In a school centered on intellectual nurture, reasoned dialogue about moral dilemmas would, in our view, constitute the most worthy approach. Nevertheless, we recognize that character may be formed more through unconscious modeling than through rational decision making, so teachers wishing to cultivate moral virtues among their students must also serve as exemplars. Of particular significance to the academic enterprise would be their modeling of virtues such as fairness, intellectual honesty, integrity, and respect for others.

Furthermore, the critical and emancipatory role that we believe teachers should play implies that they take a moral position with respect to the machinations and products of the political economy. In assuming this role, however, teachers must be particularly careful not to inculcate particular orthodoxies (left, right, or center). Instead, they should stimulate critical examination of the social world, thoughtful consideration of the meanings embedded in the various constructions of that world, and imaginative discourse about alternate possibilities.

The Intellectual School Culture

In order to accommodate an intellectual mission, schooling — no less than teaching — must change. Such change would depend on massive restructuring of schools as organizations and would implicate funding, governance, and, most notably, the roles and functions of personnel. Because our discussion attends particularly to the work of teachers, we will address specific changes in their role and in the conditions of their work.

The relationship between teachers and students. Central to the intellectual climate of schools is a certain quality to the interactions between teachers and students. These interactions, more than any other feature of the school experience, convey to students crucial messages about the nature of knowledge, sources of authority, and habits of scholarship. In most K–12 schools students acquire a naive view of knowledge as factual information whose grounding depends on authorization from inaccessible sources outside of themselves. This message has the effect of convincing students to become passive, uncritical consumers of information.

Teachers concerned with intellectual nurture, however, would encourage students to adopt a more dynamic view of knowledge and their relationship to it. By the way they treat knowledge within classroom discourse, teachers could acquaint students with a view of knowledge that places the knowing subject, rather than the object of knowledge, at the center of the interpretive process of constructing meaning.

Teachers would support learning, viewed as the social and personal construction of meaning, first by relinquishing claim to absolute authority within their classrooms. In fact, this view of learning requires students and teachers to regard all authority with appropriate skepticism. In this way students would come to scrutinize the sources of authority as well as the received wisdom authorized by those sources. By using their own reasoning processes to examine and filter competing claims, students would learn to trust intellect as an accessible, even liberating (though obviously imperfect) arbiter of truth.

For teachers to engage students in this intellectual work, they must be released from many of the constraints imposed by external sources — administrators, local boards, state education agencies. They must take charge of the construction and delivery of the curriculum, by attending both to the concerns of local community members and to the requirements of the larger communities of learning of which they are a part. Moreover, to assure their stewardship over the curriculum, teachers must take control of the school policies and organizational arrangements that influence the content and presentation of the curriculum. In collaboration with colleagues and parents, each teacher needs the freedom to shape school experiences in ways that bring together favorably the important sources of meaning found in local and intellectual culture.

Freedom, autonomy, and collaboration. In some senses, however, teachers already have considerable freedom to put into place instructional practices of their own choosing. Why, then, does this autonomy so often lead teachers to select conventional rather than innovative practices? And why does it reinforce rather than break down teachers' isolation from one another?

These circumstances result from the mechanistic way in which schooling is most often conceived. Under this construction, teachers' freedom of choice is limited to preordained options. Teachers have autonomy to "choose" instructional practices in much the same way that consumers have the "choice" to purchase one or another brand of soap. In fact, under this regimen, vendors frequently package instructional practices as products and target teachers as a ready (and presumably naive) market. Furthermore, as with other markets, vendors have a material interest in structuring individual tastes so as to manipulate collective determinations of value.

The marketplace conception of freedom is an impoverished one, even as it pertains to soap. But its application to teaching is a thorough misconstruction: The type of freedom that teachers require is of a wholly different sort than mere choosing.

For teachers to engage an intellectual mission, they *must* have the autonomy to sponsor dialogue (among themselves and with community members) that examines the value of educational aims and the merits of instructional practices. Linda McNeil and others who advocate teacher empowerment capture some of what we intend when they emphasize the role of autonomy in giving teachers scope to "place their students and their subjects at the center of their teaching" (McNeil, 1988, p. 482).

Along with these educators, we believe teaching entails a necessary balance between individual decision making within the classroom and collaborative decision making within the school and community. This sense of what is meant by "autonomy" assumes that teachers will work collaboratively with peers and community members to examine educational beliefs and practices and to recast them in accord with a consensual vision of the school's aims and pedagogy. Autonomy of this sort implies that teachers will play a significant but not domineering role in shaping the culture of the schools in which they work.

The role of teachers in school governance. A body of literature about "good schools" suggests that this type of autonomy works to transform school culture in ways that support an intellectual mission. Lightfoot (1986, p. 24) describes the culture of six schools that have undergone such transformation:

> In these good schools the image is one of teachers with voice and vision. Teachers are knowledgeable and discerning school actors who are the primary shapers of the educational environment. They are given a great deal of autonomy and authority in defining the intellectual agenda, but their individual quests are balanced against the requirement that they contribute to the broader school community.

Although Lightfoot and others have found schools where teachers assume a central role in governance, schools typically are not organized to accommodate the involvement of teachers in schoolwide decision making. Most schools can give teachers neither the time nor the ultimate control over programs and resources to assure their ongoing participation in governance. And schools are so overburdened with externally imposed requirements that governance is more a matter of identifying routes to compliance than of shaping the features of a coherent educational program.

An intellectual mission for schools, however, requires teachers to collaborate in formulating programs that are coherent yet responsive to the needs of particular students and groups. Programs that embody these features must be constructed, monitored, and reworked at the school site by the teachers who deliver them. Entrusting teachers with stewardship of this sort will, of course, require substantial increases in the funding of schools; it will also require changes in the way that time and resources are allocated within schools themselves.

Educating Intellectual Teachers

There is no readily identifiable group of people who could become teachers of the sort we imagine or function in the roles we envision. Neither practicing teachers (as a group) nor those individuals currently preparing to become teachers have the background or, for that matter, the inclination to make the necessary changes. Moreover, no other group (for example, liberal arts majors) is any better able to match the characteristics or understand the role that we propose for teachers.

For such teachers to come into being, therefore, colleges and universities must cultivate them by substantially altering programs that educate teachers. These programs need to become more exclusive with regard to entry requirements as well as more intellectually challenging. In addition to studies in the liberal arts, these programs should incorporate the foundation studies that acquaint prospective teachers with significant theories underlying pedagogical practice. Further, these programs should give education students experiences teaching children and adolescents in the ways that best work to nurture talent. Providing this kind of background to prospective teachers can be accomplished through the careful combination of particular sorts of liberal arts and pedagogical studies.

The role of the liberal arts. As we suggested earlier, the liberal arts—especially when taught from a critical vantage—offer important insights into the human condition and some of its myriad interpretations. Additionally, grounding in the liberal arts furnishes experience with modes of inquiry and analysis that can help individuals make sense out of their own lives and those of their compatriots. Moreover, the liberal arts sharpen and elaborate discourse, better enabling people to participate in the dialogues that shape interpersonal relations and inform political participation.

These outcomes provide the rationale for our proposal to incorporate study of the liberal arts into K–12 schools as a principal means to develop the intellectual talents of schoolchildren. But clearly, if such studies are to become a significant part of the education of public school students, they must first infuse the programs that educate teachers. We believe further that the intellectual mentoring that is crucial to the development of intellect in children must also be demonstrated first to teachers by their college professors. Since most teachers will be providing instruction in subjects other than those foundational to pedagogy, their liberal arts—not their education—professors ought to be the ones to serve in this mentoring role.

Of course, most teacher education programs already require students to complete general education requirements, most of which entail study in the liberal arts. In addition, such programs require prospective teachers of academic subjects in secondary school to complete majors in liberal arts fields. These requirements, however, have not resulted in the types of learning that we would hope for. We believe, therefore, that in order for such studies to become central to the education of teacher-scholars, colleges must revisit their liberal arts curricula with the intention of sharpening the focus on interpretation, inquiry, and critique.

Pedagogy as reasoning. A program to educate prospective teacher-scholars needs also to incorporate foundation studies and practical experiences. These parts of the teacher education program ought to accomplish two major objectives. First, they should offer insight into the scholarly traditions that support instructional practice: philosophy, for its consideration of the aims of education; psychology, for its study of child development and learning theory; and sociology, for its study of the relationship between schools and society. Second, these parts of the program should acquaint prospective teacher-scholars with the processes of pedagogical reasoning and give them opportunities to engage in such reasoning as they plan and deliver instruction to school-aged children.

Viewing teaching as pedagogical reasoning conceives it as an intellectual process involving informed, ethical judgment in the choice of content and technique and continual inquiry into and reflection about the effects of such content and technique in accomplishing instructional aims (see e.g., Feiman-Nemser & Buchmann, 1986; Onosko, 1989; Schaefer, 1967; Shulman, 1987). Conceived in this way, the teaching process interposes action and reasoning. According to Shulman (1987, p. 13), "teaching begins with an act of reason, continues with a process of reasoning, culminates in performances of imparting, eliciting, involving, or enticing, and is then thought about some more until the process can begin again."

To give prospective teacher-scholars occasion to reason in these ways, teacher education programs must provide opportunities for practice teaching and reflection about that teaching. Typical student teaching experiences, however, tend to subvert rather than promote this aim. They socialize prospective teachers to accept an instrumental view of the purposes of education and to develop a pragmatic reliance on conventional classroom routines.

Because we believe that the cultivation of a new sort of teacher must prefigure changes in the culture of schools, we are suggesting that student teaching experiences should be quite carefully designed to assure that prospective teachers have the chance to engage in reflective practice: to discover the character and background of their students, to experiment with instructional content and method, and to critique their own teaching and that of others.

In Chapter 2, we argued that teachers play a central role in determining the intellectual focus of schools, yet we noted that most practicing teachers do not particularly value intellectual work or contribute to a school culture that sustains it. Here we have described teachers who, by virtue of their characteristics, could nurture the intellect of students if they were provided the support to do so. We have also suggested the nature of the roles that such teachers should play in schools and the types of educational experiences that they would need in order to assume these roles. In the next section, which parallels Chapter 4, we observe that intellectual stewardship cannot be practiced unless equity is assured.

ASSURING EQUITY

Stewardship of the intellect entails more than simple fairness. For instance, certain pedagogical assumptions — such as the hereditarian premise of innately different levels of intelligence — can be implemented fairly in ways that nonetheless lead to outcomes that destroy talent and subvert intellect. And certain liberal programs — such as life adjustment, career education, and leadership training — can also lead to similarly disabling outcomes.

In our conception of intellect, however, equity is inherent. Lacking equity, intellect cannot survive. Indeed, the threat under which intellect persists in our culture is one of the symptoms of the inequality that pervades our society, an affluent society that has chosen to sacrifice or suppress much that has value. Intellect continues to be numbered among the victims.

Egalitarian Premises

Care for the intellect rests on egalitarian premises. Humans *are* created equal, though they do not enter this world in equally secure environments. Their familiar circumstances (homes, neighborhoods, schools) differ so dramatically that it is easy to forget humans' essential similarities. Both care for the intellect and faith in human potential require that we remember these similarities.

Human potential is not principally a phenomenon of individuals, but within and among cultures. Intellect, moreover, is a construction of culture and not principally of individuals, no matter how great their particular contributions may seem. Intellect derives its strength from many sources. The strong voices of individual intellects are essential, but we often forget that such voices are neither completely self-created nor can they, once mature, achieve full self-sufficiency. When schooling fails to develop intellectual capacity widely among rising generations, construction of intellect falters. This circumstance is already well upon us (Postman, 1992).

Three egalitarian premises underlie our view of schooling for the intellect:

- All humans have substantial intellectual capacity.
- A decent life requires intellectual development.
- Developing the intellect is a shared responsibility.

The first premise acknowledges something like the optimism of the reform-minded bromide, "All children can learn." But it more strongly asserts that all children are capable of the intellectual development that constitutes the realization of their human potential. Schooling that would give job training to some students and liberal learning to others violates this premise.

The second premise addresses the relevance of care for the intellect to the good life. It insists that the good life cannot be defined by the requirements of jobholding, capital accumulation, or restoration of America's postwar global economic dominion. Making meaning is the most essential part of leading an ethical life.

The third premise concerns stewardship. Care for the intellect, as we have seen, entails involvement with past and future generations. In the present, it especially concerns the conversation we enact with each other about ethical, political, and aesthetic issues as we attempt to understand the natural and human world.

These premises have implications for schooling, especially in view of the fact that American bureaucrats and politicians have so badly misconstrued the mission of schooling. Both intellect and liberal learning, in their construction, are featured as adornments of the elite, with acknowledged status value for the few. The implications of intellect for a just society are regarded at best as an impractical matter; at worst, intellect is regarded as the enemy of good order and a source of pointless discontent (e.g., Hofstadter, 1963; Wiener, 1950).

Egalitarian premises have much more to do with according respect to individuals whose circumstances differ than with the presumption of conformity to a mythical norm. This respect entails giving every human liberty to implement a distinct individuality. Humans, of course, differ in the ways in which they accomplish their own development (assisted or frustrated by schooling and other features of their environments), as well as in the meaning they derive from their educations. Egalitarian premises allow for differences in the individuation of intellect, but they nonetheless make the commitment of intellectual stewardship incumbent on every human individually and on humanity generally.

Care for the intellect suffers under autocratic premises precisely because such premises exhibit disrespect for (1) the individuality of divergent intellects, and (2) the general stewardship of the mind's critical faculty. The autocratic view, instead, specifies certain bodies of knowledge, skills, or attitudes hypothetically to serve normatively useful ends: problem-solving skills to restore economic competitiveness, for instance. Autocratic premises cultivate the instrumental view of education that dominates so much of the official discourse about schooling in America. This discourse and its valued instrumentalities obscure intellect as an educational issue, as well as the egalitarian premises on which intellectual stewardship must rest.

The Problem of Readiness

Liberal learning does not constitute elite culture except when appropriated most fully — as in the present — by a ruling class. Our way of schooling reinforces this appropriation by relegating education for employability to the masses and a vitiated liberal education, as a high-status adornment, to the ruling elite. Schooling helps most people to regard themselves as unworthy of liberal learning, while restraining the profoundly subversive character of liberal learning (Marcuse, 1978) by restricting its access to the ruling elite.

The concept of "readiness" has been applied by American educators to generations of children to suggest that children from some origins are not prepared to benefit from instruction. Typically, educators interpret the concept in relation to early learning, as in the construct "reading readiness."

But in the first National Education Goal, the term is used somewhat more broadly to refer to "school readiness." This goal — "All children in America will start school ready to learn" — refers principally to children from backgrounds recognized as so impoverished that they endanger young children's well-being. No reasonable person can interpret this goal as lying within the province of schooling. The danger into which "unready" children are born is an issue of political and economic justice. When the government interprets this circumstance as an issue of *schooling*, it deflects critique of the economic forms and social policies that allocate danger to these young children.

The concept of readiness, then, can apply to any person significantly endangered by the circumstances of life. When no program of social change or economic entitlement addresses the dangers, the government can claim that underprivileged children are not "ready" for the rigors of schooling. This lack of readiness, of course, pertains to the *instrumental form of education* offered by American schools to working-class and underprivileged children, not to an education that practices intellectual stewardship. Common sense would dictate that only the elite are "ready" for such an experience. This conclusion is convenient, since it is the elite, principally, who are exposed to this sort of education. Many teachers in elite schools, of course, report that among their students are those who are not "ready" for what they have to offer (e.g., Katchadourian & Boli, 1985).

Despite the cynicism inherent in the metaphor of readiness, which presents injustice as lack of preparedness, the observation that desperate straits distract or devastate the mind (as with in utero drug addiction) is abundantly clear. What might schools do better under conditions of desperation?

Early language. Facility with language is a prerequisite of intellectual development. Intellectual stewardship among young children implies the cultivation of all sorts of linguistic reception and expression. Maria Montessori understood this principle well in the program she devised for children of Italy's urban slums (a program now widely used with America's most affluent youngsters). The manners and forms of linguistic exchange may follow quite different conventions among different cultural groups, but the principle remains the same. Children need to observe, practice, and master increasingly complex linguistic forms. These observations apply throughout the elementary years, not just to early childhood education. The Montessori example illustrates that linguistically rich environments need *not* be unstructured, even though children do acquire language incidentally in such environments.

The richness of environments intentionally structured to cultivate language development depends more on the linguistic engagement and commitment of the teacher with students than on any particular method. In typical American classrooms, convention dictates that teachers consider only familiar circumstances with children, that new vocabulary be introduced slowly and carefully. In view of the way children learn language (at very young ages, without systematic instruction), this practice is peculiar. It serves to retard intellectual growth, rather than to advance it. We would have teachers use unfamiliar vocabulary, and entice children with stories of things and ideas unfamiliar to them. We do not suggest, of course, that teachers purposely baffle their students, but that they intrigue them with new words and expressions that will represent to children where their minds can take them.

These observations, of course, apply principally to children who are not facing extraordinary challenges (addiction, mental impairment, severe emotional difficulties). But the basic principle of using language to enrich and intrigue *will* apply even in many of these cases. In too many American classrooms the range of permissible expression is unnaturally curtailed (Brown, 1993).

Critical literacy. Intellect, we have said, is the critical faculty of the mind. Its development requires cross-generational nurture, and reading is the richest route to such nurture. Literacy is not by any means required, though, for the development of an individual intellect. One can develop critical faculties that represent the wisdom of generations without the ability to read and write. In indigenous cultures throughout the world elders articulate wisdom in other ways—apprenticeships, trials of experience, observation and practice, and disciplined action.

Learning to read and write, however, is the traditional purpose of going to school—employability, but not intellectual stewardship, requires it. Schooling to prepare students for jobs, however, cannot engage and in fact must subvert *critical* literacy: Its instrumentality necessarily construes reading and writing mostly as a mechanism for information exchange. Intellectual stewardship, when carried on as a literate process, however, understands reading and writing to serve the purposes of critique. Literacy functions to constitute, preserve, disband, and reconceive the world at the behest of the intellect (in its individual and cultural forms).

Critical literacy, we believe, cannot be nurtured in students unless they write. Most students learn to read well, in the sense that they can read to acquire information. Seldom do they learn to read critically, however, because reading critically can only be enacted in the context of an immanent production. That is, rather than extracting information, students must read in order to formulate (and warrant) their own interpretations of a phenomenon. American schooling has not been constructed to nurture students in this skill. Teachers write less well than they read, and few choose to write as a way to make sense of their experience as teachers or as persons (Mitchell, 1979).

A great deal of good work has been done in the last decade to describe the processes by which students can learn to write well (and thereby read more critically). But, in fact, no reasonable amount of staff development can convert masses of teachers into critical readers, unless, in the process, they become careful writers. The apprenticeship for careful writing will be as long for most teachers as for most students. Teachers who can show students how to write well, who will spend hours providing well-considered editorial comments to students, who can set up and direct cooperative writing teams, and who can exhibit their own productions to students are very rare. They are a scarce resource whose allocation to the privileged is wrongly justified by the concept of "readiness."

Because of the way Americans run public schools, most students will never be "ready" for critical literacy construed in this way. In our view, however, nearly everyone who can read functionally is ready for critical literacy. Our schooling need only supply the conditions necessary — mainly, capable teachers committed to stewardship of intellect.

Lived experience. American schooling is presented by politicians and bureaucrats (and many educational functionaries) as something practical for the masses — job training, functional literacy, problem-solving skills, indoctrination in attitudes useful in employment. Common people can do well without the adornments of the elite, in this view. Schooling ought instead to prepare average people for highly skilled jobholding. This misconstruction de-emphasizes intellectual development throughout our culture and society; worse still, it misrepresents liberal learning as inapplicable to lived experience.

Public schools in wealthy neighborhoods *can* provide a more elite education than schools in impoverished neighborhoods. The public nature even of wealthy schools, however, also ensures that jobholding will remain a prominent aim, and that liberal learning will persist as a status adornment. Only in elite private schools, whose traditions parallel those of elite colleges, is patriotic jobholding held in contempt as an educational aim (e.g., Jackson, 1981).

Democracy cannot be sustained by either part — elite or common — of such an educational system. Too few people will be able to approach the wisdom that a vigorous democracy requires. Instead, they will consume their lives in performing jobs and shopping, if their lives are favored. If their lives are unfavored, then envy, resentment, and self-destructive practices will consume them.

The practices and devotions that democracy requires in order to flourish do not emerge from thoughtless patriotism or the uncritical performance of jobs. If we are to maintain a democracy, stewardship of the intellect of all citizens is essential. Through schooling, the state can further the aims of democracy by supporting the conditions that make dialogue possible, but the state can neither shape intellect nor create democracy. Intellectual stewardship and democratic participation are committed actions that citizens take on behalf of one another.

Access to a Curriculum for the Intellect

The best curricula retain an "academic" focus. By this expression we mean to indicate curricula that aim to develop critical literacy, not merely functional literacy as now cultivated by mass education (i.e., drill-and-kill instructional routines). Students should quickly pick up the functional skills of reading and calculating, and there is no reason inherent in American students that this accomplishment should take anything near 8 or 12 years. We remain convinced that all "average" students can learn these functional skills in 5 or 6 years at most. This accomplishment usually takes much longer in this most affluent of countries — even among the privileged — because our real concerns have to do with cultivating conformity and ensuring custodial care.

Care for the intellect should, however, become the primary concern for all educators and for all students, but we would hardly commend a single academic curriculum (cf. Adler, 1982; Bennett, 1988). Whether all students should read *Julius Caesar* (or, indeed, even one play by Shakespeare) or whether they should all take shop, a second language, or geometry seems like an absurd question to us. Our 1986 text, *Teaching Gifted Children*, contains some recommendations about curriculum planning for individual gifted students in conventional schools. Our point there was to ensure some balance between school subjects related to the humanities and those related to the natural sciences. In general, the idea that students could exercise some latitude in choosing a course of study, but should not be permitted to ignore one form of knowledge still strikes us as quite reasonable.

In this book, however, we are discussing the broad characteristics of an education that would nurture intellect. And we think that schools of this sort should construct academic curricula that are intellectually pertinent to the lives of the students attending them. In African-American schools, for instance, the literature curriculum could well concentrate on African and

African-American literature, though we think it would be foolish to ignore altogether literature in other traditions. The same observation can apply to schools that serve a preponderance of any ethnic group. Nor would we have any difficulty endorsing a school that offered a variety of sections of a literature course, with sections divided along ethnic lines. The real issues with us are these: What is the quality of instruction? Are students learning to read critically? To write well?

These issues seem less contentious — even less relevant — in the natural sciences, but the seeming lack of ambiguity and relevance is merely apparent. The nature of scientific knowledge is changing rapidly (e.g., Gleick, 1987; Hawking, 1988), and concern about the social role of science has occupied thoughtful science teachers for over a decade (AAAS, 1989). The work of the National Council of Teachers of Mathematics (NCTM), moreover, is reconstructing mathematics instruction and curriculum dramatically. The nature of these changes, in fact, is to point up the importance of critical literacy for instruction in the natural sciences.

Keeping journals, writing as a way to participate in distance education projects, oral defenses and explications of one's own thought processes — such activities are recommended to mathematics and science teachers. Indeed, the importance of analysis, introspection, and various forms of reflection to the substance of scientific and mathematical thinking may mean that such activities will find a more ready acceptance among many teachers in the natural sciences than in subjects of the humanities (whose relevance the culture so discredits).

Value of assuring access. Education inevitably consists of much more than preparation for a job, whether or not we practice a schooling that nurtures intellect. And beyond ourselves, perhaps only a few people exert a memorable effect on the development of each of us. A form of schooling that provided a curriculum for the intellect, however, would cultivate habits of mind that allowed students to continue to implement their own intellectual development continuously, by virtue of their own authority and under their own power.

Both the canon and the anticanon seem equally important to us as constructive of such a curriculum. Ideally, all students would learn that the world differs radically from the one they think they see just over the sills of the classroom windows, the one they know so well. In constructing curriculum, however, wise educators bind themselves to their students' origins, that is, to where their students are coming from. By examining and building on the meanings that seem familiar, students learn that the world they think they know so well — their immediate world — differs somewhat from their image of it. Access to a curriculum for the intellect must exploit such openings so that students can begin to construct bridges between the narrow worlds that seem so familiar and the wider ones that seem so foreign.

The most difficult circumstances that human beings face are questions related to identity and justice; an education that fails to equip students who can apply reason to the consideration of these circumstances is *profoundly* useless (Bell, 1976). Useful ideas with which to approach these questions come from all historical periods — and, in this view, Greek philosophy and drama may easily be more pertinent than contemporary social criticism (cf. Arendt, 1954/1968, 1958).

In fact, an education of this sort would cultivate two "useful" outcomes among many students. First, it would help all students to distinguish between work and jobholding. Work concerns a calling, some answer to higher purpose, to a worldview or to an idea around which one organizes one's life. Jobs or careers can be part of the exercise of a calling, of course, but work as a calling answers principally to the ideas a person understands and the things a person finds of value.

The second useful outcome is more nearly instrumental. People schooled under a regimen of intellectual stewardship would be more academically competent than those schooled under the current authoritarian regimen of patriotic jobholding. A schooling that practiced intellectual stewardship and cultivated critical literacy widely would seemingly endow people with many of the traits that business interests say the coming century will demand. The drawback is that though such people *will* be more adaptable, they are also likely to be more broadly critical of the social and political positions that business interests represent. Part of the fear that businesses have of this sort of education stems from the comparatively well established leftist tendencies of the professorate, especially in the humanities and social sciences (Hamilton & Hargens, 1993).

Challenging social forces that limit access. Most of our discussion about the intellectual potentials of schooling has concerned the dilemmas of curriculum and instruction — the substance and processes of schooling. We have acknowledged how very difficult it will be to build a system of schooling capable of an intellectual mission. Isolated individuals can, and do, practice this sort of pedagogy even within existing schools. They are the exceptions. Multiplying these exceptions in order to ensure widespread access, however, requires two sorts of equality, of financial support ("inputs") and accomplishment ("outputs").

Equity, we noted, is a condition of intellectual stewardship and of respect for human potential. Historical concern for educational equity, however, has more to do with the shift from provisioning the educational enterprise, or inputs, to a concern for its results, or outputs (Margolis &

Moses, 1992). The Coleman Report of 1966 marks this change, for Coleman reported that inputs had very little influence on the results of schooling. Educators — particularly researchers — widely misinterpreted this finding to mean that schools were somehow useless, that they were not the path to upward mobility that the American ideology had always held them to be. As a result of this shift, inequity became a much more serious threat to the legitimacy of schooling.

Educators since that time have tended to regard Coleman as somehow unpatriotic. The school effectiveness "movement" of the late 1970s and early 1980s was the direct ideological result — based only in part on research, much of it a project of high-inference reasoning derived from the study of statistical outliers (exceptions to the general tendencies) — and its key object was *equity of outcomes*. The movement faltered, however, largely as a result of its inability to generalize the claims it made for the research on which its program of improvement was based. Lack of generalizability, of course, is easily attributed to the idiosyncratic nature of outliers and the difficulty of reproducing the conditions that characterize them.

Fundamental principles of equity dictate that funding (e.g., on a per-pupil basis) of schools ought to be equal, but some researchers (e.g., Hanushek, 1989) conclude that the level of resources devoted to operating schools has little, if any, systematic influence on students' learning. The instrumental view of education warrants existing, observable differences in funding levels as a matter of taste: If wealthy districts spend money on amenities and adornments, at least no one is thereby harmed (according to the verifiable findings of scientific research). The rich, in this view, can maintain symbols of their high status with no damage to the common good.

But we observe, by contrast, that cultivation of the intellect requires equal access to pleasant surroundings, highly qualified teachers, and ample instructional equipment and supplies. Access to equally good resources lets all students (and their parents) know that they are equally important to the commonweal. The courts seem to agree, because, in state after state, they have regarded unequal funding with suspicion. In spite of the tenuous empirical connection between the "inputs" and "outcomes" of education, the courts nevertheless fault state education agencies for tolerating such inequalities among districts.

Faith in human potential also suggests to us that a schooling based on care for the intellect of all students would succeed in cultivating accomplishments of equal value among all students. This goal, however, does not impose any particular body of knowledge (canon) or any particular level of achievement on individuals. It *does* suggest that achievement levels among *groups* of students ought to be very nearly the same. This "output" cannot emerge, over many years, without equality of funding that is adequate for schooling with an intellectual mission and educational practice that implements that mission. [2]

The hidden resources that might support education in the United States — that *do*, in part, support education in nations such as Norway, Sweden, Germany, Switzerland, and Japan (where educational performance on international tests is arguably superior to that in the United States) — reside principally in two quarters: in the military budget and in transfer payments. Jacobs (1984) refers to these two classes of expenditure as "transactions of decline," notable sources of political economic suicide principally because they are economically counterproductive.

The United States maintains the largest standing professional army in the world, augmented by citizen militias ("the National Guard" and "the Reserves") in virtually every community in the nation. Mr. Eisenhower warned the nation that this relationship ("the military-industrial complex") was politically and economically destructive. It persists nonetheless.

Transfer payments include what Turner and Starnes (1976) have called "wealthfare" payments (domestic transfers to the wealthy) and welfare payments (to the indigent). The unadvertised fact is that aggregate entitlements to "wealthfare" exceed, by a factor of three, aggregate entitlements to welfare. This situation has worsened considerably — principally during 12 years of conservative rule — since Turner and Starnes coined their ironic term (Lichter & Eggebeen, 1993).

Developing political access to these resources will be very difficult. Carnoy (1982) reminds us that the availability of educational funds is a function of political contest with business interests, who exercise dominant power, and that the state is hardly a neutral arbiter in the contest. This internal economic domination is the domestic equivalent of the sought-after international economic hegemony explicitly represented in *Nation at Risk* and the National Education Goals. Rather than diverting their attention to issues of readiness, educators ought to participate in political struggles to wrest the resources that adequate and equitable funding for schooling requires.

RETHINKING GIFTED EDUCATION

Even in schools that make conscious and thoughtful efforts to widen access to intellectual traditions, there will be students who find such traditions particularly compelling and those who do not. In addition, efforts to offset economic and social barriers to cognitive development will succeed in equalizing academic aptitude only to a certain degree: Some students will still learn faster than others, even if the discrepancy between the most and least rapid learners is decreased.

In Chapter 3, we discussed the association between rapid learning and receptivity to intellectual studies in schools as we currently know them; and we defined gifted students as those who, by virtue of their rapid learning, are particularly well-prepared to engage in challenging intellectual work. We are not certain, however, if this association will obtain in schools of the sort we imagine. In fact, we are hopeful that it will not. We hope, rather, that such schools will accommodate rapid learners, giving them every opportunity to expand their intellectual horizons and, at the same time, will so dilate the experiences of less rapid learners as to prepare them to pursue to the depth and breadth that they wish intellectual studies of any sort.

We suspect that these altered conditions in schools will necessitate gifted education that is quite different from that required now. Our previous writings have argued that, given the way schools currently function, gifted education ought to provide difficult intellectual work for the most academically apt (e.g., Howley et al., 1986; Pendarvis et al., 1990). Our vision in this book has been, however, of schools that nurture the talents of all students. The development of intellect ought, in this view, to be the birthright of all children; and challenging but satisfying intellectual work ought to be a privilege that all students enjoy.

Special Arrangements for the Gifted

If schools were to change in the ways we imagine, we believe they would better serve most children. Nonetheless, particular arrangements would still be required for certain groups of children. Schools, for example, would need to identify the best ways to educate children with disabilities, and clearly, for children with moderate and severe mental impairments the intellectual focus appropriate for most students would be unsuitable. We suspect, however, that concerned teachers would find ways to support the intellectual development of those disabled students for whom academic studies might provide significant benefit and that they would find appropriate alternatives for the very few students unlikely to benefit from such study. Our discussion here, however, will not examine these possibilities. Instead, it will focus on the special education necessary for two groups of children who, in schools as we imagine them, would still be identified as unusually talented: exceptionally rapid learners and learners with pronounced artistic talents.

The education of rapid learners. As a result of some, as yet unspecified, concordance of native proclivity and early stimulation, certain children will continue to learn some things at an extremely rapid pace. Among these children, many will learn rapidly most academic subjects, but some will advance especially rapidly in just one domain—either the verbal or the mathematical. All such children will need to receive instruction that matches the pace of their learning, however.

Ironically, accelerated instruction will be harder to provide in the sorts of schools we envision than it is in schools as they are currently structured. Most schools now conceptualize the curriculum as sequences of increasingly more complex skills and facts. Acceleration involves placing students further along in these sequences than they would normally be placed as a result of chronological age. In schools with an intellectual focus, this basis for acceleration would probably make sense in the early elementary years when instruction involves considerable attention to skill acquisition; it might also make sense in subjects like mathematics, where the sequence of the curriculum is based, at least in theory, on the hierarchical structure of the discipline itself.

In general, however, instruction designed to cultivate intellectual talent will not be organized on the basis of artificial hierarchies. Particular works of literature will not, for example, be arranged sequentially according to some arbitrary developmental plan. Instead, the possibilities for inquiry and critique will be explored at every point in the curriculum that provides them an opening. Moreover, the increasing sophistication of discourse at higher grade levels is likely to be associated more with maturation and emerging wisdom than with precocious verbal mastery.

Given these circumstances, acceleration for rapid learners may involve some combination of features: curriculum compacting in the early grades, fast-paced instruction in some subjects (e.g., math and foreign language), and modifications of expectations within the uniform curricular sequence in other subjects (e.g., literature and history). We imagine, however, that teacher-scholars, attuned to the relationship between intellectual challenge and intellectual growth, will make the adjustments necessary to assure that rapid learners, like other students, routinely engage in difficult but rewarding intellectual work. A commitment to equity demands intellectual challenge in the education of rapid learners not only so that these students accomplish all that they possibly can but also so that they come to respect the limits of what they, as individuals, can accomplish.

The education of artistically talented students. We have discussed the role of the arts in the construction of meaning and advocate a curriculum that explores aesthetic as well as scholarly interpretations of the human condition. In our view, schools should give all students access to the understandings made possible through the arts. We believe, further, that schools should provide students with opportunities to learn the symbol systems that support various artistic forms. Just as writing promotes insights about literature, so too are insights about the artistic legacy derived from experiences with drawing, painting, sculpting, dancing, playing a musical instrument, and acting. Because the processes are both active and synthetic, artistic production and interpretation may provide frequent access to the sorts of revelatory experiences that transform children's understanding of the world and its possibilities.

We do not believe, however, that incorporating study of the arts into the school curriculum will be sufficient to meet the needs of students who, at an early age, demonstrate particular talents in the arts. These children will require special instruction with opportunities for frequent, intensive practice. Whereas schools may not have the resources to provide such instruction, they can help parents make arrangements for it. Further, they can assist artistically talented students to organize their schedules in ways that accommodate both their academic and their artistic studies.

As well as providing occasion for self-expression of a highly personal nature, the performing arts especially offer a kind of intrinsic communality lacking in many other intellectual endeavors. The thoughtful artistic interpretation that represents the potential of an orchestra, jazz band, choir, drama company, or dance troupe depends on the competent craft of many performers disciplined to work together, but it also depends on the artistic brilliance of the few, most capable, soloists. In our view, this supportive interaction between the many competent and the few brilliant performers reflects the sort of synergy that ought to characterize intellectual, and perhaps political, life generally. It suggests a dialectic rather than a conflictual relationship between the interests of talented individuals and the well-being of the community.

The Special Responsibilities of Talent

The conventional rationale for gifted education links academic promise in childhood and potential for leadership in adulthood. This association suggests that a primary aim of gifted education should be the training of future leaders. According to this reasoning, public schools ought to guide their most academically capable students toward leadership roles in business, government, and the professions.

We have claimed, both in this book and elsewhere, that such a narrow and instrumental basis for gifted education degrades learning, sets up conditions for exploiting talent, and supports elitist modes of rule. This view of gifted education perpetuates myths that, in our opinion, are unconscionable: that the nation depends for its survival on the willingness of an elite to accept the responsibilities of leadership, that leadership ought to be in the hands of those with appropriate technical training and social grooming, and that the responsibilities of leadership sanction rich rewards.

These myths, in fact, obscure important questions about ends and means. What of enduring worth should we seek to preserve? What meaningful roles should citizens play in shaping our society? What does our society owe its citizens? On what basis should we distribute society's benefits? How can the interests of the individual be accommodated without damaging the commonweal?

We presume that questions such as these ought to form the cornerstone for the dialogue that constitutes democratic governance. Moreover, we believe that individuals with exceptional talents *do* have a special moral responsibility with regard to this dialogue. In our view, their responsibility involves both restraint and action. They must restrain themselves from allowing self-interest to subvert the dialogue, and they must actively care for the life of the mind.

Resisting blandishments. The just distribution of society's goods and the sharing of power will not come about easily by means either of gradual processes or violent ones. Evolutionary change in our society has tended to worsen the discrepancies between rich and poor, powerful and powerless. Violence, while possibly shifting the sites of wealth and power, may well leave their structure undisturbed. This circumstance provides few openings for hope.

Still, there are such openings, in our view. We have suggested earlier that intellect plays a crucial role in ethical and political deliberation. The quest for meaning that it supports necessarily entails contemplation of the human condition—and such contemplation necessarily confronts inequality, injustice, and abuse. This confrontation of the history and conditions of our society is essential for the informed participation of all citizens, but for a select few—those with exceptional talents—such contemplation may occasion personal sacrifice constructive of the common good.

In our society, individuals with particular talents are recruited and exploited by the ruling class to advance its interests. Yet their exploitation is masked by the rewards given them for their service. In the idiom of the marketplace, such individuals exchange their valuable services for a fair price, and capitalist ideology exalts the rationality of this transaction. We believe, however, that examination of this transaction reveals its irrationality not only in terms of the maintenance of peace and the survival of democracy but also in terms of the survival of the species. Our hope is that talented individuals who confront these irrationalities will choose to reject the blandishments offered them by the ruling elite, that they will choose, more often than at present, to sacrifice a life of privilege for one of value.

Giftedness and intellectual stewardship. The starting point for such sacrifice is the desire to embrace values other than material ones, and its process is the action that derives from those values. Action on behalf of such values (i.e., those with higher than instrumental purpose) implicates the sort of "calling" about which we spoke earlier. As applied to the life of the mind, this calling ought to become the special province of intellectuals.

We have, however, proclaimed our hope that schools will break, but certainly not reverse, the association between rate of learning and involvement with intellectual work. Clearly by expressing this hope, we did not mean to imply that the most rapid learners would or should choose to renounce the life of the mind, while others embrace it. Rather we believe that rapid learners and many others—less quick perhaps but no less capable—will and should choose the intellectual life. These individuals will be the ones to practice the most active stewardship over intellectual culture: They will be the teachers, scholars, writers, commentators, researchers, and vocal critics of our future.

In our view individuals who choose this life require an education that prepares them for stewardship of the intellectual traditions and the institutions that perpetuate these traditions. Special education for such students might begin in secondary schools for those who demonstrate early interest in particular academic studies, but its sustained effort ought to take place in colleges and universities. In fact, we contend that the most important mission of institutions of higher education is to advance the intellectual studies of such students. In the next section of the chapter we will articulate two prospects for postsecondary education, each with the potential to accommodate the special needs of emergent intellectuals.

TWO PROSPECTS FOR POSTSECONDARY EDUCATION

The discussion so far has provided quite decisive proposals for changing public K–12 schools in ways that would support a primarily intellectual mission. We will, however, be much less decisive in our recommendations for postsecondary schools. Our reluctance comes from difficulties we have imagining the match between the graduates of K–12 schools shaped according to our vision and the political economy of the future. Our best guess is that the *mismatch* will be discomfiting.

To discuss higher education here, however, we will need to assume that K–12 education will indeed be transformed according to the principles that we have thus far outlined. Furthermore, we will need to situate our recommendations in a context that, given what we know about our society, is improbable. Our recommendations fit a society that gives all its members the chance to pursue in their personal lives activities that are of enduring worth as well as to contribute meaningfully to various sorts of collective enterprise. These recommendations make sense in a society decent enough to provide for the material needs of all people and sane enough to prevent greed from interfering with democratic governance: a society that attends thoughtfully to the stewardship of the earth and its people.

In this context two approaches to postsecondary education might bridge the experiences of youth and those of adult life. One approach construes higher education as a diversified enterprise, accessed by most citizens to meet any of a variety of needs. The other conceives it as an experience more narrowly focused on particular social needs and available on a much more exclusive basis. Both approaches, however, view higher education as a public good, supported by the society that reaps its benefits rather than as a commodity available as the prerogative of, or prerequisite to, wealth and privilege.

Diversified Postsecondary Education

In K–12 schools of the sorts we imagine, students will have experiences with manual work; such experiences are productive of and compatible with intellectual development. Students will not, however, receive training in skills required for the performance of specific jobs. Such training will occur after secondary school in apprenticeships, formal school programs, or some combination of the two. Although this training will be sufficient to prepare students for specific jobs, it will not necessarily contribute to their personal fulfillment. We are suggesting, however, that a decent society might want to assure that recent high school graduates and adults, generally, have avenues for meeting both sorts of needs.

One approach to postsecondary education would accommodate the educational needs of adults, construed as both a public and an individual good. This approach would provide an array of options for practical training as well as opportunities for more intensive academic scholarship. These opportunities would be available widely — in local communities and even at job sites — and they would be available to citizens throughout their adult lives. This approach would permit those people whose jobs could not afford them sufficient chance for meaning-making to elaborate such intellectual constructions during their leisure time.

Postsecondary education of this type would, of course, implicate a massive investment of society's resources. Not only would it entail maintenance of an extensive network of educational services, it would also necessitate support for workers to have more discretionary time, including opportunities for sabbaticals from work to accommodate extended periods of study. Moreover, within this system of postsecondary options, society would need to make provision for a group of full-time teachers and scholars whose roles would include guardianship, promulgation, extension, and transformation of the traditions of intellectual culture.

Exclusive Postsecondary Education

We are not sure, however, if such a use of society's resources would be possible or even advisable. Efforts to distribute essential benefits more equitably may command such a large share of the available resources that extended educational opportunities cannot be offered universally. Nevertheless, some form of postsecondary education will be necessary for two groups: those pursuing work that requires a high level of technical expertise (e.g., medicine, computer science) and those choosing work that requires a lengthy period of scholarship (e.g., teaching, research). We believe that a decent society, confronted by finite resources, will nevertheless make provision for these two groups because technical and scholarly work, each in its way, improves the quality of life for all.

Under such constraints, we believe it will be particularly important for society to find fair and equitable methods to select candidates for postsecondary opportunities. We believe, moreover, that those who are fortunate enough to receive such exclusive benefits ought to be willing to serve their communities without demanding special status or rewards. Because their advanced training itself represents a benefit and because the intrinsic value of their work is a second sort of reward, we believe that such individuals have no special claim to material advantages greater than those accorded their fellows. Where the opportunities for advanced education are limited, those individuals who accept this special benefit are, by virtue of that choice, committing themselves to serve others, not to exploit them: They are accepting the responsibilities of a "calling," not the unwarranted entitlements of a sinecure.

Regardless of the form postsecondary education takes, colleges and universities ought to be places that shelter and nurture the culture of the intellect. Their primary mission should be to protect the life of the mind — both its history and its future — from the instrumental interests that seek to deflect or coopt it. Only through such protection will the intellect of individuals, variously talented, and the range of possibilities of a people retain vitality. Furthermore, as sanctuaries for the intellectual culture, colleges and universities have a particular obligation to those individuals whose capabilities and interests dispose them to follow an intellectual or artistic calling. A society that cultivates the talents of all its citizens will surely give special care to those individuals with the exceptional talent or the extraordinary will to commit their lives in service of intellect.

CONCEIVING POSSIBILITIES

Our discussion here — and, in fact, throughout the entire book — has proceeded from an inherent faith in possibilities. We have joined our faith in the potential of each human being with a more encompassing faith in the potential of society to nurture, and through such care to realize, human potential for the common good. Yet we have made quite clear that our faith is confronted, in virtually every realm of life, by the inhibiting conspiracy of social circumstances to trivialize such possibilities.

Like some of our compatriots, we call upon the "language of possibility" to alter the ways that we as a people speak about circumstance. This invocation does, in the final analysis, collide with the potential of material reality — and the social circumstances built on it — to accommodate fundamental changes. In our view, making such material changes will impose upon humans' potential for decency a much greater challenge than the recasting of discourse ever might. Implicit in these changes are adaptations to the human condition that transcend personal circumstance by linking individual destiny to that of the culture and, ultimately, the species. For us, however, "the language of possibility" carries an abiding faith in intellect to imagine and to fashion such adaptations. Discourse about a better world serves, then, to stir the imagination, calling on the intellect of a people to examine and attend to its circumstances.

We presume that intellect, a broader capacity than discourse alone, but one surely encompassing it, contains a hidden source of power to transform the world that we know. For the individual, that presumption associates new ways of conceiving the world with the ongoing process of self-formation. Intellect, thus, gives us some way to gauge the force as well as the impermanence of our contributions. For culture, it warrants the vitality of traditions whose origins in the past may no longer appear relevant but whose continuity allows humans to transcend the limits of the individual life span.

The transformative power of intellect expands the collective imagination and, hence, the power to forge new ways of being in the world. We hope that sometime in the not too distant future, humans, imagining more promising ways of being in the world, will seek to build a just and equitable society, shaping its future on the commitment to nurture, and yet take sustenance from, the possibilities for the common good inherent in every one of its members.

Notes

NOTES TO CHAPTER 1

1. In this set agenda, the character of wise democracy and good economic steward-ship are not matters for continuing debate among educators. Teacher organizations, however, are among the few professional groups that, from time to time, do exhibit public concern for social and economic justice. Teachers, unfortunately, are not among those who set the agenda; they *are* chief among those to be held accountable (DeYoung, 1989). Note, too, that in this formulation prosperity is a condition of democracy, as if a decline in the standard of living implied that people could not govern themselves. In fact, some astute observers have maintained exactly the opposite viewpoint (e.g., Arendt, 1958).
2. Except in the Hegelian sense of "world-mind."
3. For example: academic literacy, adolescent literacy, agricultural literacy, civic literacy, content literacy, document literacy, family literacy, geography literacy, historical literacy, home literacy, information literacy, legal literacy, library literacy, mathematical literacy, media literacy, multicultural literacy, newspaper literacy, political literacy, psychological literacy, visual literacy, vocational literacy, workforce literacy, and workplace literacy. This multiplication of literacies has also created a role for terms like "literacy education," "literacy curriculum," and "literacy learning." For a discussion of "literacy literacy," see Kintgen (1988).
4. These five ideologies are most useful for considering the purposes of intellect and literacy. See Kliebard (1986) for a scheme based on types of curriculum. We could have as easily distinguished three or seven separate ideologies, but the five are sufficient to represent the range of thought about the aims of education in the United States.
5. *Social efficiency* is actually a concept that derives from scientific management, through the work of Charles Prosser, a figure influential in vocational education early in the century. Hofstadter (1963) links the concept to the life adjustment curriculum that dominated American educational thinking after World War II.
6. Coleman was a sociologist by training; school effectiveness researchers were educationists by training. The differences in academic specialization probably contributed to the rift in the liberal perspective. The two liberal camps — the sociologists and the educationists — tended to concentrate on looking at different parts of the same question. Coleman had studied the possible influence of "input variables," for example, funding, facilities, instructional materials. He

discovered that once socioeconomic background variables are controlled, input variables do not explain additional amounts of the variance in achievement. Because input variables are, however, strongly related to student background variables (in simple terms: wealthy communities tend to fund schools well), this finding is not very surprising. The educational researchers, however, looked more closely at what went on inside schools – the processes used to run schools. Both sets of variables, input and process, are still important in studies of educational equity. Moreover, the question of adequate and equitable funding ("input variables") is a continuing source of friction in many states. In fact, litigation on this issue may have an impact that equals that of the legislated reforms of the 1980s, which provided little or no additional aid to needy schools.

7. There were "conservative progressive" educators, according to Cremin (1961). These included the scientific managers, but more particularly the researchers who developed the principles of psychological measurement, standardized tests, and methods of systematic oversight. In the long run, Cremin notes, the conservative progressives had a more substantial effect on American education than the liberal progressives or the more radical social reconstructionists like George Counts.

8. In most instances, "hegemony" refers to domination, especially the unilateral domination of one class or nation over another. In critical theory it refers especially to domination of discourse. The perception is an old one: Plato noted that those who tell a nation's stories control the polity. The unilateral power to set agendas, for example, is "hegemonic."

9. Under current schemes, vouchers would be funded at approximately $1,000 to $3,000 per child; tuition at elite private schools is priced at upwards of $15,000.

10. The issue of the "canon" and its authority will be considered later in this book. The question of what the best texts may be, however, is also a question that must be considered by the intellect. New works emerge continuously, and they must be subject to interpretation and debate. Quite different bodies of work, may, in fact, serve equally meaningful ends, but only if they are considered by students and teachers as objects for reason and for the understanding. As an assemblage of cultural artifacts to inspire a worshipful attitude (cf. Bloom, 1987; Hirsch, 1987) a canon can as easily serve an anti-intellectual purpose as an intellectual one (Moretti, 1993).

11. As Bracey (1991) and Berliner (1992) pointed out, however, the United States actually invests less in K–12 schooling (and more in higher education) than many nations. Overall, funding for education is substantial – in large measure due to the fact that postsecondary experiences are so widely available.

12. American rights are founded on the idea that liberty is bounded only by mutual restraint. That is, the restraint on liberty is that our mutual rights not interfere with one another. Liberty is not a right *to* something, it is a right *from* something – namely, from the unwarranted intrusion of the state. In consequence, for example, the struggle for the educational franchise – the unqualified *right* to good schooling – is still not over, as the proposals to let the free market determine educational services show. The positive right to schooling requires equity. A negative right to education does not: "Learn whatever you may,

however you will; the State is not fundamentally interested." Litigation is changing this perspective, but only within each state system. For a discussion of this issue as it pertains to the education of able students, see Howley, Howley, & Pendarvis, 1986, pp. 359–363.

13. Frederick W. Taylor, the originator of scientific management, invented the phrase to characterize the goal of task analysis: to discover the single, most efficient way of carrying out a particular task.

14. We do not refer to the "innovative" curricula that had their roots in the post-Sputnik frenzy, but to the excesses of such efforts as affective education, career education, creative problem solving, leadership training for children, and so forth.

15. We personally believe that global dominion is a very questionable goal for either national foreign policy or the international economic practice of corporations. But, with respect to schooling, this particular question—or any single critical question—is far too restrictive a basis to give intellect its proper scope.

16. Hofstadter (1963) traces sentimentality to its historical origins in American evangelism, in which movement spiritual rebirth was not a rational experience (as it had been for the Puritans). Instrumentalism and sentimentality fuse, in Hofstadter's account, in such evangelists as Billy Sunday (ca. 1935), who established religious emotionalism as big business.

17. Lilian Katz (1993) and Frank Smith (1990), however, write of the need to cultivate dispositions. One needs not only to learn to read, for instance, but actually to read; disposition is the link between knowing how and actually doing. The person who is disposed to read sees the value of reading. Dispositions cannot be reformed or restructured as skills, but instead reveal themselves as habits of great intellectual relevance. Indeed, a disposition to read puts one in the way of nurturing one's own mind.

NOTES TO CHAPTER 2

1. Political orientations of intellectuals, however, are quite variable. Intellectuals in some fields, for example sociology and fine arts, tend to identify their political orientations as liberal or radical, whereas those in other fields, for example business and engineering, rate themselves as quite conservative.

2. Some of these "cynics" doubtless understand the workings of the system that oppresses them, but many of them do not, blaming themselves instead for the failure of their aspirations to be realized (see Fine, 1986).

NOTES TO CHAPTER 3

1. Unlike procedures to identify disabled children, methods for selecting students for gifted programs need not adhere to standards of statistical validity and reliability. The federal mandate for serving disabled students addresses issues of

assessment as do some state mandates for serving the gifted. Only a few states
have mandates with such provisions. Hence, most states permit districts to use
"eccentric" identification methods.

2. SMPY uses the Scholastic Aptitude Test as a high-ceilinged group test of achievement for seventh-grade students. The Woodcock-Johnson Tests of Achievement,
sometimes used to assess the achievement of gifted students, might also be used
to infer the learning rate of elementary-age students.

3. See Howley and Howley (1989) for an illustration of the use of standardized test
scores for this purpose in schools in poor, rural districts.

4. Guilford proposes the relatedness of process and content. For instance, his model
classifies divergent productive operations on semantic material as relatively independent from divergent productive operations on symbolic, figural, or behavioral content.

NOTES TO CHAPTER 4

1. The West Virginia case illustrates well the relationship between adequacy and
equity. A more equitable distribution of *inadequate* funds does *not* provide
equity, because adequate funding is a prerequisite of equity (Honeyman, Thompson, & Wood, 1989; Wise, 1982).

2. Contemporary interest in "resilient children" represents the most recent attempt
to institutionalize this perspective on the basis of scientific investigation. These
investigations do help explain how some children overcome the dangers that
beset them. The problem is that programs to foster resiliency rely on charity *and*
fail to attack the root causes of the dangers.

3. Interestingly, similar arguments have been used for a long time to explain conditions in rural education (Bickel, Banks, & Spatig, 1991).

4. West (1994) has commented on the danger for African-American intellectuals,
who, if they are to achieve recognition and status, must immerse themselves in
the "very culture and society which degrade and devalue" the community from
which they come. Consequently, materially successful intellectuals from African-
American and other minority groups may find that they have distanced themselves from a most significant community, their community of origin. According
to West, this distancing is detrimental to both the intellectual and his or her
community.

NOTES TO CHAPTER 5

1. Many theorists of both the left and right have tried, at least since the 1930s, to
show that technical rationality is a diminished and dangerous form of thinking.
They often distinguish "reason" from technical rationality. Reason, according
to many of these thinkers, helps us understand the complicated relation that
exists between our conceptions of the good life and what is true (McCarthy,
1990). Technical rationality, on the other hand, banishes just such issues (com-

mitment to ideas, people, and things) from its formal consideration — as Weizenbaum's story, repeated in Chapter 1, so clearly indicated. This banishment, however, allows the *hidden commitments* of technical rationality (e.g., truth as a collection of facts and a false posture of neutrality) to discredit all other commitments. In this way, technical rationality "totalizes" — everything that is must eventually submit to its commitments (Bell, 1976). The point is that much that is important to the world can by no means be understood by technical rationality, and, left unchecked, technical rationality will destroy (has *already* destroyed) much that is important to our very survival (Postman, 1992).

2. *Societal progress* refers to the development of society, as opposed to *social progress*, which refers to the development of social relations. The former term encompasses the latter. Such a distinction allows for societal "progress" that may produce dysfunctional social relations.

3. In his discussion of "technopoly" (the totalizing regime of technology), Postman (1992, p. 63) writes, "Indeed, one way of defining a Technopoly is to say that its information immune system is inoperable. Technopoly is a form of cultural AIDS. . . . This is why it is possible to say almost anything without contradiction provided you begin your utterance with the words, 'A study has shown . . . ' or 'Scientists now tell us that . . . '"

4. *Gesellschaft* is most frequently translated as "society," but English-speaking people are often unaware that both translations — as society and as corporation — reveal different aspects of Tönnies's concept. Arendt (1958) explains that societies were originally private associations; the idea of a general society (*societas sui generis*) came later. Society is a kind of mutual-benefit corporation, a fact reflected in the Enlightenment's enduring notion of the "social contract." A key difference between community and corporation (society) is that in community people remain together despite their differences, whereas in society (or the corporation) people remain separate despite their common interests (cf. Nisbet, 1966, p. 75).

5. Other accounts are numerous (e.g., Best & Kellner, 1991; Foucault, 1988; Freire, 1970; Giroux, 1983; Keizer, 1988).

6. Bell attributes the changes that we attribute to loss of intellectual distance to loss of social distance. Although our view differs from Bell's, his observations are relevant: "The loss of social distance means the loss of manners and the erosion of civility, which has made contact between persons manageable and allowed individuals to have a 'walking space' of their own" (Bell, 1976, p. 117). Bell refers rather obliquely in this passage to the conformism of mass society. Meaning devolves to fashion and fashion is a matter of private taste, but, at the same time, the narrowed "walking space" that remains to the intellect cannot reconstruct the meaning thus lost. In this way, people defend the "right" to arbitrary choices at the expense of conversation, reason, and meaning.

7. As Lilian Katz (1993) points out, schooling starts early to cultivate the narcissism that pervades modernist society.

8. Smith (writing at the time of the American revolution) was the inventor of modern economics. According to Robert Heilbroner (1960, pp. 32–33), "In Adam Smith's great conception, an 'invisible hand,' directed the entirety of

society toward its economic destiny. The economic mechanism as a whole was thus embarked on a long upward gradient whose prospects stretched far into the future, and whose slow but perceptible benefits attended even the meanest of society's classes. And all of this propitious vista needed for its realization nothing more than a continuation of the economic process to which men were in any case driven and from which they could not escape."

9. The term "progressive," of course, is not appropriate to the postmodern circumstance. Not only does social progress not follow technological progress, neither does "improvement" necessarily flow from the development or use of more sophisticated tools. In Dewey's day, this circumstance was not yet clear.

10. Arendt refused to speculate about human nature, which she viewed as indeterminate for the very reason under discussion: Human nature depends on the development of humanity over many generations. Guesses about the outcome of this development are hazardous at best. A nature capable of articulating ideas of good and evil and of carrying out good and evil acts does seem typical of humans, however. The salient point is that humans do not possess a *fixed* nature. This perception is a comparatively parsimonious ground on which to establish faith in human potential.

11. Goods constitute both things and services useful to individuals or to the commonweal in general.

NOTES TO CHAPTER 6

1. The literature on the relationship between teacher characteristics and student achievement reveals little consistency, except for the positive association with teachers' verbal ability, according to Stockard and Mayberry (1992). Most of the applicable research, however, is dated, because it is not considered fashionable to investigate this phenomenon.

2. The state trials of the National Assessment of Educational Progress (NAEP) suggest that a wide variety of performance levels exists—at the level of state aggregation—among students from all ethnic backgrounds. In selected states, groups that in most states perform badly do very well indeed.

References

Acker, A. L. (1988). A medical school fellowship program for minority high school students. *Journal of Medical Education, 63*(3), 171–175.

Adler, M. (1982). *The Paidea proposal: An educational manifesto.* New York: Macmillan.

Adler, M. (1993). *Intellect: Mind over matter.* New York: Collier Books.

Albert, H. (1985). *Treatise on critical reason* (M. V. Rorty, Trans.). Princeton, NJ: Princeton University Press.

Allardyce, G. (1982). The rise and fall of the western civilization course. *American Historical Review, 87*, 695–725.

American Association for the Advancement of Science. (1989). *Science for all Americans: A Project 2061 report on literacy goals in science, mathematics, and technology.* Washington, DC: Author. (ERIC Document Reproduction Service No. ED 309 059)

Anderson, L. (1981). *Student response to seatwork: Implications for the study of students' cognitive processing.* Lansing, MI: Michigan State University, Institute for Research on Teaching. (ERIC Document Reproduction Service No. ED 207 709)

Anyon, J. (1980). Social class and the hidden curriculum of work. *Journal of Education, 162*(4), 68–92.

Anyon, J. (1987). Social class and the hidden curriculum of work. In E. Stevens & G. Woods (Eds.), *Justice, ideology, and education: An introduction to the social foundations of education* (pp. 210–226). New York: Random House.

Apple, M. (1982). Education and cultural reproduction: A critical reassessment of programs for choice. In R. Everhart (Ed.), *The public school monopoly: A critical analysis of education and the state in American society* (pp. 503–541). Cambridge, MA: Ballinger.

Apple, M. (1987). The de-skilling of teachers. In F. S. Bolin & J. M. Falk (Eds.), *Teacher renewal: Professional issues, personal choices* (pp. 59–75). New York: Teachers College Press.

Apple, M. (1988). Redefining equality: Authoritarian populism and the conservative restoration. *Teachers College Record, 90*(2), 167–186.

Apple, M. (1993). The politics of official knowledge: Does a national curriculum make sense? *Teachers College Record, 95*(2), 222–241.

Apple, M., & Weis, L. (1986). Seeing education relationally: The stratification of culture and people in the sociology of school knowledge. *Journal of Education, 168*(1), 7–34.

Archambault, Jr., F. X., Westberg, K. L., Brown, S. W., Hallmark, B.W., Emmons, C. L., & Zhang, W. (1993). *Regular classroom practices with gifted students: Results of a national survey of classroom teachers* (Research Monograph 93102). Storrs: University of Connecticut, National Research Center on the Gifted and Talented.

Arendt, H. (1958). *The human condition*. Chicago: University of Chicago Press.

Arendt, H. (1968). The crisis in education. In *Between past and future: Eight exercises in political thought* (rev. ed., pp. 173–196). New York: Viking Press. (Original work published 1954)

Arendt, H. (1977). *The life of the mind: Thinking* (Vol. 1). New York: Harcourt Brace Jovanovich.

Arendt, H. (1981). *The life of the mind*. New York: Harcourt Brace Jovanovich.

Aronowitz, S. (1988). *Science as power: Discourse and ideology in modern society*. Minneapolis: University of Minnesota Press.

Aronowitz, S., & Giroux, H. A. (1985). *Education under siege: The conservative, liberal and radical debate over schooling*. South Hadley, MA: Bergin & Garvey.

Atwell, R. H. (1993). [Invited essay]. In The Wingspread Group, *An American imperative: Higher expectations for higher education* (Appendix D). Racine, WI: Johnson Foundation. (ERIC Document Reproduction Service No. ED 364144)

Bacon, F. (1944). *Advancement of learning and novum organum*. New York: Willey Book Company. (Original work published 1620)

Barker, B. (1992). *The distance education handbook*. Charleston, WV: ERIC Clearinghouse on Rural Education and Small Schools. (ERIC Document Reproduction Service No. ED 340 547)

Barnet, R. J. (1974). *Global reach: The power of the multinational corporations*. New York: Simon & Schuster.

Barrow, C. W. (1990). *Universities and the capitalist state: Corporate liberalism and the reconstruction of American higher education, 1894–1928*. Madison: University of Wisconsin Press.

Barzun, J. (1959). *The house of intellect*. New York: Harper & Row.

Barzun, J. (1989). *The culture we deserve*. Middletown, CT: Wesleyan University Press.

Barzun, J. (1991). *Begin here*. Chicago: University of Chicago Press.

Baumrind, D. (1971). Current patterns of parental authority. *Developmental Psychology Monograph, 4,* 1–103.

Bean, F., & Tienda, M. (1987). *The Hispanic population of the United States* (The population of the United States in the 1980s: A census monograph series). New York: Russell Sage Foundation.

Beck, C. (1988). Education for spirituality. *Interchange, 17*(2), 148–158.

Becker, G. (1964). *Human capital*. New York: Columbia University Press.

Belenky, M. F., Clinchy, B. M., Goldberger, N. R., & Tarule, J. M. (1986). *Women's ways of knowing: The development of self, voice, and mind*. New York: Basic Books.

Bell, D. (1973). *The coming of post-industrial society: A venture in social forecasting*. New York: Basic Books.

Bell, D. (1976). *The cultural contradictions of capitalism*. New York: Basic Books.

Bell, D. (1990). Resolving the contradictions of modernity and modernism. *Society*, *27*(3), 43-50.

Bellack, A., Kliebard, H., Hyman, R., & Smith, F. (1966). *The language of the classroom*. New York: Teachers College Press.

Bellah, R. N., Madsen, R., Sullivan, W. M., Swidler, A., & Tipton, S. M. (1985). *Habits of the heart: Individualism and commitment in American life*. New York: Harper & Row.

Benbow, C. (1986). Physiological correlates of extreme intellectual precocity. *Neuropsychologia*, *24*, 719-725.

Bennett, E. W. (1987). *James Madison High School: A curriculum for American students*. Washington, DC: U. S. Department of Education. (ERIC Document Reproduction Service No. ED 287 854)

Bennett, E. W. (1988). Moral literacy and the formation of character. *NASSP Bulletin*, *72*(512), 29-34.

Bennett, K. P., & LeCompte, M. D. (1990). *The way schools work: A sociological analysis of education*. New York: Longman.

Berg, T. (1980). The smart man's burden. *Peabody Journal of Education*, *58*(1), 31-33.

Berliner, D. (1992, February). *Educational reform in an era of disinformation*. Paper presented at the annual meeting of the American Association of Colleges for Teacher Education, San Antonio, Texas. (ERIC Document Reproduction Service No. ED 34870)

Berliner, D. (1993). Educational reform in an era of disinformation. *Education Policy Analysis Archives*, *1*(1). (Electronic journal available from listserv@ asucad.bitnet)

Bernstein, H. T. (1985). The new politics of textbook adoption. *Phi Delta Kappan*, *66*, 463-466.

Berry, W. (1989). *The hidden wound*. San Francisco: North Point Press. (Original work published 1970)

Berry, W. (1990). *What are people for?* San Francisco: North Point Press.

Best, S., & Kellner, D. (1991). *Postmodern theory: Critical interrogations*. New York: Guilford Press.

Betz, M., & Garland, J. (1974). Intergenerational mobility rates of urban school teachers. *Sociology of Education*, *47*, 511-522.

Bhola, H. (1987, May). *Adult literacy for development in Zimbabwe: The third phase of the revolution examined*. Paper presented at the Canadian Association of African Studies, Edmonton, Alberta. (ERIC Document Reproduction Service No. ED 279 898)

Bickel, R., Banks, S., & Spatig, L. (1991). Bridging the gap between high school and college in an Appalachian state: A near-replication of Florida research. *Journal of Research in Rural Education*, *7*(2), 75-87.

Bishop, J., & Carter, S. (1991). The worsening shortage of college-graduate workers. *Educational Evaluation and Policy Analysis*, *13*(3), 221-246.

Bledstein, B. J. (1976). *The culture of professionalism: The middle class and the development of higher education in America*. New York: W. W. Norton.

Bloom, A. (1987). *The closing of the American mind.* New York: Simon & Schuster.

Bloom, B. (Ed.). (1956). *Taxonomy of educational objectives, handbook 1: Cognitive domain.* New York: David McKay.

Bloom, B. (Ed.). (1985). *Developing talent in young people.* New York: Ballantine.

Bloom, B., & Sosniak, L. (1981). Talent development vs. schooling. *Educational Leadership, 39*(2), 86–94.

Blum, J. M. (1978). *Pseudoscience and mental ability.* New York: Monthly Review Press.

Boli, J., Ramirez, F., & Meyer, J. (1985). Explaining the origins and expansion of mass education. *Comparative Education Review, 29*(2), 145–170.

Bollier, D. (1991). *Electronic media regulation and the first amendment: A perspective for the future.* Queenstown, MD: Aspen Institute. (ERIC Document Reproduction Service No. ED 343 168)

Borland, J. (1978). Teacher identification of the gifted: A new look. *Journal for the Education of the Gifted, 2*(1), 22–32.

Borland, J. (1986). What happened to them all? In C. J. Maker (Ed.), *Critical issues in gifted education: Defensible programs for the gifted* (pp. 91–106). Austin, TX: PRO-Ed.

Bourdieu, P., & Passeron, J. (1977). *Reproduction in education, society, and culture.* Beverly Hills: Sage.

Bowen, J. (1981). *As history of western education* (Vol. 3). New York: St. Martin's Press.

Bowles, S., & Gintis, H. (1976). *Schooling in capitalist America.* New York: Basic Books.

Bracey, G. (1991). Why can't they be like we were? *Phi Delta Kappan, 73*(2), 104–117.

Britzman, D. P. (1986). Cultural myths in the making of a teacher: Biography and social structure in teacher education. *Harvard Educational Review, 56*(4), 442–456.

Brown, B. B., & Steinberg, L. (1991). *Noninstructional influences on adolescent engagement and achievement* (Final Rep., Project 2). Madison, WI: National Center on Effective Secondary Schools. (ERIC Document Reproduction Service No. ED 340 641)

Brown, R. (1993). *Schools of thought: How politics shape literacy in the classroom.* San Francisco: Jossey-Bass

Bruner, J. (1960). *The process of education.* New York: Vintage Books.

Bruner, J. (1966). Teaching a native language. In *Toward a theory of instruction* (pp. 102–112). Cambridge, MA: Harvard University Press.

Bryk, A., & Driscoll, M. (1988). *The high school as community: Contextual influences and consequences for students and teachers.* (ERIC Document Reproduction Service No. ED 302 539)

Bryk, A., Holland, P., Lee, V., & Carriedo, R. (1984). *Effective Catholic schools: An exploration.* Washington, DC: National Center for Research in Total Catholic Education, National Catholic Education Association. (ERIC Document Reproduction Service No. ED 251 365)

Brym, R. (1980). *Intellectuals and politics*. London: George Allen & Unwin.

Burbules, N., & Densmore, K. (1991). The persistence of professionalism: Breakin' up is hard to do. *Educational Policy, 5*(2), 150–157.

Burgess, C., & Borrowman, M. L. (1969/1980). John Dewey and the great community. In E. Steiner, R. Arnove, & B. E. McClellan (Eds.), *Education and American culture* (pp. 34–49). New York: Macmillan.

Bush, G. (1991). President's remarks. In *America 2000: An education strategy* (Sourcebook). Washington, DC: U. S. Department of Education. (ERIC Document Reproduction Service No. ED 327 985)

Callahan, R. E. (1962). *Education and the cult of efficiency: A study of the social forces that have shaped the administration of the public schools*. Chicago: University of Chicago Press.

Caplan, N., Choy, M. H., & Whitmore, J. K. (1992, February). Indochinese refugee families and academic achievement. *Scientific American*, pp. 36–42.

Carlsen, W. (1991). Questioning in classrooms: A sociolinguistic perspective. *Review of Educational Research, 61*(2), 157–178.

Carnoy, M. (1982). Educational adequacy: Alternative perspectives and their implications for educational finance. In E. Tron (Ed.), *Adequate education: Issues in its definition and implementation* (pp. 34–58). Washington, DC: Office of Educational Research and Improvement. (ERIC Document Reproduction Service No. ED 226 489)

Carnoy, M., & Levin, H. (1985). *Schooling and work in the democratic state*. Stanford, CA: Stanford University Press.

Casey, K. (1992). Why do progressive women activists leave teaching? Theory, methodology, and politics in life-history research. In I. F. Goodson (Ed.), *Studying teachers' lives* (pp. 187–208). New York: Teachers College Press.

Cetron, M., Rocha, W., & Lucken, R. (1988). *Long-term trends affecting the United States*. Bethesda, MD: World Future Society.

Chall, J.S., & Conard, S. S. (1991). *Should textbooks challenge students? The case for easier or harder textbooks*. New York: Teachers College Press.

Cheney, L. (1990). *Tyrannical machines: A report on educational practices gone wrong and our best hopes for setting them right*. Washington, DC: National Endowment for the Humanities. (ERIC Document Reproduction Service No. ED 326 533)

Childs, R. E. (1981). A comparison of the adaptive behavior of normal and gifted five and six year old children. *Roeper Review, 4*(2), 41–43.

Chubb, J., & Moe, T. (1990). *Politics, markets, and America's schools*. Washington, DC: Brookings Institute.

Cixous, H. (1975/1988). Sorties. In D. Lodge (Ed.), *Modern criticism and theory* (pp. 287–293). New York: Longman.

Clark, G., & Zimmerman, E. (1984). *Educating artistically talented students*. Syracuse, NY: Syracuse University Press.

Clifford, G. J., & Guthrie, J. W. (1988). *Ed school*. Chicago: University of Chicago Press.

Clinchy, E. (1989). Public school choice: Absolutely necessary but not wholly sufficient. *Phi Delta Kappan, 71*(4), 289–294.

Cochran-Smith, M. (1991). Learning to teach against the grain. *Harvard Educational Review, 61*(3), 279–310.

Cogan, J. J., & Anderson, H. (1977). Teachers' professional reading habits. *Language Arts, 54,* 254–258.

Cohen, D. K., & Ball, D. L. (1990). Relations between policy and practice: A commentary. *Educational Evaluation and Policy Analysis, 12*(3), 331–338.

Cohen, J. (1987). Parents as educational models and definers. *Journal of Marriage and Family, 49,* 339–351.

Cohen, R. M. (1991). *A lifetime of teaching: Portraits of five veteran high school teachers.* New York: Teachers College Press.

Coleman, J. (1961). *Adolescent society: The social life of the teenager and its impact on education.* New York: Free Press.

Coleman, J. (1966). *Equality of educational opportunity* (Summary Rep.). Washington, DC: U. S. Office of Education, Department of Health, Education, and Welfare. (ERIC Document Reproduction Service No. ED 012 275)

Coleman, J. (1966/1987). Equal schools or equal students. In E. Stevens & G. Wood (Eds.), *Justice, ideology, and education* (pp. 32–37). New York: Random House.

Coleman, J., & Hoffer, T. (1987). *Public and private high schools: The impact of communities.* New York: Basic Books.

Coles, R. (1977). *Privileged ones: The well-off and rich in America.* Boston: Little, Brown.

Colvin, M., & Pauly, J. (1983). A critique of criminology: Toward an integrated structural-Marxist theory of delinquency production. *American Journal of Sociology, 89*(3), 513–551.

Commission on the Reorganization of Secondary Education. (1918). *Cardinal principles of secondary education.* Washington, DC: National Education Association.

Committee for Economic Development. (1985). *Investing in our children: Business and the public schools.* New York: Committee for Economic Development. (ERIC Document Reproduction Service No. ED 261 117)

Conant, J. (1953). *Modern science and modern man.* Garden City, NY: Doubleday.

Conant, J. (1959). *The American high school today: A first report to citizens.* New York: McGraw-Hill.

Counts, G. (1930). *The American road to culture: A social interpretation of education in the United States.* New York: John Day. (Facsimile reprint ed. by Arno Press-New York Times, 1971)

Counts, G. (1932/1987). Dare the school build a new social order? In E. Stevens & G. Wood (Eds.), *Justice, ideology, and education* (pp. 200–205). New York: Random House.

Cox, J., Daniel, N., & Boston, B. (1985). *Educating able learners: Promising programs and practices.* Austin: University of Texas Press.

Cremin, L. (1961). *The transformation of the school.* New York: Vintage Books.

Csikszentmihalyi, M., & Robinson, R. E. (1986). Culture, time, and the development of talent. In R. J. Sternberg and J. E. Davidson (Eds.), *Conceptions of giftedness* (pp. 264–284). New York: Cambridge University Press.

Cuban, L. (1982). Persistence of the inevitable: The teacher-centered classroom. *Education and Urban Society, 15*(1), 26–41.

Cuban, L. (1992). Managing dilemmas while building professional communities. *Educational Researcher, 20*(4), 4–11.

Cummings, S., & Taebel, D. (1978). The economic socialization of children: A neo-Marxist analysis. *Social Problems, 26*(2), 198–210.

Curti, M. (1943). *The growth of American thought*. New York: Harper & Brothers.

Cusick, P. A. (1973). *Inside high school: The student's world*. New York: Holt, Rinehart & Winston.

Cusick, P. A. (1982). *A study of networks among professional staffs in secondary schools*. East Lansing, MI: Institute for Research on Teaching. (ERIC Document Reproduction Service No. ED 218 772)

Cusick, P. A. (1983). *The egalitarian ideal and the American high school: Studies of three schools*. New York: Longman.

Daines, D. (1982). *Teachers' oral questions and subsequent verbal behaviors of teachers and students*. Provo, UT: Brigham Young University, College of Education. (ERIC Document Reproduction Service No. ED 225 979)

Darwin, C. (1859). *The origin of species and the descent of man*. New York: Modern Library.

Daurio, S. (1979). Educational enrichment versus acceleration. A review of the literature. In W. George, S. Cohn, & J. Stanley (Eds.), *Educating the gifted: Acceleration and enrichment* (pp. 13–63). Baltimore, MD: Johns Hopkins University Press.

Deaton, B., & McNamara, K. (1984). *Education in a changing rural environment: The impact of population and economic change on the demand for and costs of public education in rural America*. Mississippi State, MS: Southern Rural Development Center. (ERIC Document Reproduction Service No. ED 241 210)

Deci, E. L., & Ryan, R. M. (1985). *Intrinsic motivation and self-determination in human behavior*. New York: Plenum.

Denton, C., & Postlethwaite, K. (1982). *The identification of more able pupils in comprehensive schools* (Final Rep.). Oxford: Oxford University, Oxford Educational Research Group. (ERIC Document Reproduction Service No. ED 229 359)

Devaney, K., & Sykes, G. (1988). Making the case for professionalism. In A. Lieberman (Ed.), *Building a professional culture in schools* (pp. 3–22). New York: Teachers College Press.

Dewey, J. (1916). *Democracy and education*. New York: Macmillan.

Dewey, J. (1956). *The child and the curriculum*. Chicago: University of Chicago Press. (Original work published 1902)

DeYoung, A. J. (1986). Educational "excellence" vs. teacher "professionalism": Towards some conceptual clarity. *Urban Review, 18*(1), 71–84.

DeYoung, A. (1989). *Economics and American education: A historical and critical overview of the impact of economic theories on schooling in the United States*. New York: Longman.

DeYoung, A., & Howley, C. (1992). The political economy of rural school consolidation. *Peabody Journal of Education, 67*(4), 63–89.

Dirks, J., & Quarfoth, J. (1981). Selecting children for gifted classes: Choosing for breadth vs. choosing for depth. *Psychology in the Schools, 18*(4), 437–449.

Dorans, N. J., & Livingston, S. A. (1987). Male-female differences in SAT-Verbal ability among students of high SAT-Mathematical ability. *Journal of Educational Measurement, 24*(1), 65–71.

Dorfman, C. (Ed.). (1987). *Japanese education today: A report from the U.S. Study of Education in Japan.* Washington, DC: U.S. Department of Education, Office of Educational Research and Improvement. (ERIC Document Reproduction Service No. ED 275 620)

Dornbusch, S. M., Ritter, P. L., Leiderman, P. H., Roberts, D. F., & Fraleigh, M. J. (1987). The relation of parenting style to adolescent school performance. *Child Development, 58*, 1244–1257.

Douthitt, V. L. (1992). A comparison of adaptive behavior in gifted and nongifted children. *Roeper Review, 14*(3), 149–151.

Drews, E. M. (1964). *A study of non-intellectual factors in superior (average and slow) high school students: The creative intellectual style in gifted adolescents: Motivation to learn—attitudes, interests, and values.* East Lansing, MI: Michigan State University. (ERIC Document Reproduction Service No. ED 011 979).

Ducharme, E. R., & Agne, R. M. (1989). Professors of education: Uneasy residents of academe. In R. Wisniewski & E. R. Ducharme (Eds.), *The professors of teaching: An inquiry* (pp. 67–86). Albany: State University of New York Press.

Duckworth, E. (1986). Teaching as research. *Harvard Educational Review, 56*(4), 481–495.

Duffey, R. V. (1973). Teacher as reader. *Reading Teacher, 27,* 132–133.

Duffey, R. V. (1974, October/November). *Elementary school teachers' reading.* Paper presented at the annual meeting of the College Reading Association, Bethesda, Maryland. (ERIC Document Reproduction Service No. ED 098 554)

Dungan, R. A. (1970). Higher education: The effort to adjust. In S. R. Graubard & G. A. Ballotti (Eds.), *The embattled university* (pp. 141–153). New York: George Braziller.

Durkheim, E. (1964). *The division of labor in society.* New York: Free Press of Glencoe. (Original work published 1933)

Dusewicz, R., & Beyer, F. (1988). *Dimensions of excellence scales: Survey instruments for school improvement.* Philadelphia: Research for Better Schools.

Edelstein, F., & Schoeffe, E. (1989). *A blueprint for business on restructuring education.* Washington, DC: National Alliance of Business.

Edmonds, R. (1979). Effective schools for the urban poor. *Educational Leadership, 37*, 15–24.

Edwards, A., & Furlong, V. (1978). *The language of teaching.* London: Heinemann.

Ehrenreich, B. (1987). The new right attack on social welfare. In F. Block, R. A. Cloward, B. Ehrenreich, & F. F. Piven (Eds.), *The mean season: The attack on the welfare state* (pp. 161–193). New York: Pantheon.

Eisner, E. W. (1983). The kind of schools we need. *Educational Leadership, 41*(2), 48–55.

Elmore, R., & McLaughlin, M. (1988). *Steady work: Policy, practice, and the reform of American education.* Santa Monica, CA: Rand Corporation.

Engler, R. (1967). Social science and social consciousness: The shame of the universities. In T. Roszak (Ed.), *The dissenting academy* (pp. 182–207). New York: Random House.

Epstein, J. L. (1988). *Homework practices, achievements, and behaviors of elementary school students* (Rep. No. 26). Baltimore, MD: Center for Research on Elementary and Middle Schools. (ERIC Document Reproduction Service No. ED 301 322)

Erickson, F. (1982). Classroom discourse as improvisation: Relationships between academic task structure and social participation structure in lessons. In L. Wilkinson (Ed.), *Communicating in the classroom* (pp. 153–181). New York: Academic Press.

Etzioni, A. (1985). *Self-discipline, schools, and the business community.* Washington, DC: Chamber of Commerce of the United States. (ERIC Document Reproduction Service No. ED 249 335)

Eubanks, E. E., & Parish, R. I. (1990). Why does the status quo persist? *Phi Delta Kappan, 72*(3), 196–197.

Faia, M. A. (1974). The myth of the liberal professor. *Sociology of Education, 47,* 171–202.

Fallows, J. (1987, March). Gradgrind's heirs. *The Atlantic,* pp. 16–24.

Fay, B. (1987). *Critical social science: Liberation and its limits.* Ithaca, NY: Cornell University Press.

Feiman-Nemser, S. (1990). Teacher preparation: Structural and conceptual alternatives. In W. R. Houston (Ed.), *Handbook of research on teacher education* (pp. 212–233). New York: Macmillan.

Feiman-Nemser, S., & Buchmann, M. (1986). The first year of teacher preparation: Transition to pedagogical thinking? *Journal of Curriculum Studies, 18,* 239–256.

Feldman, D. (1984). The mysterious case of extreme giftedness. In A. H. Passow (Ed.), *The gifted and talented: Their education and development* (Seventy-Eighth Yearbook of the National Society for the Study of Education, Part 2, pp. 335–351). Chicago: University of Chicago Press.

Fetterman, D. M. (1988). *Excellence and equality.* Albany: State University of New York Press.

Filson, G. (1988). Ontario teachers' deprofessionalization and proletarianization. *Comparative Education Review, 32*(3), 298–317.

Fine, M. (1986). Why urban adolescents drop into and out of public high school. *Teachers College Record, 87,* 393–410.

First, J. M. (1988). Immigrant students in public schools: Challenges with solutions. *Phi Delta Kappan, 70*(3), 205–210.

Ford, D. Y., & Harris, J. J. (1992). The American achievement ideology and achievement differentials among preadolescent gifted and nongifted African American males and females. *Journal of Negro Education, 61*(1), 45–64.

Foster, G. E. (1991). *New York and New Jersey directory of independent schools owned by African-Americans*. New York: Toussaint Institute Fund.

Foster, J. B. (1993). "Let Them Eat Pollution": Capitalism and the world environment. *Monthly Review, 44*(8), 10–20.

Foucault, M. (1973). *Madness and civilization: A history of insanity in the age of reason* (R. Howard, Trans.). New York: Random House.

Foucault, M. (1979). *Discipline and punish: The birth of the prison* (A. Sheridan, Trans.). New York: Pantheon.

Foucault, M. (1988). *The final Foucault* (J. Bernauer and D. Rasmussen, Eds.). Cambridge, MA: MIT Press.

Fox, L. H. (1976). Sex differences in mathematical precocity: Bridging the gap. In D. Keating (Ed.), *Intellectual talent research and development* (pp. 183–214). Baltimore, MD: Johns Hopkins University Press.

Freire, P., & Macedo, D. (1987). *Literacy: Reading the word and the world*. South Hadley, MA: Bergin & Garvey.

French, J. L., & Cardon, B. W. (1968). Characteristics of high mental ability dropouts. *Vocational Guidance Journal, 16*(3), 162–168.

French, T. (1993). *South of heaven: Welcome to high school at the end of the twentieth century*. New York: Doubleday.

Friedenberg, E. (1965). *Coming of age in America: Growth and acquiescence*. New York: Vintage Books.

Friedkin, N., & Necochea, J. (1988). School system size and performance: A contingency perspective. *Educational Evaluation and Policy Analysis, 10*(3), 237–249.

Friedrich, C. (1972). *Tradition and authority*. New York: Praeger.

Gage, N. (1979). *The scientific basis of the art of teaching*. New York: Teachers College Press.

Galambos, E. C., Cornett, L. M., & Spitler, H. D. (1985). *An analysis of transcripts of teachers and arts and sciences graduates*. Atlanta, GA: Southern Regional Education Board.

Gall, M. (1984). Synthesis of research on teachers' questioning. *Educational Leadership, 42*(3), 40–47.

Gallagher, J. (1993) [Invited essay]. In The Wingspread Group, *An American imperative: Higher expectations for higher education* (Appendix D). Racine, WI: Johnson Foundation. (ERIC Document Reproduction Service No. ED 364 144)

Gallagher, J. (1985). *Teaching the gifted child* (3rd ed.). Boston: Allyn & Bacon.

Gallagher, J., & Courtright, R. D. (1986). The educational definition of giftedness and its policy implications. In R. J. Sternberg and J. E. Davidson (Eds.), *Conceptions of giftedness* (pp. 93–111). New York: Cambridge University Press.

Galton, F. (1972). *Hereditary genius*. London: Fontana. (Original work published 1869)

Gamoran, A. (1992). The variable effects of high school tracking. *American Sociological Review, 57*(6), 812–828.

Gardner, H. (1983). *Frames of mind: The theory of multiple intelligences*. New York: Basic Books.

Gardner, J. (1961). *Excellence*. New York: Harper & Row.

Gardner, S. (1982). *Status of the American public school teacher, 1980-81*. Washington, DC: National Education Association.

Garibaldi, A. M. (1992). Educating and motivating African American males to succeed. *Journal of Negro Education, 61*(1), 4-11.

Garman, N. (1986, March). *Leadership and the educative act: Looking toward the next century to ensure quality*. John Dewey Society Memorial Lecture presented at the annual conference of the Association for Supervision and Curriculum Development, San Francisco. (ERIC Document Reproduction Service No. ED 270 857)

Gaventa, J. (1982). *Power and powerlessness: Quiescence and rebellion in an Appalachian valley*. Chicago: University of Illinois Press.

Gearing, F., & Epstein, P. (1982). Learning to wait: An ethnographic probe into the operations of an item of hidden curriculum. In G. Spindler (Ed.), *Doing the ethnography of schooling: Educational anthropology in action* (pp. 241-267). New York: Holt, Rinehart & Winston.

Geschwind, N., & Behan, P. (1982). Left-handedness: Association with immune disease, migraine, and developmental learning disorder. *Proceedings of the National Academy of Sciences, 79*, 5097-5100.

Geschwind, N., & Galaburda, A. (1984). *Cerebral dominance: The biological foundations*. Cambridge, MA: Harvard University Press.

Gibboney, R. A. (1991). The killing field of reform. *Phi Delta Kappan, 72*(9), 682-688.

Gilliland, H. (1986). The need for an adapted curriculum. In J. Reyhner (Ed.), *Teaching the Indian child: A bilingual/multicultural approach* (2nd ed., pp. 29-41). Billings: Eastern Montana College. (ERIC Document Reproduction Service No. ED 283 628)

Gintis, H., & Bowles, S. (1988). Contradiction and reproduction in educational theory. In M. Cole (Ed.), *Bowles and Gintis revisited* (pp. 16-32). New York: Falmer Press.

Giroux, H. (1983). *Theory and resistance in education: A pedagogy for the opposition*. South Hadley, MA: Bergin & Garvey.

Giroux, H. (1988). *Teachers as intellectuals: Toward a critical pedagogy of learning*. Granby, MA: Bergin & Garvey.

Glass, G. (1987). What works: Politics and research. *Educational Researcher, 16*(4), 5-10.

Gleick, J. (1987). *Chaos: Making a new science*. New York: Penguin.

Glenn, C. (1989). Putting school choice in place. *Phi Delta Kappan, 71*(4), 295-300.

Glickman, C. D. (1990). *Supervision of instruction: A developmental approach* (2nd ed.). Boston: Allyn & Bacon.

Goodlad, J. I. (1991). *Teachers for our nation's schools*. San Francisco: Jossey-Bass.

Goodlad, J. I., Soder, R., & Sirotnik, K. A. (1990). *Places where teachers are taught*. San Francisco: Jossey-Bass.

Goodman, J. (1989). Education for critical democracy. *Journal of Education, 171*(2), 88-116.

Goodman, P. (1964). *Compulsory miseducation.* New York: Vintage Books.

Gottfried, A. E., & Gottfried, A. W. (1991, April). *Parents' reward strategies and children's academic intrinsic motivation and school performance.* Paper presented at the biennial meeting of the Society for Research in Child Development, Seattle, Washington. (ERIC Document Reproduction Service No. ED 335 144)

Gould, S. (1981). *The mismeasure of man.* New York: W. W. Norton.

Gouldner, A. (1979). *The future of intellectuals and the rise of the new class.* New York: Oxford University Press.

Gramsci, A. (1971). *Selections from the prison notebooks* (Q. Hoare & G. Smith, Eds. and Trans.). New York: International Publishers.

Grant, G. (1982). The character of education and the education of character. *American Education, 18*(1), 37–46.

Grant, V., & Snyder, T. (1986). *Digest of education statistics, 1985–86* (22nd ed.). Washington, DC: U.S. Department of Education, National Center for Education Statistics. (ERIC Document Reproduction Service No. ED 270 903)

Greene, M. (1982). Educational adequacy: A philosophical approach. In E. Tron (Ed.), *Adequate education: Issues in its definition and implementation* (pp. 93–109). Washington, DC: Office of Educational Research and Improvement. (ERIC Document Reproduction Service No. ED 226 489)

Greene, M. (1986). How do we think about our craft? In A. Lieberman (Ed.), *Rethinking school improvement: Research, craft, and concept* (pp. 13–25). New York: Teachers College Press.

Guilford, J. P. (1959). Three faces of intellect. *American Psychologist, 14*, 469–479.

Guilmet, G. J. (1983). *The inappropriateness of standardized testing in a culturally heterogeneous milieu: A Navajo example.* Los Angeles: University of California Press. (ERIC Document Reproduction No. ED 261 830)

Gutman, H. G. (1987). Schools for freedom: The post-emancipation origins of Afro-American education. In I. Berlin (Ed.), *Power and culture: Essays on the working class* (pp. 260–297). New York: Pantheon.

Guttmann, A. (1987). *Democratic education.* Princeton, NJ: Princeton University Press.

Habermas, J. (1971). *Knowledge and human interests* (J. Shapiro, Trans.). Boston: Beacon Press.

Habermas, J. (1973). *Theory and practice* (J. Viertel, Trans.). Boston: Beacon Press.

Habermas, J. (1975). *Legitimation crisis* (T. McCarthy, Trans.). Boston: Beacon Press.

Habermas, J. (1985). *Theory of communicative action* (T. McCarthy, Trans.). Boston: Beacon Press.

Hagen, E. (1980). *Identification of the gifted.* New York: Teachers College Press.

Hallinan, M. T., & Sorensen, A. B. (1987). Ability grouping and sex differences in mathematics achievement. *Sociology of Education, 60*, 63–72.

Halsey, A. H., & Trow, M. (1971). *The British academics.* Cambridge, MA: Harvard University Press.

Hamilton, R. F., & Hargens, L. L. (1993). The politics of the professors: Self-identifications, 1969-1984. *Social Forces, 71*(3), 603-627.

Hampshire, S. (1983). *Morality and conflict.* Cambridge, MA: Harvard University Press.

Haney, W. (1993). Testing and minorities. In L. Weis & M. Fine (Eds.), *Beyond silenced voices: Class, race, and gender in United States schools* (pp. 25-73). Albany: State University of New York Press.

Hanushek, E. (1989). The impact of differential expenditures on school performance. *Educational Researcher, 18*(4), 45-62.

Hardeo, S. (1989). Relations of sociodemographic variables and cognitive ability: A comparative analysis of the cognitive scores of high school seniors. *Perceptual and Motor Skills, 69*(3), 1139-1158.

Harvey, D. (1989). *The condition of postmodernity.* Cambridge, MA: Basil Blackwell.

Hawking, S. (1988). *A brief history of time.* New York: Bantam.

Hearnshaw, L. S. (1979). *Cyril Burt: Psychologist.* London: Hodder & Stoughton.

Heilbroner, R. (1960). *The future as history.* New York: Vintage Books.

Heilbroner, R. (1985). *The nature and logic of capitalism.* New York: W. W. Norton.

Heilbroner, R. (1993). *Twenty-first century capitalism.* New York: W. W. Norton.

Heilbroner, R., & Thurow, L. (1985). *Understanding macroeconomics* (8th ed.). Englewood Cliffs, NJ: Prentice-Hall.

Herberg, W. (1955). *Protestant, Catholic, Jew.* Garden City, NY: Doubleday.

Hill, P., Foster, G., & Gendler, T. (1989). *High schools with character.* Santa Monica, CA: Rand Corporation.

Hirsch, E. D. (1987). *Cultural literacy: What every American needs to know.* Boston: Houghton Mifflin.

Hirst, P. (1973). Liberal education and the nature of knowledge. In R. S. Peters (Ed.), *Philosophy of education* (pp. 87-111). Oxford: Oxford University Press.

Hofstadter, R. (1955). *Academic freedom in the age of the college.* New York: Columbia University Press.

Hofstadter, R. (1963). *Anti-intellectualism in American life.* New York: Knopf.

Hollis, M. (1982). The social destruction of reality. In M. Hollis & S. Lukes (Eds.), *Rationality and relativism* (pp. 67-86). Cambridge, MA: MIT Press.

Holzer, H. (1989). *Labor force participation and employment among young men: Trends, causes, and policy implications* (Background Paper No. 21). Washington, DC: Commission of Workforce Quality and Labor Market Efficiency, U. S. Department of Labor. (ERIC Document Reproduction Service No. ED 317 688)

Honeyman, D., Thompson, D., & Wood, C. (1989). *Financing rural and small schools: Issues of adequacy and equity.* Charleston, WV: ERIC Clearinghouse on Rural Education and Small Schools. (ERIC Document Reproduction Service No. ED 314 225)

House Select Committee on Children, Youth, and Families. (1987). *U.S. children and their families: Current conditions and recent trends.* Washington, DC:

U.S. Government Printing Office. (ERIC Document Reproduction Service No. ED 288 611)

Howley, A. (1986). Gifted education and the spectre of elitism. *Journal of Education*, *168*(1), 117-125.

Howley, A., & Covaleskie, J. (1993, November). *The professionalization of teachers: Democratic empowerment or ruling class ruse?* Paper presented at the annual meeting of the American Educational Studies Association, Chicago.

Howley, A., Ferrell, S., Bickel, R., & Leary, P. (1994). *Teachers' values and the prospect for school reform*. Unpublished manuscript, Marshall University, Huntington, West Virginia.

Howley, A., & Hartnett, R. (1994). Recalcitrance and the canon wars: A Foucaultian genealogical study. *Journal of Thought*, *29*(1), 51-67.

Howley, A., Howley, C., & Pendarvis, E. (1986). *Teaching gifted children: Principles and strategies*. Boston: Little, Brown.

Howley, A., Pendarvis, E., & Howley, C. (1993). Anti-intellectualism in U. S. schools. *Education Policy Analysis Archives*, *1*(6). (Electronic journal available from listserv@asucad.bitnet)

Howley, C. (1987a). Anti-intellectualism in programs for able students (beware of gifts): An application. *Social Epistemology*, *1*(2), 175-181. (ERIC Document Reproduction Service No. ED 321 431)

Howley, C. (1987b). It's controversial, but "acceleration" could bring gifted kids up to full speed. *American School Boards Journal*, *174*(6), 32-33, 40.

Howley, C. (1990). *Cultural contradictions and the institutional dilemma of education in capitalist America*. Unpublished paper, West Virginia University, Morgantown. (ERIC Document Reproduction Service No. ED 320 217)

Howley, C. (1991). Economics and education: Instrumentalism and the dilemma of learning in rural areas. In A. DeYoung (Ed.), *Rural education: A resource book* (pp. 73-145). New York: Garland.

Howley, C. (1992). Early entry is essential for young gifted children. *The ERIC Review*, *4*(1). (ERIC Document Reproduction Service No. 343 583)

Howley, C. (1993, July). *Absent without leave: Solitude and the scheme of schooling*. Paper presented at the Third Invitational Conference on Thoughtful Teaching and Learning, Brigham Young University, Provo, Utah.

Howley, C., & Howley A. (1989). Gifted programs: Equal access in rural areas. *Rural Special Education Quarterly*, *8*(4), 3-8.

Hoy, W., & Miskel, C. (1987). *Educational administration: Theory, research, and practice* (3rd ed.). New York: Random House.

Hoy, W., & Woolfolk, A. (1990). Socialization of student teachers. *American Educational Research Journal*, *27*(2), 279-300.

Hoyt, K., & Hebler, J. (1974). *Career education for gifted and talented students*. Salt Lake City, UT: Olympus.

Hudson-Ross, S. (1989). Student questions: Moving naturally into the student-centered classroom. *Social Studies*, *80*(3), 110-113.

Hughes, M. (1993). *The fair share dilemma*. Charleston: West Virginia Education Fund. (ERIC Document Reproduction Service No. 356 119)

Hutchins, R. (1968). *The learning society*. New York: Praeger.

Ilika, J. (1974, May). *A critical review of the teacher readership characteristics research and the implications for performance based teaching.* Paper presented at the annual meeting of the International Reading Association, New Orleans. (ERIC Document Reproduction Service No. ED 092 912)

Illich, I. (1971). *Deschooling society.* New York: Harper and Row.

Imig, D. G., & Imig, D. R. (1987). Strengthening and maintaining the pool of qualified teachers. In C. P. Magrath & R. L. Egbert (Eds.), *Strengthening teacher education: The challenges to college and university leaders* (pp. 36–54). San Francisco: Jossey-Bass.

Inkeles, A., & Smith, D. (1974). *Becoming modern.* Cambridge, MA: Harvard University Press.

Irvine, J. J. (1986). Teacher-student interactions: Effects of student race, sex, and grade level. *Journal of Educational Psychology, 78*(1), 14–21.

Jackson, J. (1992). Deviance and change in the urban African American community. *Western Journal of Black Studies, 16*(3), 123–131.

Jackson, P. (1981). Secondary schooling for the privileged few: A report on a visit to a New England boarding school. *Daedelus, 110*(4), 117–130.

Jacobs, J. C. (1971). Effectiveness of teacher and parent identification of gifted children as a function of school level. *Psychology in the Schools, 6*, 140–142.

Jacobs, J. (1984). *Cities and the wealth of nations: Principles of economic life.* New York: Random House.

Jacobs, J. (1992). *Systems of survival: A dialogue on the moral foundations of commerce and politics.* New York: Vintage Books.

James, H., & Levin, H. (1970). Financing community schools. In H. Levin (Ed.), *Community control of schools* (pp. 250–274). New York: Simon & Schuster.

James, W. (1915). *Talks to teachers on psychology and to students on some of life's ideals.* New York: H. Holt and Company. (Original work published 1899)

Jarrell, R. H., & Borland, J. H. (1990). The research base for Renzulli's three-ring conception of giftedness. *Journal for the Education of the Gifted, 13*, 288–308.

Jaspers, K. (1970). *Philosophy* (Vol. 2, E. B. Ashton, Trans.). Chicago: University of Chicago Press. (Original work published 1932)

Jencks, C., Bartlett, S., Corcoran, M., Crouse, J., Eaglesfield, D., Jackson, G., McClelland, K., Mueser, P., Olneck, M., Schwarz, J., Ward, S., & Williams, J. (1979). *Who gets ahead? The determinants of economic success in America.* New York: Basic Books.

Jencks, C., Smith, M., Acland, H., Bane, M., Cohen, D., Gintis, H., Heyns, B., & Michelson, S. (1972). *Inequality: A reassessment of the effect of family and schooling in America.* New York: Harper & Row.

Jensen, A. (1973). *Educability and group differences.* New York: Harper & Row.

Johansen, B. (1989). William James Sidis' "Tribes and States": An unpublished exploration of Native American contributions to democracy. *Northeast Indian Quarterly, 6*(3), 24–29.

Johnson, J. L. (1979). An essay on incarcerated youth: An oppressed group. *Exceptional Children, 45*(7), 566–571.

Jones, M. G. (1989). Gender issues in teacher education. *Journal of Teacher Education*, *40*, 33–38.

Jones-Wilson, F. C., Arnez, N. L., & Asbury, C. A. (1992). Why not public schools? *Journal of Negro Education*, *61*(2), 125–137.

Joseph, P. B., & Efron, S. (1991, April). *Moral choices/moral values: Self-perceptions of schoolteachers*. Paper presented at the annual meeting of the American Education Research Association, Chicago. (ERIC Document Reproduction Service No. ED 332 376)

Kane, P. R. (1990). Just ask liberal arts graduates to teach. *Phi Delta Kappan*, *71*(10), 805–807.

Kanevsky, L. (1990). Pursuing qualitative differences in the flexible use of problem-solving strategy by young children. *Journal for the Education of the Gifted*, *13*(2), 115–140.

Katchadourian, H., & Boli, J. (1985). *Careerism and intellectualism among college students*. San Francisco: Jossey-Bass.

Katz, L. (1993). *Dispositions as educational goals* (ERIC Digest EDO-PS-93-10). Urbana, IL: ERIC Clearinghouse on Elementary and Early Childhood Education. (ERIC Document Reproduction Service No. ED 363 454)

Katz, L., & Raths, J. (1992). Six dilemmas in teacher education. *Journal of Teacher Education*, *43*(5), 376–385.

Katz, M. (1968). *The irony of early school reform*. Cambridge, MA: Harvard University Press.

Katz, M. (1971). *Class, bureaucracy, and schools*. New York: Praeger.

Kauffman, J. M. (1992). *Characteristics of emotional and behavioral disorders of children and youth* (5th ed.). Columbus, OH: Charles E. Merrill.

Keating, D. P. (1988). *Adolescents' ability to engage in critical thinking* (Monograph published by the National Center on Effective Secondary Schools). Madison: University of Wisconsin Center for Education Research. (ERIC Document Reproduction Service No. 307 508)

Keith, T. Z. (1982). Time spent on homework and high school grades: A large-sample path analysis. *Journal of Educational Psychology*, *74*, 248–253.

Keizer, G. (1988). *No place but here*. New York: Viking Press.

Kellogg, J. B. (1988). Forces of change. *Phi Delta Kappan*, *70*(3), 199–204.

Kerchner, C. T., & Mitchell, D. E. (1988). *The changing idea of a teachers' union*. New York: Falmer Press.

Kerr, C. (1963). *The uses of the university*. Cambridge, MA: Harvard University Press.

Kerr, C. (1991). *The great transformation of higher education: 1960–1980*. Albany: State University of New York Press.

Kintgen, E. (1988). Literacy literacy. *Visible Language*, *22*(2/3), 149–168.

Kliebard, H. M. (1986). *The struggle for the American curriculum*. Boston: Routledge and Kegan Paul.

Koballa, T. R. (1987). The professional reading patterns of Texas life science teachers. *School Science and Mathematics*, *87*(2), 118–124.

Kolander, C., & Chandler, C. (1990, March). *Spiritual health: A balance of all dimensions*. Paper presented at the annual meeting of the American Alliance for Health, Physical Education, Recreation, and Dance, New Orleans. (ERIC Document Reproduction Service No. ED 323 172)

Kozol, J. (1985). *Illiterate America*. New York: Anchor Press.

Kozol, J. (1991). *Savage inequalities: Children in America's schools*. New York: Crown.

Krymkowski, D., & Krauze, T. (1992). Occupational mobility in the year 2000: Projections for American men and women. *Social Forces, 71*(1), 145–157.

Kulik, J., & Kulik, C. (1984). Effects of accelerated instruction on students. *Review of Educational Research, 54*(3), 409–425.

Kurtz, P. (1974). Excellence and irrelevance: Democracy and higher education. In S. Hook, P. Kurtz, & M. Todorovich (Eds.), *The idea of a modern university* (pp. 185–202). Buffalo, NY: Prometheus Books.

Labov, W. (1972). *Language in the inner city: Studies in the Black English vernacular*. Philadelphia: University of Pennsylvania Press.

Ladd, E. C., & Lipset, S. M. (1975). *The divided academy*. New York: McGraw-Hill.

Lareau, A. (1989). *Home advantage: Social class and parental intervention in elementary education*. Philadelphia: Falmer Press.

Lasch, C. (1979). *The culture of narcissism: American life in an age of diminishing expectations*. New York: W. W. Norton.

Lasch, C. (1991). *The true and only heaven: Progress and its critics*. New York: W. W. Norton.

Lawson, H. A. (1992). Beyond the new conception of teacher induction. *Journal of Teacher Education, 43*(3), 163–172.

Ledent, J. (1982). Rural-urban migration, urbanization, and economic development. *Economic Development and Cultural Change, 30*, 507–538.

Lehman, D. (1992). Refuting Howard Gardner's theory of multiple intelligences. In M. Leue (Ed.), *Challenging the giant* (pp. 240–256). Albany, NY: Down-to-Earth Books.

Leman, N. (1986, June). The origins of the underclass. *The Atlantic, 257* (6), 31–43,47–55.

Leontief, W. (1982, September). The distribution of work and income. *Scientific American*, pp. 188–204.

Levin, B. (1993). Students and educational productivity. *Education Policy Analysis Archives, 1*(5). (Electronic journal available from listserv@asucad.bitnet)

Levin, H. M. (1970). A cost-effective analysis of teacher selection. *Journal of Human Resources, 1*, 24–33.

Levin, H. M. (1991). *Accelerating the progress of all students* (Rockefeller Institute Special Rep., No. 31). Albany, NY: Nelson A. Rockefeller Institute of Government. (ERIC Document Reproduction Service No. ED 334 313)

Levine, D. O. (1986). *The American college and the culture of aspiration, 1915–1940*. Ithaca, NY: Cornell University Press.

Lewontin, R. C., Rose, S., & Kamin, L. J. (1984). *Not in our genes: Biology, ideology, and human nature*. New York: Random House.

Lichter, D., & Eggebeen, D. (1993). Rich kids, poor kids: Changing income inequality among American children. *Social Forces, 71*(3), 761–780.

Liebert, R. M., & Sprafkin, J. (1988). *The early window: Effects of television on children and youth* (3rd ed.). New York: Pergamon.

Lightfoot, S. L. (1986). On goodness in schools: Themes of empowerment. *Peabody Journal of Education, 63*(3), 9–28.

Liston, D. P., & Zeichner, K. M. (1990). Teacher education and the social context of schooling: Issues for curriculum development. *American Educational Research Journal, 27*(4), 610–636.

Liston, D. P., & Zeichner, K. M. (1991). *Teacher education and the social conditions of schooling.* New York: Routledge, Chapman & Hall.

Lortie, D. C. (1975). *School teacher: A sociological study.* Chicago: University of Chicago Press.

Lowe, R. (1992). Choosing inequality in the schools. *Monthly Review, 44*(1), 2134.

Lucas, A. (1979). *Educational goals and values of students and teachers: An exploratory study.* (Unpublished paper, ERIC Document Reproduction Service No. ED 175 801)

Lucas, S., & Gamoran, A. (1993). *Race and track assignment: A reconsideration with course-based indicators of track locations.* Madison, WI: Center on Organization and Restructuring of Schools. (ERIC Document Reproduction Service No. ED 357 455)

Lucking, R. A. (1977, March). *Teachers' classroom questioning skills.* Paper presented at the annual meeting of the Conference on English Education, Knoxville, Tennessee. (ERIC Document Reproduction Service No. ED 150 615)

Lukes, S. (1974). *Power: A radical view.* London: Macmillan.

Luria, S. E., & Luria, Z. (1970). The role of the university: Ivory tower, service station, or frontier post. In S. R. Graubard & G. A. Ballotti (Eds.), *The embattled university* (pp. 75–83). New York: George Braziller.

Lyotard, J. (1984). *The postmodern condition: A report on knowledge* (G. Bennington & B. Massumi, Trans.). Minneapolis: University of Minnesota Press. (Original work published 1979)

Lyotard, J. (1989). *The Lyotard reader* (A. Benjamin, Ed.). Cambridge, MA: Basil Blackwell.

Mace-Matluck, B. (1987). *The effective schools movement: Its history and context.* Austin, TX: Southwest Educational Development Laboratory. (ERIC Document Reproduction Service No. ED 304 781)

MacIntyre, A. (1984). *After virtue: A study in moral theory* (2nd ed.). Notre Dame, IN: University of Notre Dame Press.

Maharidge, D. (1992, January 13). And the rural poor get poorer. *The Nation,* pp. 10–12.

Maker, C. J. (1987). Assessment of the gifted learner. In W. H. Berdine and S. A. Meyer (Eds.), *Assessment in special education.* Boston: Little, Brown.

Marcuse, H. (1955). *Eros and civilization: A philosophical inquiry into Freud.* New York: Viking Press.

Marcuse, H. (1978). *The aesthetic dimension.* New York: Beacon Press.

Margolin, L. (1994). *Goodness personified: The emergence of gifted children.* New York: Aldine De Gruyter.

Margolis, E., & Moses, S. (1992). *The elusive quest: The struggle for equality of educational opportunity*. New York: Apex Press.

Marland, S. (1972). *Education of the gifted and talented: Report to the Congress of the United States by the US Commissioner of Education*. Washington, DC: U. S. Government Printing Office.

Martin, J. (1970). *Explaining, understanding, and teaching*. New York: McGraw-Hill.

Martinson, R. (1979). *The identification of the gifted and talented*. Reston, VA: Council for Exceptional Children.

Maslow, A. H. (1968). *Toward a psychology of being*. Princeton, NJ: Van Nostrand.

Maslow, A. H. (1970). *Motivation and personality*. New York: Harper & Row.

Massialas, B. G. (1969). *Education and the political system*. Reading, MA: Addison-Wesley.

Matthews, N. (Ed.). (1985). *West Virginia women: In perspective, 1970–1985*. Charleston: West Virginia Women's Commission.

McCarthy, C. (1990). Rethinking liberal and radical perspectives on racial inequality in schooling: Making the case for nonsynchrony. In N. M. Hidalgo, C. L. McDowell, & E. V. Siddle (Eds.), *Facing racism in education* (pp. 35–49). Cambridge, MA: Harvard University Press. (Reprint Series No. 21, *Harvard Educational Review*)

McClelland, D., Atkinson, J., Clark, R., & Lowell, E. (1953). *The achievement motive*. New York: Appleton-Century-Crofts.

McDill, E. L., & Coleman, J. (1965). Family and peer influences in college plans of high school students. *Sociology of Education, 38*(2), 112–126.

McDonald, J. P. (1986). Raising the teacher's voice and the ironic role of theory. *Harvard Educational Review, 56*(4), 355–378.

McGinn, N., & Pereira, L. (1992). Why states change the governance of education: An historical comparison of Brazil and the United States. *Comparative Education, 28*(2), 167–180.

McLaughlin, M. W., Pfeifer, R. S., Swanson-Owens, D., & Yee, S. (1986). Why teachers won't teach. *Phi Delta Kappan, 67*(6), 420–426.

McNeil, L. M. (1988). Contradictions of control, part 3: Contradictions of reform. *Phi Delta Kappan, 69*(7), 478–485.

McPeck, J. E. (1986, October). *Teaching critical thinking through the disciplines: Content versus process*. Paper presented at the annual meeting of the South Atlantic Philosophy of Education Society, Baltimore, Maryland. (ERIC Document Reproduction Service No. ED 283 823)

Meckley, R., Hartnett, R., & Yeager, J. (1987). The year of education: That dog won't hunt. *Journal of Education Finance, 13*, 182–188.

Meeker, M. (1969). *The structure of intellect*. Columbus: Charles E. Merrill.

Metropolitan Life Survey of the American Teacher. (1985). *Strengthening the profession*. New York: Metropolitan Life Insurance Company. (ERIC Document Reproduction Service No. ED 268 076)

Meyer, J., Tyack, D., Nagel, J., & Gordon, A. (1979). Public education as nation-building in America: Enrollments and bureaucratization in the American states, 1870–1930. *American Journal of Sociology, 85*(3), 591–613.

Mickelson, R. A. (1989). Why does Jane read and write so well? The anomaly of women's achievement. *Sociology of Education, 62*, 47–63.

Mill, J. S. (1956). *On liberty.* New York: Bobbs-Merrill. (Original work published 1859)

Miller, G. E. (1988). *The meaning of general education: The emergence of a curriculum paradigm.* New York: Teachers College Press.

Mitchell, C. (1988). Paralleling cognitive and moral development with spiritual development and denominational choice. *Psychology: A Journal of Human Behavior, 25*(1), 1–9.

Mitchell, R. (1979). *Less than words can say.* Boston: Little, Brown.

Montour, K. M. (1977). William James Sidis: The broken twig. *American Psychologist, 32*(4), 265–279.

Moretti, F. (1993). Who controls the canon? A classicist in conversation with cultural conservatives. *Teachers College Record, 95*(1), 113–126.

Muller, T., & Espanshade, T. J. (1985). *The fourth wave: California's newest immigrants.* Washington, DC: Urban Institute Press.

Mumford, L. (1961). *Technics and civilization.* New York: Harcourt Brace Jovanovich. (Original work published 1934)

Murphy, J. (1989). Educational reform in the 1980s: Explaining some surprising success. *Educational Evaluation and Policy Analysis, 11*(3), 209–221.

Murphy, K., & Finis, W. (1989). Wage premiums for college graduates: Recent growth and possible explanations. *Educational Researcher, 18*(4), 17–26.

National Alliance of Business. (1984). *A nation at work: Education and the private sector.* Washington, DC: National Advisory Council on Vocational Education and National Alliance of Business. (ERIC Document Reproduction Service No. ED 246 201)

National Center for Education Statistics. (1991). *Digest on a disk* (computerized version of the 1991 *Digest of education statistics*). Washington, DC: Author.

National Center for Education Statistics. (1993). *Time to complete baccalaureate degree* (Indicator of the Month, October). Washington, DC: Author. (ERIC Document Reproduction Service No. ED 366 657)

National Center for Research on Teacher Education. (1991). *Findings from the teacher education and learning to teach study* (Final Rep.). East Lansing, MI: Author. (ERIC Document Reproduction Service No. ED 359 168)

National Center on Education and the Economy. (1990). *America's choice: High skills or low wages.* National Center on Education and the Economy, Commission on the Skills of the American Workforce. (ERIC Document Reproduction Service No. ED 323 297)

National Commission on Excellence in Education. (1983). *A nation at risk: The imperative for educational reform.* Washington, DC: U. S. Department of Education. (ERIC Document Reproduction Service No. ED 226 006)

National Council of Teachers of Mathematics (NCTM). (1991). *Professional standards for teaching mathematics.* Reston, VA: National Council of Teachers of Mathematics. (ERIC Document Reproduction Service No. ED 344 779)

National Governors' Association. (1990, March 2). Education goals, objectives. *Governors' Weekly Bulletin*, p. 2.

Navarro, V. (1991). Class and race: Life and death situations. *Monthly Review*, *43*(4), 1-13.

Newman, J. (1959). *The idea of a university*. New York: Doubleday. (Original work published 1852)

Nisbet, R. (1966). *The sociological tradition*. New York: Basic Books.

Nisbet, R. (1971). *The degradation of the academic dogma: The university in America, 1945-1970*. New York: Basic Books.

Nystrand, M., & Gamoran, A. (1989). *Instructional discourse and student engagement*. Madison, WI: National Center on Effective Secondary Schools. (ERIC Document Reproduction Service No. ED 319 780)

Nystrand, M., & Gamoran, A. (1991). Instructional discourse, student engagement, and literature achievement. *Research in the Teaching of English*, *25*(3), 261-290.

Oakes, J. (1985). *Keeping track: How schools structure inequality*. New Haven, CT: Yale University Press.

Oakeshott, M. (1962). *Rationalism in politics and other essays*. New York: Basic Books.

Odiorne, G. (1965). *Management by objectives: A system of managerial leadership*. New York: Pitman.

Office of Technology Assessment. (1989). *Linking for learning: A new course for education* (OTA-SET-430). Washington, DC: U. S. Government Printing Office. (ERIC Document Reproduction Service No. ED 310 765)

Ogbu, J. (1978). *Minority education and caste*. New York: Academic Press.

Onosko, J. (1989). Comparing teachers' thinking about promoting students' thinking. *Theory and Research in Social Education*, *17*(3), 174-195.

Orlich, D. C. (1989). Education reforms: Mistakes, misconceptions, miscues. *Phi Delta Kappan*, *70*(7), 512-517.

Orr, J., & Klein, F. (1991). Instruction in critical thinking as a form of character education. *Journal of Curriculum and Supervision*, *6*(2), 130-144.

Ortiz, V., & Gonzalez, A. (1989). Validation of the short form of the WISC-R with accelerated and gifted Hispanic students. *Gifted Child Quarterly*, *33*(4), 152-156.

O'Tuel, F. (1983). The SOI as an identification tool for the gifted: Windfall or washout? *Gifted Child Quarterly*, *27*(3), 126-134.

Ouchi, W. (1981). *Theory Z: How American business can meet the Japanese challenge*. Reading, MA: Addison-Wesley.

Oxford English Dictionary (compact ed.). (1971). London: Oxford University Press. (Original work published 1928)

Ozga, J., & Lawn, M. (1981). *Teachers, professionalism and class: A study of organized teachers*. Sussex: Falmer Press.

Pajares, M. F. (1992). Teachers' beliefs and educational research: Cleaning up a messy construct. *Review of Educational Research*, *62*(3), 307-332.

Parish, R., & Arends, R. I. (1982, March). *Discontinuation of innovative programs*. Paper presented at the annual meeting of the American Educational

Research Association, New York. (ERIC Document Reproduction Service No. ED 218 758)

Parker, A. A. (1992, January/February). Choosing sides on school choice. *Dollars and Sense*, pp. 6–8.

Passmore, J. (1966). *A hundred years of philosophy*. New York: Penguin Books.

Passow, A. H. (1984). *Reforming schools in the 1980s: A critical review of the national reports*. New York: ERIC Clearinghouse on Urban Education. (ERIC Document Reproduction Service No. ED 242 859)

Pauley v. Kelley, 255 SE 2d 859 (1979). Civil Action No. 75–1268, Circuit Court of Kanawha County.

Pearson, J. (1989). Myths of choice: The governor's new clothes? *Phi Delta Kappan, 70* (10), 821–823.

Pegnato, C. W., & Birch, J. W. (1959). Locating gifted children in junior high school. *Exceptional Children, 25*(7), 300–304.

Pendarvis, E., Howley, A., & Howley, C. (1990). *The abilities of gifted children*. Englewood Cliffs, NJ: Prentice-Hall.

Perelman, L. (1992, December 10). Hyperlearning: Clinton's greatest opportunity for change. *Discovery Institute Inquiry*, pp. 1–12.

Perkinson, H. J. (1968). *The imperfect panacea: American faith in education, 1865–1965*. New York: Random House.

Perrine, J. (1989). Situational identification of gifted Hispanic students. In C. J. Maker & S. W. Schiever (Eds.), *Critical issues in gifted education: Defensible programs for cultural and ethnic minorities* (pp. 5–18). Austin, TX: Pro-Ed.

Pink, W. T. (1982). Academic failure, student social conflict, and delinquent behavior. *Urban Review, 14*(3), 141–180.

Porter, A. C., & Freeman, D. J. (1986). Professional orientations: An essential domain for teacher testing. *Journal of Negro Education, 55*, 284–292.

Postman, N. (1992). *Technopoly: The surrender of culture to technology*. New York: Knopf.

Poulantzas, N. (1980). *State, power, socialism*. London: Verso.

Prawat, R. S. (1991). Conversations with self and settings: A framework for thinking about teacher empowerment. *American Educational Research Journal, 28*(4), 737–757.

Pringle, M. K. (1970). *Able misfits*. London: Longman.

Rand, A. (1965). *The virtue of selfishness: A new concept of egoism*. New York: New American Library.

Raph, J. B., Goldberg, M. L., & Passow, A. H. (1966). *Bright underachievers*. New York: Teachers College Press.

Ratteray, J. D. (1992). Independent neighborhood schools: A framework for the education of African-Americans. *Journal of Negro Education, 61*(2), 138–147.

Ravitch, D. (1991, November). *My goals for OERI*. Speech delivered at the OERI Forum, Washington, DC. (ERIC Document Reproduction Service No. ED 355 911)

Reed, R. J. (1988). Education and achievement of young black males. In J. T.

Gibbs (Ed.), *Young, black, and male in America: An endangered species* (pp. 37–96). New York: Auburn House.

Reid, N. (1992, July). *Correcting cultural myopia: The discovery and nurturance of the culturally different gifted and talented in New Zealand.* Paper presented at the Asian Conference on Giftedness, Taipei, Taiwan. (ERIC Document Reproduction Service No. ED 357 532)

Reis, S. M., Westberg, K. L., Kulikowich, J., Caillard, F., Hebert, T., Plucker, J., Purcell, J. H., Rogers, J. B., & Smist, J. M. (1993). *Why not let high ability students start school in January? The curriculum compacting study* (Research Monograph No. 93105). Storrs: University of Connecticut, National Research Center on the Gifted and Talented.

Reisman, D. (1981). *On higher education: The academic enterprise in an era of rising student consumerism.* San Francisco: Jossey-Bass.

Renzulli, J. (1977). *The enrichment triad model: A guide for developing defensible programs for the gifted and talented.* Wethersfield, CT: Creative Learning Press.

Renzulli, J. (1978). What makes giftedness? *Phi Delta Kappan, 60*(3), 180–184, 261.

Rhodes, R. (1989). Native American learning styles: Implications for teaching and testing. In *Proceedings of the eighth annual international Native American Language Issues Institute.* Choctaw, OK: Native American Language Issues Institute.

Richards, I. (1942). *How to read a page: A course in effective reading, with an introduction to a hundred great words.* New York: W. W. Norton.

Robinson, A. (1990). Cooperation or exploitation? The argument against cooperative learning for talented students. *Journal for the Education of the Gifted, 14*(1), 9–27.

Rodriguez, L. S. (1989). Reaction to "Promoting Pluralism and Power." In C. J. Maker and S. W. Schiever (Eds.), *Critical issues in gifted education: Defensible programs for cultural and ethnic minorities* (pp. 37–40). Austin, TX: Pro-Ed.

Rogers, K. B. (1986a). Do the gifted learn and think differently? A review of recent research and its implications for instruction. *Journal for the Education of the Gifted, 10*(1), 17–39.

Rogers, K. B. (1986b). *Review of research on the education of intellectually and academically gifted students.* St. Paul, MN: Minnesota State Department of Education. (ERIC Document Reproduction Service No. ED 268 761)

Rogers, K. B. (1989). A content analysis of the literature on giftedness. *Journal for the Education of the Gifted, 13*(1), 78–88.

Rosenholtz, S. J. (1989). *Teachers' workplace: The social organization of schools.* New York: Longman.

Rudolph, F. (1977). *Curriculum: A history of the American undergraduate course of study since 1636.* San Francisco: Jossey-Bass.

Ruiz, R. (1989). Considerations in the education of gifted Hispanic students. In C. J. Maker & S. W. Schiever (Eds.), *Critical issues in gifted education:*

Defensible programs for cultural and ethnic minorities (pp. 60–64). Austin, TX: Pro-Ed.

Rumberger, R. W., & Willms, J. D. (1992). The impact of racial and ethnic segregation on the achievement gap in California high schools. *Educational Evaluation and Policy Analysis, 14*(4), 377–396.

Russett, C. E. (1976). *Darwin in America: The intellectual response, 1865–1912.* San Francisco: W. H. Freeman.

Ryan, W. (1971). *Blaming the victim.* New York: Pantheon.

Sadker, M., Sadker, D., & Steindan, S. (1989). Gender equity and educational reform. *Educational leadership, 46*(1), 44–48.

Safer, D. J. (Ed.). (1982). *School programs for disruptive adolescents.* Baltimore, MD: University Park Press.

Salvia, J., & Ysseldyke, J. E. (1991). *Assessment in special and remedial education* (5th ed.). Boston: Houghton Mifflin.

Sapon-Shevin, M. (1993). Gifted education and the protection of privilege: Breaking the silence, opening the discourse. In L. Weis and M. Fine (Eds.), *Beyond silenced voices: Class, race, and gender in United States schools* (pp. 25–44). Albany: State University of New York Press.

Sapon-Shevin, M. (1994). *Playing favorites: Gifted education and the disruption of community.* Albany: State University of New York Press.

Sarason, S. (1971). *The culture of school and the problems of change.* Boston: Allyn & Bacon.

Sashkin, M., & Egermeier, J. (1993). *School change models and processes: A review and synthesis of research and practice.* Washington, DC: U. S. Department of Education, Office of Educational Research and Improvement. (ERIC Document Reproduction Service No. ED 362 960)

Schaefer, R. J. (1967). *The school as a center of inquiry.* New York: Harper & Row.

Schlechty, P. C., & Vance, V. S. (1981). Do academically able teachers leave education? The North Carolina case. *Phi Delta Kappan, 63,* 106–112.

Schneider, J. M., & Brookover, W. B. (1974, April). *Academic environments and elementary school achievement.* Paper presented at the annual meeting of the American Educational Research Association, Chicago. (ERIC Document Reproduction Service No. ED 091 858)

Schor, J. (1991). *The overworked American: The unexpected decline of leisure.* New York: Basic Books.

Schroeder, K. (1991). Minorities in college. *Education Digest, 56*(7), 74.

Sealey, J. (1985). *Curriculum development projects of the sixties.* Washington, DC: National Institute of Education. (ERIC Document Reproduction Service No. ED 272 378)

Secretary's Commission on Achieving Necessary Skills (SCANS). (1991). *What work requires of schools: A SCANS report for America 2000.* Washington, DC: U. S. Department of Labor.

Sedlak, M., & Schlossman, S. (1986). *Who will teach? Historical perspectives on the changing appeal of teaching as a profession.* Santa Monica, CA: The Rand Corporation. (ERIC Document Reproduction Service No. ED 292 184)

Sedlak, M., Wheeler, C. W., Pullin, D. C., & Cusick, P. A. (1986). *Selling students short: Classroom bargains and academic reform in the American high school.* New York: Teachers College Press.

Seligman, D. (1992). *A question of intelligence: The IQ debate in America.* New York: Birch Lane Press.

Sennett, R., & Cobb, J. (1972). *The hidden injuries of class.* New York: Vintage Books.

Sharp, B., & Watson, P. (1981). *Evaluation of the gifted and talented program, 1980-1981.* Oklahoma City: Oklahoma City Public Schools, Department of Planning, Research, and Evaluation. (ERIC Document Reproduction Service No. ED 221 010)

Shea, C. (1989). Pentagon vs. multinational capitalism: The political economy of the 1980s school reform movement. In C. Shea, E. Kahane, & P. Sola (Eds.), *The new servants of power: A critique of the 1980s school reform movement* (Contributions to the Study of Education, No. 28). New York: Greenwood.

Sheffler, I. (1985). *Of human potential: An essay in the philosophy of education.* London: Routledge & Kegan Paul.

Shils, E. (1980). *Tradition.* Chicago: University of Chicago Press.

Shore, B. M., Cornell, D. G., Robinson, A., & Ward, V. S. (1991). *Recommended practices in gifted education: A critical analysis.* New York: Teachers College Press.

Shulman, L. S. (1987). Knowledge and teaching: Foundations of the new reform. *Harvard Educational Review, 57*(1), 1-22.

Silverman, L. (1986). Whatever happened to the gifted girl? In J. Maker (Ed.), *Critical issues in gifted education* (pp. 43-89). Rockville, MD: Aspen.

Sirotnik, K., & Clark, R. (1988). School-centered decision making and renewal. *Phi Delta Kappan, 69*(9), 660-664.

Slavin, R. E. (1990). *Cooperative learning: Theory, research and practice.* Englewood Cliffs, NJ: Prentice-Hall.

Smith, F. (1990). *To think.* New York: Teachers College Press.

Smith, M., & O'Day, J. (1990). Systemic school reform. In S. Fuhrman & B. Malen (Eds.), *The politics of curriculum and testing* (Politics of Education Association Yearbook 1990, pp. 233-267). Bristol, PA: Falmer Press.

Smyth, J. (1992). Teachers' work and the politics of reflection. *American Educational Research Journal, 29*(2), 267-300.

Sockett, H. (1993). *The moral base for teacher professionalism.* New York: Teachers College Press.

Soder, R. (1991). The ethics of the rhetoric of teacher professionalization. *Teaching & Teacher Education, 7*(3), 295-302.

Solano, C. (1976, September). *Teacher and pupil stereotypes of gifted boys and girls.* Paper presented at the annual meeting of the American Psychological Association, Washington, DC. (ERIC Document Reproduction Service No. ED 137 667)

Spatig, L. (1995). Student teaching as social reproduction: An Appalachian ethnography. In M. Ginsburg & B. Lindsay (Eds.), *The political dimension in teacher education: Comparative perspectives on policy formation, socialization, and society.* London: Falmer.

Spencer, H. (1963). *Education: Intellectual, moral and physical.* Patterson, NJ: Littlefield Adams. (Original work published 1860)

Spring, J. (1975). *A primer of libertarian education.* New York: Free Life Editions.

Spring, J. (1986). *The American school 1642-1985.* New York: Longman.

Stallard, K., Ehrenreich, B., & Sklar, H. (1983). *Poverty in the American dream: Women and children first.* Boston: South End Press.

Stanley, J. C. (1976, September). *Brilliant Youth: Improving the quality and speed of their education.* Paper presented at the annual conference of the American Psychological Association, Washington, DC. (ERIC Document Reproduction Service No. ED 136 536)

Stanley, J. C. (1981). Rationale of the Study of Mathematically Precocious Youth (SMPY) during its first five years of promoting educational acceleration. In W. Barbe & J. Renzulli (Eds.), *Psychology and education of the gifted* (pp. 248-283). New York: Irvington.

Stanley, J. C. (1986, April). *The urgent need for an academic focus.* Paper presented at the annual conference of the American Educational Research Association, San Francisco. (ERIC Document Reproduction No. ED 277 205)

Stedman, L. C. (1987). It's time we changed the effective schools formula. *Phi Delta Kappan, 69*(3), 215-224.

Steele, C. M. (1992, April). Race and the schooling of black Americans. *The Atlantic*, pp. 68-78.

Stephens, E. R. (1991). *A framework for evaluating state policy options for the reorganization of rural, small school districts.* Charleston, WV: ERIC Clearinghouse on Rural Education and Small Schools and Appalachia Educational Laboratory. (ERIC Document Reproduction Service No. ED 332 855)

Sternberg, R. (1985). *Beyond IQ: A triarchic theory of human intelligence.* New York: Cambridge University Press.

Sternberg, R. (1986). A triarchic theory of intellectual giftedness. In R. J. Sternberg and J. E. Davidson (Eds.), *Conceptions of giftedness* (pp. 223-243). New York: Cambridge University Press.

Sternberg, R., Subotnik, R., Karp, D., & Morgan, E. R. (1989). High IQ children at midlife: An investigation into the generalizability of Terman's genetic studies of genius. *Roeper Review, 11*(3), 139-144.

Stevenson, C. L. (1966). The emotive meaning of ethical terms. In J. Margolis (Ed.), *Contemporary ethical theory* (pp. 81-102). New York: Random House.

Stockard, J., & Mayberry, M. (1992). *Effective educational environments.* Newbury Park, CA: Corwin Press. (ERIC Document Reproduction Service No. ED 350 674)

Stogdill, R. (1974). *Handbook of leadership: A survey of theory and research.* New York: Free Press.

Storr, A. (1988). *Solitude: A return to the self.* New York: Free Press.

Street, S., & Licata, J. W. (1988, April). *Supervisor expertise, teacher autonomy, and environmental robustness.* Paper presented at the annual meeting of the American Educational Research Association, New Orleans. (ERIC Document Reproduction Service No. ED 299 697)

Strike, K. A. (1993). Professionalism, democracy, and discursive communities:

Normative reflections on restructuring. *American Educational Research Journal, 30*(2), 255–275.

Subotnik, R. F., Karp, D. E., Morgan, E. R. (1989). High IQ children at midlife: An investigation into the generalizability of Terman's Genetic Studies of Genius. *Roeper Review, 11*(3), 139–144.

Sweezy, P. (1992). Globalization – to what end? *Monthly Review, 43*(10), 1–19.

Swisher, K., & Deyhle, D. (1987). Styles of learning and learning of styles: Educational conflicts for American Indian/Alaskan Native youth. *Journal of Multilingual and Multicultural Development, 8*(4), 345–360.

Szasz, M. (1992). Current conditions in American Indian and Alaska Native communities. In P. Cahape & C. Howley (Eds.), *Indian nations at risk: Listening to the people* (pp. 1–5). Charleston, WV: ERIC Clearinghouse on Rural Education and Small Schools. (ERIC Document Reproduction Service No. ED 339 538)

Taba, H. (1965). Learning by discovery: Psychological and educational rationale. In J. Gallagher (Ed.), *Teaching gifted students: A book of readings* (pp. 177–186). Boston: Allyn & Bacon.

Tabachnick, B. R., & Zeichner, K. (1984). The impact of the student teaching experience on the development of teacher perspectives. *Journal of Teacher Education, 35*, 28–36.

Tannenbaum, A. (1981). Pre-Sputnik to post-Watergate concern about the gifted. In W. Barbe & J. Renzulli (Eds.), *Psychology and education of the gifted* (3rd ed., pp. 20–37). New York: Irvington.

Taylor, R. L., & Richards, S. B. (1991). Patterns of intellectual differences of Black, Hispanic, and white children. *Psychology in the Schools, 28*(1), 5–9.

Terman, L. M. (1925). *Mental and physical traits of a thousand gifted children*: Vol. 1. *Genetic studies of genius*. Stanford, CA: Stanford University Press.

Thanksgiving Statement Group. (1984). *Developing character: Transmitting knowledge*. Posen, IL: Thanksgiving Statement Group. (ERIC Document Reproduction Service No. ED 251 381)

Thomas, G. E. (1992). Participation and degree attainment of African American and Latino students in graduate education relative to other racial and ethnic groups: An update from office of Civil Rights data. *Harvard Educational Review, 62*(1), 45–66.

Thurow, L. C. (1987, May). A surge in inequality. *Scientific American*, pp. 30–37.

Tippeconnic, J. W., III. (1989). *Educational neglect: Reform reports and the schooling of American Indians*. Unpublished manuscript, Arizona State University, Tempe. (ERIC Document Reproduction Service No. ED 319 555)

Tönnies, F. (1957). *Community and society* (C. Loomis, Trans.). East Lansing: Michigan State University Press. (Original work published 1887 as *Gemeinschaft und Gesellschaft*)

Torrance, E. P. (1971). Are the Torrance tests of creative thinking biased against or in favor of disadvantaged children? *Gifted Child Quarterly, 15*, 75–80.

Torrance, E. P. (1974). *Torrance tests of creative thinking*. Princeton, NJ: Personnel Press.

Trumpbour, J. (1989). *How Harvard rules: Reason in the service of ideology*. Boston: South End Press.

Turner, J., & Starnes, C. (1976). *Inequality: Privilege and poverty in America.* Pacific Palisades, CA: Goodyear.

Tyack, D. (1974). *The one best system: A history of American urban education.* Cambridge, MA: Harvard University Press.

Tye, B. B. (1985). *Multiple realities: A study of 13 American high schools.* Lanham, MD: University Press of America.

Tyree, A. (1993). Examining the evidence: Have states reduced local control of curriculum? *Educational Evaluation and Policy Analysis, 15*(1), 34–50.

Uchitelle, S. (1989). What it really takes to make school choice work. *Phi Delta Kappan, 71*(4), 301–303.

United States Department of Education. (1991). *America 2000.* (Sourcebook) Washington, DC: U. S. Government Printing Office. (ERIC Document Reproduction Service No. ED 327 985)

Urmson, J. O. (1968). *The emotive theory of ethics.* New York: Oxford University Press.

Valli, L. (1990). Moral approaches to reflective practice. In R. T. Clift, W. R. Houston, & M. C. Pugach (Eds.), *Encouraging reflective practice in education: An analysis of issues and programs* (pp. 39–56). New York: Teachers College Press.

Vance, V. S., & Schlechty, P. C. (1982). The distribution of academic ability in the teaching force: Policy implications. *Phi Delta Kappan, 64*, 22–27.

Vann, A. (1988). Let's give values clarification another chance. A special report: Developing character. *Principal, 68*(2), 15–16, 18.

Veblen, T. (1979). *Theory of the leisure class.* New York: Penguin Books. (Original work published 1899)

Verstegen, D., & McGuire, K. (1991). The dialectic of reform. *Educational Policy, 5*(4), 386–411.

Veysey, L. (1965). *The emergence of the American university.* Chicago: University of Chicago Press.

Vieth, M. (1981). *Time teachers spend reading versus time they spend watching TV.* Unpublished master's thesis, Kean College of New Jersey, Union. (ERIC Document Reproduction Service No. ED 200 922)

Virginia Department of Education. (1993). *The Virginia common core of learning.* Richmond, VA: Author. (Draft)

von Bertalanffy, L. (1968). *General systems theory: Foundations, development, application.* New York: George Braziller.

Wallace, A. (1986). *The prodigy.* New York: E. P. Dutton.

Wallach, M. A. (1970). Creativity. In P. H. Mussen (Ed.), *Carmichael's manual of child psychology* (pp. 1211–1271). New York: John Wiley & Sons.

Wallerstein, I. (1984). *Historical capitalism.* London: Verso.

Weaver, W. T. (1978). Educators in supply and demand: Effects on quality. *School Review, 86*(4), 522–593.

Weaver, W. T. (1979). In search of quality: The need for talent in teaching. *Phi Delta Kappan, 61*(1), 29–33.

Webb, C. (1992). *What do we mean by thoughtfulness in education?* Unpublished manuscript, Brigham Young University, Provo, UT.

Weber, G. (1971). *Inner-city children can be taught to read: Four successful schools* (Occasional Paper No. 18). Washington, DC: Council for Basic Education. (ERIC Document Reproduction Service No. ED 057 125)

Weber, M. (1958). *The Protestant ethic and the spirit of capitalism* (T. Parsons, trans.). New York: Charles Scribner's Sons. (Original work published 1904)

Weber, M. (1947). *The theory of social and economic organizations* (T. Parsons, Ed.; A. Henderson & T. Parsons, Trans.). New York: Free Press.

Weiler, D. (1978). The alpha children: California's brave new world for the gifted. *Phi Delta Kappan, 60*(3), 185–187.

Weiner, L. (1990, May). *The "triumph of commercialism": The corporate ethos and educational reform.* Paper presented at the annual meeting of the New England Educational Research Organization, Rockport, Maine. (ERIC Document Reproduction Service No. ED 322 647)

Weinstein, C. S. (1989). Teacher education students' perceptions of teaching. *Journal of Teacher Education, 40*(2), 53–60.

Weizenbaum, J. (1976). *Computer power and human reason: From judgment to calculation.* New York: William Freeman.

West, C. (1989). *The American evasion of philosophy: A genealogy of pragmatism.* Madison: University of Wisconsin Press.

West, C. (1994). The dilemma of the black intellectual. *Journal of Blacks in Higher Education,* (2), 59–67. (Originally published 1985 in *Cultural Critique,* (1), 109–124)

West, E. G. (1982). The prospects for education vouchers: An economic analysis. In R. B. Everhart (Ed.), *The public school monopoly: A critical analysis of education and the state in American society* (pp. 369–389). Cambridge, MA: Ballinger Publishing Company.

Westberg, K. L., Archambault, Jr., F. X., Dobyns, S. M., & Salvin, T. J. (1993). *An observational study of instructional and curricular practices used with gifted and talented students in regular classrooms* (Research Monograph No. 93103). Storrs: University of Connecticut, National Research Center on the Gifted and Talented.

Whitmore, J. (1980). *Giftedness, conflict, and underachievement.* Boston: Allyn & Bacon.

Wiener, N. (1950). *The human use of human beings: Cybernetics and society* (rev. ed.). Boston: Houghton Mifflin.

Wigginton, E. (1985). *Sometimes a shining moment.* Garden City, NY: Anchor Press/Doubleday.

Wilcox, K. (1982). Differential socialization in the classroom: Implications for equal opportunity. In G. Spindler (Ed.), *Doing the ethnography of schooling* (pp. 268–309). New York: CBS College Books.

Wilcox, K., & Moriarity, P. (1977). Schooling and work: Social constraints on equal educational opportunity. *Social Problems, 24*(2), 204–213.

Wiley, J., & Goldstein, D. (1991). Sex, handedness, and allergy: Are they related to academic giftedness? *Journal for the Education of the Gifted, 14*(4), 412–422.

Williams, J. (1952). *What Americans believe and how they worship.* New York: Harper & Row.

Williams, J., & Muehl, S. (1978). Relations among student and teacher perceptions of behavior. *Journal of Negro Education, 47*(4), 328–336.

Willis, P. (1977). *Learning to labor: How working class kids get working class jobs.* New York: Columbia University Press.

Wilshire, B. (1990). *The moral collapse of the university: Professionalism, purity, and alienation.* Albany: State University of New York Press.

Wilson, E. O. (1975). *Sociobiology: The new synthesis.* Cambridge, MA: Harvard University Press.

Wilson, S. M. (1990). The secret garden of teacher education. *Phi Delta Kappan, 72*(3), 204–209.

Winchester, I. (1987). Literacy and intellect. *Interchange, 18*(1/2), 23–31.

Windmiller, M. (1967). The new American mandarins. In T. Roszak (Ed.), *The dissenting academy* (pp. 110–134). New York: Random House.

Wingspread Group. (1993). *An American imperative: Higher expectations for higher education.* Racine, WI: Johnson Foundation.

Wise, A. (1982). Educational adequacy: A concept in search of meaning. In E. Tron (Ed.), *Adequate education: Issues in its definition and implementation* (pp. 111–124). Washington, DC: Office of Educational Research and Improvement. (ERIC Document Reproduction Service No. ED 226 489)

Wollstonecraft, M. (1986). *A vindication of the rights of woman.* New York: Penguin Books. (Original work published 1792)

Wright, E. O. (1979). *Class, crisis, and the state.* London: Verso.

Wright, E. O. (1985). *Classes.* London: Verso.

Wuthrick, M. A. (1990). Blue jays win! Crows go down in defeat. *Phi Delta Kappan, 71*(7), 553–556.

Wynne, E. (1988). Balancing character development and academics in the elementary school. *Phi Delta Kappan, 69*(6), 424–426.

Young, R. (1990). *A critical theory of education: Habermas and our children's future.* New York: Teachers College Press.

Young, T. A. (1990). Alternatives to ability grouping in reading. *Reading Horizons, 30*(3), 169–183.

Young, T. A., & McCullough, D. (1992). Looking out for low-achieving readers. *Reading Horizons, 32*(5), 394–402.

Zeichner, K., & Liston, D. (1987). Critical pedagogy and teacher education. *Journal of Education, 169*(3), 117–137.

Zeichner, K., Tabachnick, B., & Densmore, K. (1987). Individual, institutional and cultural influences on the development of teachers' craft knowledge. In J. Calderhead (Ed.), *Exploring teachers' thinking* (pp. 21–59). London: Cassell.

Zinn, H. (1980). *A people's history of the United States.* New York: Harper & Row.

Name Index

Acker, A., 128
Adler, M., 2, 4, 5, 14, 42
Adorno, T., 17
Agne, R., 50
Albert, H., 173, 174, 175
Allardyce, G., 71
Anderson, H., 55
Anderson, L., 62
Anyon, J., 62, 122, 123
Apple, M., 3, 10, 18, 19, 23, 26, 29, 36, 45, 51
Archambault, , F., 106
Arends, R., 48
Arendt, H., 7, 10, 11, 31, 37, 38, 39, 41, 103, 104, 146, 147, 150, 157, 168, 172, 173, 175, 206
Arnez, N., 130
Aronowitz, S., 14, 19, 46, 47, 75, 159
Asbury, C., 130
Atkinson, J., 146
Atwell, R., 66, 75

Bachmann, M., 131
Bacon, F., 146
Baldwin, J., 131
Barker, B., 23
Barnet, R., 139
Barrow, C., 7, 10, 71
Barzun, J., 2, 5, 6, 7, 8, 10, 29, 31, 32, 37, 38, 63, 66, 67, 73, 74, 75, 76, 98, 142, 143, 147, 153, 162
Baumrind, D., 65
Bean, F., 132
Beck, C., 31
Becker, G., 141, 170
Behan, P., 126
Belenky, M., 128
Bell, D., 2, 4, 6, 10, 12, 29, 36, 38, 141, 142, 143, 144, 154, 163, 183, 184, 206
Bellack, A., 39

Bellah, R., 73, 123, 176, 177
Benbow, C., 126–127
Bennett, E., 14, 24, 31, 204
Bennett, K., 181
Berg, T., 165
Berliner, D., 2, 6, 24, 139
Bernstein, H., 106
Berry, W., 38, 153–154, 155, 169, 170, 185
Best, S., 73, 142, 146, 151, 169
Betz, M., 50
Beyer, F., 146
Bhola, H., 165
Bickel, R., 50
Binet, A., 87
Birch, J., 90
Bishop, J., 26, 32
Bledstein, B., 72, 74
Bloom, A., 73, 156, 160
Bloom, B., 63, 94, 97, 107
Boli, J., 3, 53, 73, 101, 201
Bollier, D., 23
Borland, J., 78, 90
Borrowman, M., 16
Boston, B., 86
Bourdieu, P., 163
Bowen, J., 27
Bowles, S., 34, 81, 89
Bracey, G., 24
Britzman, D., 47, 49
Brookover, W., 15
Brown, B., 65
Brown, R., 2, 4, 6, 7, 10, 27, 33, 40, 44, 106, 122, 123, 130, 176, 192, 202
Brown, S., 106
Brownson, O., 32
Bruner, J., 39, 94, 96
Bryck, R., 170
Brym, R., 8
Buchmann, M., 197
Burbules, N., 52

Subject Index

About the Authors

Craig B. Howley works for the Appalachia Educational Laboratory, where he directs the ERIC Clearinghouse on Rural Education and Small Schools. His main interest is the cultural and political-economic circumstance of schooling.

Aimee Howley is professor of educational administration at Marshall University, where she currently serves as associate dean of the College of Education. Her chief concern is the academic substance of the institutions of schooling.

Edwina D. Pendarvis is a professor of special education at Marshall University, Huntington, West Virginia. Her education and teaching experience are primarily in gifted education; and within that field her interests are economically disadvantaged gifted students, assessment, and advocacy for gifted students.